THE
HIRING, FIRING
(AND EVERYTHING IN BETWEEN)
PERSONNEL
FORMS BOOK

James Jenks

Round Lake Publishing
Ridgefield, Connecticut

Round Lake Publishing Co.
31 Bailey Avenue
Ridgefield, CT 06877

Printed in the United States of America

0987654321

ISBN 0-929543-24-6

This publication is designed to provide accurate and authoritative information in regard to the subject matter covered. It is sold with the understanding that the publisher is not engaged in rendering legal, accounting or other professional service. If legal advice or other expert assistance is required, the services of a competent professional person should be sought. *From a Declaration of Principles jointly adopted by a Committee of the American Bar Association and a Committee of Publishers.*

The publisher cannot in any way assure that the forms in this book will be used for the purposes intended and accordingly does not assume any responsibility for their use.

Other Helpful Books from Round Lake Publishing

The following books are available from your bookseller. If they are not in stock, you may order directly from Round Lake Publishing.

The Complete Book of Contemporary Business Letters
400 model letters for all areas of business, including customer relations, handling customer complaints, credit and collections, personnel relations, memos and reports, job search, personal letters and much more. 470 pages, soft cover, 6" x 8 3/4" $19.95

The Only Personal Letter Book You'll Ever Need
Over 400 letters cover all areas of personal correspondence, including apologies and thank you's, complaints to companies and individuals, congratualtions and invitations, saying no, sympathy and condolences, and much more. 460 pages, soft cover, 6" x 8 3/4" $19.95

Encyclopedia of Money Making Sales Letters
Over 300 letters covering all phases of selling, from prospecting for new customers to closing sales. Includes responses to objections, keeping the customer buying, selling yourself, plus much more. *"Helps sell anything"*—The New York Times. 370 pages, soft cover, 6" x 8 3/4" $19.95

Step-By-Step Legal Forms and Agreements
165 legal forms for business and personal use. Includes wills, living will, power of attorney, forms for buying and selling real estate, starting a company, corporate forms, and much more. The most comprehensive book of its kind. *"Could hardly be easier to use"*—The New York Times. 440 pages, soft cover, 6" x 8 3/4" $19.95

Encyclopedia of Job-Winning Resumes
400 resumes covering every major industry and all job levels—from entry level to CEO. Also 40 cover letters for all situations, 30 resumes for difficult situations and expert advice on preparing resumes for each field. *The most comprehensive resume book ever published.* 548 pages, soft cover, 6" x 8 3/4" $16.95

The Complete Book of Consulting
150 forms—plus expert advice— for starting and running a successful consulting practice. Includes business plans, fee calculation worksheets, sales letters, brochures and cover letters, proposals, contracts, invoices, plus much more. Maximize your income with this extremely unusual and helpful consulting resource. 300 pages, soft cover, 6" x 8 3/4" $19.95

Contents

CHAPTER 1 SKILLFUL INTERVIEWING TECHNIQUES

CHAPTER 2   HIRING AND ORIENTATION PROGRAMS THAT WORK

Recruiting

Screening and evaluating applicants

Job offers and applicant rejections

Orientation programs

Forms

CHAPTER 3 BUILDING A JOB DESCRIPTION PROGRAM

Defining a job description program and its benefits

Collecting the necessary information

Job analysis development

Forms

CHAPTER 4   DEVELOPING SUCCESSFUL TRAINING PROGRAMS

Needs analysis—the first step in training program development

The training process

Training techniques

Applying the skills on the job

CHAPTER 5   GETTING RESULTS THROUGH PERFORMANCE APPRAISAL

Getting the most from the performance appraisal program

The appraisal interview

Introducing and maintaining an effective performance appraisal program

Forms

CHAPTER 6   EVALUATING AND IMPROVING EMPLOYEE ATTITUDES

Attitude survey basics

Forms

CHAPTER 7   MANPOWER PLANNING

Manpower planning basics

The manpower planning process

CHAPTER 8   DEVELOPING SUCCESSFUL PERSONNEL
POLICIES AND PROCEDURES

CHAPTER 9 ·DEVELOPING AN EFFECTIVE WAGE AND SALARY ADMINISTRATION PROGRAM

Job evaluation methods

Establishing wages

After the evaluation process

Forms

CHAPTER 10   PERSONNEL MANAGEMENT AND THE LAW

The basics

Pay

Equal employment opportunity

Sexual harassment

Religious and sexual discrimination

Safety and health

Miscellaneous laws and regulations

Forms

CHAPTER 11   RECORD KEEPING

What this Book Will Do for You

This book is a highly effective resource for companies that are not staffed with a formal personnel department. All the major areas of personnel management are explained in a way that every one can understand—*including those with no background in personnel.* And it includes 160 forms ready to customize for virtually any personnel management requirement.

Accompanying each chapter are the necessary documents to implement the many personnel programs. The 160 forms provide a comprehensive, forms-based personnel management program that will help any business deal with the wide range of personnel matters, easily and effectively.

For example, there are forms to develop the following essential programs:

- Create a comprehensive personnel policy manual
- Establish a rewarding interviewing and hiring program
- Implement a successful performance appraisal system
- Deal effectively with the sensitive areas of discipline and termination

Whether you're new to personnel management or a personnel professional, many subjects in this book will be of interest to you, such as hiring and orientation, the subject of Chapter 2, or personnel policies, the focus of Chapter 8. Chapter 10 discusses the major federal laws and regulations affecting personnel management, and will help you avoid problems with the government—and possible employee law suits. And there are chapters on manpower planning, interviewing, wage and salary administration, and much more.

The information in this book—plus the 160 forms, checklists, letters, guides, policies and other documents—will quickly make this book your company's most valuable personnel management resource.

How to Use this Book

This book covers the major areas of personnel management. Each chapter focuses on a specific aspect, first explaining the subject in an easy to follow question and answer format. Then the pertinent forms, checklists and other documents are shown, giving the reader the necessary tools to deal effectively with that area.

If you're inexperienced in the field of personnel management, it's best to read the text before using the forms in the chapter. Even if you are a seasoned personnel professional, you're likely to find information there that will be of value.

When you need a personnel form, you can find it quickly by using the comprehensive table of contents or either of two indexes, one of which is organized alphabetically and the other by key word.

Many of the forms can be used exactly as they appear. Others, such as those in the personnel policies chapter, can be easily adapted for your company's particular needs.

Important Note

Since each state has its own laws, and both federal and state laws continually change, the reader is urged to contact an attorney familiar with personnel regulations before implementing any personnel practices or procedures.

Skillful Interviewing Techniques 1

Why are hiring interviews so important?

The hiring interview is the most critical step in the selection process. No application form, resume, letter or oral recommendation has the impact of a personal meeting with a candidate for a job. Moreover, the decision that an interviewer, supervisor or manager makes based on the interview, may affect your company for years to come. Selecting the right person for the job can strengthen an organization. Conversely, of course, the process of hiring the wrong individual can be costly in time, money and morale.

What are the advantages of hiring the right person the first time?

There are many advantages, some obvious and some not so obvious, including:

1. The right person is more productive. Experience has shown that the most productive employee in a particular position is typically more than twice as productive as the least qualified employee.
2. The right employee learns faster. The better qualified the new employee is, the shorter your wait until the newcomer begins to produce at full capacity.
3. The right person requires less supervision and training. You can spend a lot of time bringing a substandard employee up to an acceptable level of performance. Employees also benefit psychologically and financially by getting up to speed rapidly.
4. The right employee is more likely to stay on the job. Satisfaction reduces turnover.
5. The right employee frees up the manager's time to manage. Sound selection of new personnel insures that employees will do their work well, giving the manager time to turn his attention to more productive pursuits.

What are the characteristics of a good interviewer?

The successful interviewer is able to:

- put applicants at ease
- make an objective decision despite subjective reactions to the applicant's appearance, personality or background
- understand and empathize with an applicant's fears and anxieties
- make the hiring recommendation without unnecessary delay

A good interviewer can interpret an applicant's behavior, expressions and body language in an objective manner. The interviewer can engage in personal conversation without becoming emotionally involved in the subjective matter.

Good interviewers never interrupt. Interruptions send the message that what the candidate is saying isn't very important and suggests that the interviewer thinks he or she is better or smarter than the candidate. If a question arises while the candidate is speaking, it's best to wait and ask it later.

It's also not a good idea to criticize the applicant, either orally or by one's own body language and facial expressions. Always encourage positive discussions.

What is the interviewer's most useful aid?

Anyone who conducts employment interviews should use a written interview guide. It's a detailed script for conducting the interview that contains all the questions you need to ask in order to obtain a complete, reliable picture of the candidate's skill and experience.

An interview guide insures that interviews are handled in a way that makes comparisons among applicants valid and reliable. Keep in mind, though, that the form is a guide, not an authoritative document. Effective use demands flexibility. Questions need not be asked in the order shown, and some can even be omitted. Digression from time to time to retain spontaneity is a good idea.

What are the steps in structuring interviews?

Successful interviewers structure a meeting by:

- Establishing rapport
- Getting a perspective on the applicant's background
- Obtaining detailed information about the applicant's education and experience
- Evaluating special accomplishments
- Evaluating an applicant's potential to fit into the job and the company

- Evaluating personal characteristics and behavior
- Giving information about the company and the job
- Allowing the applicant to ask and answer questions
- Discussing salary
- Closing the interview

What are the features of a structured interview?

A structured interview covers the following:

1. Background information about the applicant. This helps the interviewer look for jobs and experiences that are relevant to the position being filled.
2. Questions directed at job-related behavior. The candidate is asked to describe what decisions and actions he has made in situations similar to the ones he will encounter on the job.
3. Follow-up questions. Missing information can be discovered and completed in the brief review. Sensitive questions can be asked that might have influenced the rest of the interview if asked earlier.
4. Questions about the applicant's educational background.
5. Questions relating to specialized training and skills.
6. Questions about intangible factors including the applicant's goals and attitudes.
7. A description of the job and your organization, leaving time for the candidate to ask questions.
8. Concluding the interview. It should be ended on a cordial note. There should be a description of the next steps in the process.

The Interview Guide (1-01), shown at the end of the chapter, should be used when preparing for an interview. Simply adapt the form to your needs.

What is the best way to begin an interview?

The conversation should be opened with easy, non-controversial questions. They help allay anxiety and reduce tension.

How do expert interviewers establish rapport?

Good rapport depends upon three factors: The way the interviewer greets the applicant, the atmosphere of the room in which the interview is held and the tone used during the opening minutes.

To get off to a good start, the interviewer should go personally to the reception room and greet the applicant warmly and by name. Sending someone in the interviewer's place to escort the candidate to the office can be intimidating.

Interviews should be held in a private office or conference room. That provides a more relaxed atmosphere than having a desk positioned between the interviewer and the candidate. Telephone calls should be diverted in advance and interruptions kept to a minimum.

What method of questioning elicits the most information?

All questions should be open-ended so that they get descriptive responses rather than a simple "yes" or "no." For instance, if the interviewer asks, "Are you currently a production supervisor?" that question can be answered "yes" or "no" and is a poor question. Instead, he should say, "Tell me about your job as a production supervisor." Then he should sit back and listen.

> Applicant: I supervised 12 people.
>
> Interviewer: [Remains silent]
>
> Applicant: Seven were women and five were men.
>
> Interviewer: Ah, I see [nodding].
>
> Applicant: I had some trouble disciplining the women especially
> when they were late for work.

Now the interviewer is beginning to get useful information about how the candidate performed as a supervisor. Using silence, neutral comments such as "I see," "yes," "hmm," and similar responses encourage the applicant to continue. He or she will often tell details of experiences and behavior that would not ordinarily be given.

When preparing interview guides, questions about the applicant's work history should be included, using details gleaned from the resume or the application form.

How well does past experience predict an applicant's future performance?

In judging an applicant's experience, the real question is just how relevant that experience is to the company's needs. The best way to zero in on relevant experience is to analyze an applicant's behavior on the previous job. An employee's actual behavior in past job-related situations is a good way to predict performance on the job.

How can an interviewer judge an applicant's abilities?

For every critical job requirement the interviewer wants to know: What has the applicant done in the past to meet this requirement?

The company has determined what the job requires. Look for the applicant who has met similar requirements in the past. Give the strongest consideration to those who have met the requirements often and well.

When you do this you are using past behavior to predict future behavior. No system can actually foresee the future, of course. Still, it's reasonable to expect that if someone has behaved a certain way before, this person will probably behave the same way should the same situation arise.

Finding out what an applicant has done before is at the core of the selection process. Once you know what the applicant has done, you have a reasonable guide to what can be expected in the future. The individual whose behavior comes closest to what you expect is a prime candidate for the job.

The STAR system is a way to determine past behavior. STAR stands for these three steps:

1. Determine the Situation or the Task for which the applicant was responsible.
2. Find out what Action the applicant took.
3. Determine the Results of that action.

What kinds of questions help an interviewer probe past experience?

Using the STAR system, the interviewer should ask the applicant to describe what he or she did in a particular type of situation.

The questions should be keyed to the specific job requirements you've established. You want to compile a record of what the individual actually has done in situations that are related, as closely as possible, to the job you want to fill.

A nervous applicant may not instantly recall the incident the interviewer asked about. The interviewer may have to encourage or probe for more information.

The behavior-oriented questions should be attached to the structured interview guide. Examples are found at the end of the chapter in the form Interview Questions--Behavior Oriented (1-02).

How can poor interview questions be turned into good ones?

Good questions are phrased in ways that elicit descriptive answers and avoid single word replies. Common interview questions are shown at the end of the chapter in the form Interview Questions--Weak vs. Strong (1-03). Compare the "faulty" ones to the "improved."

What kinds of questions should be asked of recent graduates or individuals who have little or no work experience?

Highly motivated people have goals, and they strive to reach them early in their lives. Students generally manifest this trait through active participation in extracurricular activities. To evaluate motivational patterns, the following questions can be used to elicit information on different kinds of behavior:

- What were your ambitions when you were in school?

- How successful were you in achieving the goals of groups you headed or were a member of?
- What are your career or professional goals?
- What steps are you taking in order to achieve these goals?

Situational questions also help when developing information on individuals without much work experience. Applicants can be asked how they might handle simulated problems they may meet on the job. For example, here is a situational question about a customer service job:

Question:	A customer is irate about a delayed shipment. How would you handle this complaint?
Poor response:	I'd apologize for the delay and report it to the shipping department for action.
Better response:	I'd apologize for the delay and tell the customer I'd check into its status and let him know when he could expect delivery. I'd assure the customer I'd do whatever I could to personally expedite it.

Performance of recent graduates can be measured by grade level or class standing; creativity can be spotted by questions on hobbies and special interests.

What are sequential interviews?

In a sequential interview, applicants are screened by other employees in the company first. If they are considered worthy of further consideration, they are interviewed by the next higher ranking person who decides either to pass them on to a more senior manager — or to hire them. This screening procedure eliminates unqualified people early, before they take a senior manager's valuable time. Sometimes, two or more lower-level interviewers compare evaluations and choose a few top applicants for interviews with the executive who will make the final choice.

What is a serialized interview?

The personnel department or an administrative assistant screens out the obviously unqualified candidates according to specific guidelines. All candidates who meet the basic qualifications are interviewed by at least two other company representatives. They may be personnel specialists, the department head or other members of the department which has the job opening.

No one interviewer can reject anyone. Each interviewer completes a written review for each candidate. When all interviews are finished, the interviewers meet, compare notes and decide which candidates to present to the final decision maker. In this way, the final decision maker can base his or her decision on the perspectives and evaluations of several managers.

Different interviewers may uncover different facts or temper one another's biases. This increases the chances for a productive hiring decision. The procedure is expensive and time consuming, however. It may lead to delays in filling the position and the loss of good candidates who decide to accept positions elsewhere.

What is a panel interview?

In a panel interview, a group of managers or supervisors interview the applicant at the same time. It's conducted like a conference with one of the managers acting as the chairman. The panelists ask questions, usually in an unplanned, spontaneous fashion.

After the interview, the panel discusses the candidate and decides to hire, not hire or delay its decision until it has seen other applicants.

The panel interview saves time for panel members, allows members to compare their impressions based on a uniform experience, and increases the chances that relevant questions missed by one interviewer will be asked by another.

A panel interview puts considerable pressure on job applicants. Some will be intimidated and not interview well. This can be offset, to some extent, by briefing the applicant in advance. Another drawback: One panel member may dominate the interview.

What areas should be covered in a job offer interview?

Come to a clear understanding with the applicant about:

1. Compensation and benefits
2. Conditions of the offer
3. Relocation requirements, if any
4. Travel requirements
5. Starting date
6. Deadline for accepting the offer
7. Special job requirements

Job offers normally are made subject to certain conditions, such as passing a physical examination, receipt and verification of references and academic degrees, proof of citizenship, etc. Most job offers are made orally, though some companies confirm them in writing, especially for senior positions.

How should compensation be discussed in the interview?

Normally, the candidate knows what compensation to expect from the source that led him to apply, such as an advertisement, executive recruiter or employment agency. Still, the subject should be brought up as soon as the company becomes satisfied that the applicant has the potential to be hired. The amounts and details of compensation should be made very clear.

If the applicant wants more money than your company is willing to pay, use other aspects of the job to persuade him or her to reconsider. Special benefits or the growth potential may outweigh starting salary considerations.

How can interviewing skills be evaluated?

Managers can improve their interviewing techniques by using the Interviewer Evaluation Checklist (1-04) shown at the end of the chapter. This is a good way to find out if managers are neglecting one or more techniques or if they are applying them inconsistently from one interview to the next. Filling out the checklist will help interviewers keep track of the multiple elements that go into productive interviews.

To evaluate their knowledge and understanding of the interviewing process, ask your managers, supervisors, personnel department people, and anyone else who conducts interviews to review the Interviewing Skills Questionnaire (1-05) located at the end of the chapter. The answers will help to determine their interviewing strengths and weaknesses and point to areas that need improvement.

INTERVIEW GUIDE

Name of applicant _____

Address _____

Telephone _____

Position _____

Interviewed by _____ Date _____

I. JOB FACTORS - GENERAL   Notes and Comments

1. On your application you indicated you
worked for _____. How long were you   _____
employed there?   _____

2. Please describe your responsibilities   _____
and duties with this company.   _____

3. Tell me what you consider to be your   _____
major accomplishment at that company.   _____

4. Tell me about some of your setbacks   _____
and disappointments on the job.   _____

5. Tell me about the progress you made   _____
while with that company.   _____

6. (If progress was significant, ask:) To
what do you attribute this fine progress?
(If progress was not impressive, ask:)
Were you satisfied with your progress? (If
not, ask:) How did you attempt to   _____
overcome this?   _____

7. What was the most valuable   _____
experience you obtained in that position?   _____

8. Why did you leave (or why do you want
to leave) this company? (Use additional   _____
paper if needed for each job covered.)   _____

Notes and Comments

II. EDUCATION (Use questions in part A
for applicants who did not attend a
college. Use questions in part B for
those who have had some college
education or who are graduates.)

A. For applicants who did not attend
college.

1. What was the highest level of schooling
you completed?

_____

_____

2. How were your overall grades?

_____

_____

3. In what extracurricular activities did you
participate?

_____

_____

4. If you worked, how many hours a
week? What kind of jobs?

_____

_____

5. Have you acquired additional education
since leaving high school?

_____

_____

6. What training did you have in school?

_____

_____

7. What was the first significant job you
held after leaving school?

_____

_____

B. For college graduates and those who
have had some college education.

1. I see that you attended
_____. Why did you select
that school?

_____

_____

2. What was your major? What
determined this choice?

_____

_____

3. What were your overall college grades?

_____

_____

Notes and Comments

4. In what types of extracurricular activities did you participate?

_____
_____

5. How did you finance your education?

_____
_____

6. If you worked at college, how many hours per week? Summers? What type of jobs?

_____
_____

7. What were your vocational plans when you were at college?

_____
_____

8. If they are different now, when did you change your thinking? Why?

_____
_____

9. What additional education have you had since you graduated from college?

_____
_____

10. (If a college education was not completed.) Why did you leave college? Have you ever planned to complete your degree? What steps have you taken? What results?

_____
_____
_____
_____
_____

11. What was the first significant job you had after leaving (graduating from) college?

_____
_____

12. How did this lead to your current career?

_____
_____

III. TECHNICAL OR SPECIAL FACTORS
Questions related to specialized skills, training and experience should be developed for each type of work for which applicants are being interviewed.

IV. INTANGIBLE FACTORS   Notes and Comments

A. GOALS AND MOTIVATION

    1. Tell me about your career goals, short-term and long-term.

    2. In what way would a job with our company meet your career objectives?

    3. What factors in the past have contributed most to your growth?

    4. What factors do you believe may have handicapped you from moving ahead more rapidly?

    5. When did you decide to go into this career area? What influenced you to make this decision?

    6. What changes would you make in your life and career?

    7. What aspects of a job are important to you?

    8. What are your present earnings expectations? How did you arrive at this figure?

B. JOB PERFORMANCE AND ATTITUDES

    1. How would you describe the most effective superior you have had? What were his or her strengths? Limitations? Describe your least effective supervisor.

Notes and Comments

2. Tell me about a significant problem you
encountered on your job. How did you
approach it? What did you actually do?

GENERAL COMMENTS AND RECOMMENDATIONS:

BEHAVIOR-ORIENTED INTERVIEW QUESTIONS

- Have you ever had an assignment that required careful attention to detail? How did you handle it?

- Tell me about a recent experience where you had to work closely with someone else on an assignment or project. What was your role? What happened?

- Describe a situation where you had to go out of your way to help someone. What did you do? What was involved?

- I'd like to hear about an instance in which you anticipated a problem or influenced a significant decision. How did it work out?

- Give me an example of how you did more than required in your job.

- Everyone has to bend or break the rules once in a while. Can you give me an example of how you handled this kind of situation?

- Can you tell me about a time when you had to be critical of someone else? What happened?

- Describe the most successful experience you have ever had in persuading someone to do something.

- Tell me about a situation in which you were under particular pressure. How did you handle it?

INTERVIEW QUESTIONS—WEAK VS. STRONG

WEAK	IMPROVED
Are you a leader?	Give me an example of a time when you emerged as the leader of a group. How did it come out?
Are you pleased with your career so far?	Where would you like to go from here in your career? How do you plan to accomplish this?
Can you learn complex material quickly?	What kinds of material do you feel you can learn best?
Did you find it easy to work with your supervisor?	In what ways did you and your supervisor think alike? How did you differ?
Did your previous job prepare you for greater responsibilities?	What did you learn from your previous job that prepared you for greater responsibilities?
Do you believe in management by objectives?	What have you done to set performance objectives for your subordinates?
Do you think you could handle this job?	How do you feel your education and experience prepare you for this job?
Do you work well with people?	Tell me about an important relationship you had to maintain. How did you handle it?
Can you take criticism?	Tell me about a time you had to take some criticism. What did you do?
Can you make decisions?	Describe a situation in which you had to make an important decision. What did you do?

INTERVIEWER EVALUATION CHECKLIST

	YES	NO
1. INTRODUCTION		
a) Did interviewer establish rapport?	_____	_____
b) Did interviewer move smoothly into body of interview?	_____	_____
2. GETTING INFORMATION		
a) Did interviewer ask open-ended questions that elicited information?	_____	_____
b) Did interviewer follow through on answers?	_____	_____
c) Did interviewer avoid telegraphing desired responses?	_____	_____
d) Did interviewer control the interview?	_____	_____
e) Did interviewer get applicant to speak freely?	_____	_____
f) Did interviewer really listen?	_____	_____
g) Did interviewer obtain adequate job factor information?	_____	_____
h) Did interviewer obtain adequate intangible factor knowledge?	_____	_____
3. GIVING INFORMATION		
a) Did interviewer describe job adequately?	_____	_____
b) Did interviewer give applicant the company's background?	_____	_____
c) Did interviewer "sell" job and company to applicant?	_____	_____
d) Did interviewer encourage applicant to ask questions?	_____	_____
4. CLOSING THE INTERVIEW		
a) Did interviewer control when interview closed?	_____	_____
b) Did interviewer inform applicant of next step in procedure? (if applicant was to be considered further)	_____	_____
c) Did interviewer leave applicant with good impression of firm?	_____	_____
d) Did interviewer make appropriate notes after applicant left?	_____	_____

INTERVIEWING SKILLS QUESTIONNAIRE

	TRUE	FALSE
1. The first step in filling a job is getting an idea of the job market for the particular skill.	_____	_____
2. A well-written resume is as good a source of information as a completed application form.	_____	_____
3. Frequent job changes do not necessarily mean that the applicant is unstable.	_____	_____
4. The first thing a good interviewer does in an interview is to establish rapport with the applicant.	_____	_____
5. The correct way to greet an applicant is to have your secretary bring him to your office as soon as he arrives.	_____	_____
6. Even when detailed information on specific areas is required, questions should be open-ended.	_____	_____
7. The interviewer should obtain information by first asking an open-ended question and then remaining silent or giving only a word or gesture to encourage the applicant to continue to talk.	_____	_____
8. The best way to ease an applicant's nervousness is to get down to business as quickly as possible.	_____	_____
9. A good way to obtain information on education and experience is by asking the six basic questions: What? When? Where? Who? Why? How?	_____	_____
10. When prior experience does not reflect managerial ability, creativity or other talents, look for them in outside activities.	_____	_____
11. While "selling" the company to an applicant may be important, exaggerations can create serious problems.	_____	_____
12. Discussing negative aspects of your company is a mistake, since it may discourage a potentially valuable person from accepting the job.	_____	_____

	TRUE	FALSE
13. Salary should not be discussed until the final interview.	_____	_____
14. Never take notes during an interview because it may distract or intimidate the applicant.	_____	_____
15. Skillful interviewers evaluate only those factors that relate to the job.	_____	_____
16. Asking a "leading" question is an interviewing mistake.	_____	_____
17. One way to make sure that you stay alert during an interview is to concentrate on the applicant's facial expressions and other non-verbal behavior.	_____	_____
18. The first clue that your mind is beginning to wander is when you begin to hear sounds rather than ideas coming from the speaker.	_____	_____
19. Talking too much is a sign of inexperience or incompetence in an applicant.	_____	_____
20. Belligerence may hide a real talent for handling authority and demonstrate a "no nonsense" approach to business.	_____	_____
21. The sequential interview has the advantage of eliminating unqualified people before they take up valuable time from top executives.	_____	_____
22. The serialized interview requires that at least two interviewers must concur before an applicant can be rejected.	_____	_____
23. The panel interview saves time, but may intimidate an applicant.	_____	_____
24. Job offers should include a reasonable deadline for a decision.	_____	_____

1. False. The first step in filling a position is a job analysis which comprises the job description, a detailed summary of the duties, responsibilities and other job factors, and the job specifications, skills and aptitudes needed to perform the job. Availability becomes a factor when determining the salary.

2. False. While a resume may supplement an application, it cannot replace it. An application asks for information the company needs to have. A resume gives only that information the applicant wants known. Applicants who attempt to submit resumes in place of the completed application should be told that they must also complete the form.

3. True. Instability may be indicated, but the interviewer should find out the reasons for the changes during the job interview. A previous employer's business reversal or a decision to leave or enter a specific field could account for the frequent moves.

4. True. The more relaxed the applicant, the more information he will give. An open, communicative candidate is also easier to evaluate in terms of his personal characteristics.

5. False. The interviewer should greet the applicant personally and by name. Having a secretary bring the candidate into the office while the interviewer sits behind his desk reading the applicant's resume or application can be very intimidating.

6. True. The descriptive response elicited by an open-ended question will include specific information. The question that requires only a "yes" or "no" answer will not get a broad, informative response. Moreover, open-ended questions can be followed by more specific ones.

7. True. Encouraging the interviewee to say what is on his mind rather than having him answer a lot of questions may reveal information that the interviewer might never have thought to ask about.

8. False. Non-controversial questions are the best way to start an interview. These permit an applicant to start talking without feeling that his future hangs on his first words. Still, make the questions productive by linking them casually to the matter at hand.

9. True. Elaborated, these questions are: "What skills were needed to accomplish the task?" "When did you do this kind of work?" "Where were these skills applicable?" "Who was responsible?" "Why did you make that decision?" "How did you solve this problem?"

10. True. The applicant's experience may not show an ability because his previous job, or previous employer, gave him no opportunity to develop it. Therefore, the interviewer should inquire about talents the candidate may have used in educational, civic, religious, trade or professional association activities. Such abilities, when directed toward work, could make an applicant with acceptable business experience an outstanding employee.

11. True. Nothing creates greater bitterness than giving false hope. The employer who creates it may find that an exciting prospect has become an embittered, resentful employee.

12. False. He'll find out about the shortcomings sooner or later anyway, and the later he finds out, the greater his resentment will be. Negative information can, however, be carefully phrased: "We've had two bad years, but we expect to do well this year."

13. False. Although the specific offer is not made until the hiring interview, general discussions about salary should take place well before then.

14. False. Taking notes helps the interviewer structure the interview, keep track of subjects he wants to know more about (without interrupting the applicant) and remember the applicant after the interview is over. However, note-taking should be done judiciously, since writing constantly interferes with both the interviewer's and the candidate's concentration.

15. True. For example, a mechanical engineer does not need to be gregarious or assertive and a salesman may not need to have a gift for finance.

16. True. It refers to rhetorical questions which indicate to the applicant the answer that the interviewer wants to hear. For example: "Don't you think that getting along with subordinates is absolutely critical to good management?"

17. True. Experienced interviewers know that it takes an overt effort to listen for extended periods of time. Concentrating on non-verbal behavior is a good way to maintain a long span of attention.

18. True. The experienced interviewer can spot this in himself almost immediately. Learning to recognize loss of attention early is an important part of becoming a good interviewer.

19. False. Some people simply express their anxiety by talking a lot and this mannerism may hide real ability. The interviewer may need to interrupt frequently to ask specific questions. In some instances, however, applicants who are not competent may try to hide their unsuitability by telling endless stories.

20. False. Applicants who try to put the interviewer on the defense or force him into an argument should not be hired.

21. True. Lower ranking persons in the company can screen out unqualified people early.

22. True. Personnel or an administrative assistant screens out the obviously unqualified according to specific guidelines. Those remaining are interviewed by two or more company representatives.

23. True. Therefore, when a group of executives is going to interview an applicant in a conference setting, i.e., a panel interview, the applicant should be briefed in advance about who will be on the panel and what its purpose is.

24. True. Otherwise, an applicant who has personal reservations or offers from other companies may stall indefinitely.

> How to score yourself:
> 24 correct answers - a superior knowledge of interviewing and selection
> 21-23 correct - excellent
> 18-20 correct - good
> 15-17 correct - average
> Below 15 - poor

Hiring and Orientation Programs that Work 2

What are the most effective ways to recruit new employees?

Among the best ways to recruit new employees are through:

- Referrals from current employees
- Recruiting at vocational schools and universities
- Advertising in classified sections of newspapers and in trade and professional publications
- Job fairs
- Employment agencies
- Executive recruiters

Recruiting is the first step in the hiring process. The goal is to attract qualified people whose skills and experience meet the demands of the job you want to fill. Once you have an initial pool of qualified people, you can use interviewing and references to screen for other desirable qualities. Later still, you can zero in on candidates who show those qualities to the highest degree.

Of course, in most companies the process begins with an employee requisition-- the written document specifying the need for a new worker. A Staff Requisition (2-01) is found at the end of the chapter.

What is the best way to describe a job that needs to be filled?

Listing all the qualities wanted in a new employee might be the best way to describe the job. But the problem with this method is that it can attract just about anyone without drawing in applicants who meet the most vital requirements. For example, you might think being "cooperative" is an important requirement for a secretarial position — and it is. But anyone can claim to be cooperative, and really believe it, too. Listing that requirement does nothing to attract individuals who have good typing, shorthand and proofreading skills, which are the skills really needed.

Instead, concentrate on the critical requirements for the job, the few qualifications that are absolutely essential, no matter which method of recruitment is used. They should be objective capabilities that anyone can easily and accurately assess in themselves. To recruit a database administrator who can provide an IDM knowledge base of both internal and external parameters for IDMS-DB/DE, say so, and you'll draw in qualified professionals. At the same time, you'll turn away people who don't know what these terms mean.

It's also important to include reasons for a prospective employee to consider joining your company. Mention your firm's reputation if it's well known, its working atmosphere, strong benefits package, desirable location — items that will be attractive to prospective employees.

How can advertising work well as a recruitment method?

Start by selecting the most effective advertising medium in your job market. You wouldn't resort to a television advertisement to recruit computer programmers, for example, because TV appeals to too broad a market. Placing an ad in a programmers' magazine, or one discussing software, would be a more likely source.

Once you've found the right medium, concentrate on the ad itself, keeping these characteristics in mind:

- Design the ad so that it is distinctive in language and appearance. Use typography and layout to make your company and the job stand out from other ads on the page.

- Highlight the major advantages you have to offer. Address a prospective employee's most important needs and concerns.

- State only the most critical job requirements. Make half the ad deal with the job itself. Devote the other half to selling your organization.

What are the specifics of a job advertisement?

The well-structured ad includes:

1. The job title. Use the most familiar term for the job to attract the most readers.
2. A strong opening statement. Use an attention-getting opening that highlights the most attractive feature your job has to offer, so people will want to read further.
3. Specifics about the job and the job requirements.
4. The additional advantages of taking this job. Include attention-getting information such as the profitability of the firm, its interesting location, advancement potential, etc.

Concentrate on benefits that are important to the type of person you're seeking. If you're looking for professionals or managers, stress a tuition payment plan for advanced degrees. Conversely, don't try to sell your pension plan to entry-level applicants.

What is a job profile and what is it used for?

A job profile outlines what the company demands from the person who holds it, expressed in terms of the type of behavior needed to do the job well. Building a job profile is one way to systematically identify a job's requirements. A Job Profile (2-02) is found at the end of the chapter.

What are the ingredients of a reliable employee selection system?

A selection system is simply an organized hiring plan. It consists of these steps, though the exact sequence will vary with the nature of the job:

1. Advertising and recruiting
2. Initial screening and evaluations
3. In-depth screening and interviews
4. Preliminary selection of a candidate to fill the job
5. Reference and medical checks
6. Job offer
7. Handling of applicants who are not hired
8. Orientation and training

How should applicants be screened?

The first step should be to eliminate obviously unqualified applicants — those who do not possess your most important job requirements — by reviewing resumes and application forms. For example, if you're looking for a sales representative who has experience selling your product line, a quick review of the resumes you receive will filter out those who don't have such experience.

Questions on the application form will vary according to the specific needs of your company but, in general, this is the kind of information you will want to ask for:

- General identification: Full name, address, telephone number.
- Work experience: Names and addresses of previous employers. Positions held, starting and ending dates. Names of immediate supervisors. Ask whether past employers may be contacted for references.
- Personal references.
- Education: Include formal schooling, special training, military training and on-the-job courses.
- Statement and signature: Have the applicant sign the form,

including a statement that gives you permission to verify the application and that the information is correct to the best of the applicant's knowledge.

A Job Application Form (2-03) and a Job Application Disclaimer and Acknowledgement (2-04) are found later in the chapter, along with a Job Application Update (2-05).

How can resumes be evaluated?

Bear in mind that a resume is a selling tool. Many of them are professionally prepared. They should be treated as a demonstration of the intelligence, organizational ability and thinking of the individual it describes.

Make notes on each resume for yourself. Indicate which areas should be probed during the interview. Keep handy the list of the job requirements and check them against the knowledge and skills claimed on the resume.

These four major areas are the most important ones:

1. Education — is it the right kind for the job?
2. Specific work experience — good resumes give details of achievements as well as descriptions of main duties and responsibilities. If anything is unclear, make a note to have it clarified in the interview.
3. Progress in each job — look at the numbers of different positions the applicant has held in each company, the kinds of positions, and whether the progressions indicate promotions, lateral moves, or even demotions. Look for signs of increasing responsibility.
4. Stability — frequent job changes suggest the candidate easily becomes dissatisfied, though there may be extenuating circumstances that you'll want to inquire about in the interview.

What questions should be asked when checking references?

Normally, you want to obtain basic work experience information: the dates of employment and positions held, attendance and performance at various schools.

This information is quite valuable. If something is inconsistent, it can be cleared up at the follow-up interview. Overt dishonesty about a past job is grounds to reject the applicant.

Expect personal references to present favorable pictures of the applicant, but they should be followed through with a phone call anyway. Specific questions about a particular job qualification may yield a useful reply. Another thing to consider: Many applicants list the most important people they know. These people are often particularly frank and objective. A Telephone Reference Checklist (2-06) is located at the end of the chapter together with an Employment Reference Response Form (2-07).

One way to get good information from a personal reference is to ask about some weakness already discovered. Normally, you'll get either a confirmation or a detailed denial.

If a reference check raises questions about a candidate you've tentatively selected, don't be too quick to reverse that selection. Be particularly cautious if the unfavorable information is inconsistent with the results of the other reference checks. It may indicate a biased or mistaken reference. Another interview should be scheduled where the applicant is asked about it. There may be a perfectly logical explanation.

An Authorization for Release of Prior Employment Information (2-08) and Request for College Transcript (2-09) round out the information needed. Forms are found at the end of the chapter.

How can applicants be compared after they've been interviewed?

Make up an Applicant Rating Form (2-10) for each applicant, similar to the one found at the end of the chapter. It calls for a numerical rating for each of the major job requirements, plus overall reaction to the candidate.

What are the differences between hiring senior executives and lower-level individuals?

The hiring process is much the same at each level, though the job requirements for senior managers are longer and more detailed. They emphasize characteristics important to top management.

You'll want to have several senior executives interview a candidate for a top-level position, while one or two interviews with the immediate supervisor is usually sufficient for lower-level personnel.

Style and personality count more when choosing an executive, as do leadership ability and the candidate's plans for the future of your company. Intangible factors like organizational chemistry and "fit" with other executives are also important considerations for executives.

What information should be covered in the job offer?

After the decision has been reached on the person to be hired, the selected applicant will be formally offered the job. At this time, all the details of the offer should be explained and any questions that the applicant may have about the offer answered.

There should be clear understanding about:

1. Compensation and benefits
2. Conditions of the offer
3. Relocation requirements (if applicable)

4. Travel requirements
5. Starting date
6. Deadline for acceptance of the offer
7. Special job requirements

Normally, an oral job offer is followed by a Job Offer Letter (2-11), located at the end of the chapter.

How should rejected candidates be handled?

It's always to the company's advantage to personally contact those individuals who have been interviewed but will not be offered a job. It's possible, for example, that you might want to make an offer at some future time to one of the applicants, either because your first choice didn't accept your offer or didn't perform up to your expectations once he or she took the job. Or you might have another opening suitable for a person you've rejected for a different job.

Beyond those practical considerations, it is unkind and unethical to totally ignore individuals who have applied and have taken the time to be interviewed. It's also extremely poor public relations.

An Applicant Rejection Letter (2-12) that can be adapted to your own needs is found at the end of the chapter.

What results should be expected from a new employee orientation program?

A good orientation program can help a new employee realize his or her full promise. Among the things an effective program can do are to:

1. Make an excellent first impression. The new employee's early reactions can set the tone for his entire career. This is when most newcomers develop their attitudes toward the company, the job and their supervisors.

2. Lead to better morale and motivation. It can prevent the errors, misunderstanding and discontent that poor communication can cause.

3. Present accurate information. It's to everyone's advantage that a new employee fully understand the company's rules and practices, and the benefits offered in return. Don't leave this important information to chance or the grapevine. Poor communications now can lead to serious misunderstandings later.

4. Improve learning. The well-briefed employee is less likely to make mistakes and will require less training and supervision on the job.

What should an orientation program cover?

The plan should have several key components, to:

1. Let the new employee know what the company expects of him or her. These are the basic policies and procedures usually found in employee handbooks and policy manuals.
2. Let the employee know what the company offers.
3. Provide information on whom to see for help or information.
4. Introduce the new employee to co-workers, supervisors, and the workplace.

What is the supervisor's role in orienting new employees?

The supervisor plays a vital role in orienting new employees. He or she should personally welcome each new employee and introduce him or her to other members of the department.

Supervisors should be trained how to carry out this important task. An Orientation Checklist for New Employees (2-13) covers the subject. It is shown later in the chapter.

A Confidentiality Agreement (2-14) should be used if confidential information will be available to the new employee. Such a form is found at the end of the chapter.

What paperwork should be filled out at the time the new employee joins the company?

A New Hire Personnel Data Sheet (2-15) should be completed and the Personnel Department should collect the items described in a Personnel File Checklist (2-16). The employee should sign a New Employee Acknowledgement Form (2-17), acknowledging receipt of personnel literature. These forms are located at the end of the chapter.

If the employee is a part time or hourly worker, he or she should be given the Part Time Employee Letter of Understanding (2-18) or Hourly Employee Information Sheet (2-19). In the case of an employee returning to the company, the Rehire Form (2-20) should be used to update records. All three forms are shown at the end of the chapter.

STAFF REQUISITION

Department _____   Date _____

Position Title _____   Position Number _____

Refer Applicant to _____   Ext. No. _____

Requested Starting Date _____   Hours _____

Position Description Summary: _____

_____

_____

Preferred Qualifications and Experience: _____

_____

_____

Will Consider: _____ Transfer Applicants   _____ Job Postings

                                             _____ Outside Applicants

Replacement: __Yes __No

      Name of person being replaced _____

      Date leaving _____

      Final salary _____

Addition to Staff __Yes __No

If yes, state why increase is needed: _____

_____

_____

Requirements

College graduate (Yes/no) _____   Typing (wpm) _____

Professional degrees (specify) _____   Shorthand (wpm) _____

_____

Other qualifications _____

_____

Job Summary

_____

_____

_____

_____

Suggested in-house candidates for position:

_____

_____

_____

_____

Approvals must be obtained prior to submission to Human Resources

Submitted by: _____ _____ Approval: _____ _____
              Immediate supervisor   Date   Department manager   Date

Approval: _____ _____
              Division head   Date

FOR HUMAN RESOURCES USE ONLY

Date received _____ Date Filled _____ By _____

JOB PROFILE FOR SECRETARY

Adaptability: Performs a variety of tasks, often changing assignments on short notice.

Administration: Keeps other members of the organization informed of progress and problems. Monitors the progress of delegated assignments and makes corrections when necessary.

Cooperation: Works well with other people. Takes time to help co-workers, customers and others achieve their goals and assignments.

Grammar, Proofreading: Writes, transcribes and proofreads written material with a high level of accuracy.

Information Retrieval: Develops a system of filing that provides access to specific information. Shows ability to retrieve and deliver information.

Initiative: Actively tries to influence events to achieve goals. A self-starter, working well without close supervision. Tries to achieve goals beyond minimal level of performance.

Learning Ability: Learns and applies new skills and knowledge with routine training.

Motivation: Activities on the job match personal interests and goals. Can take personal satisfaction in performance and accomplishments.

Typing: Types a minimum of _____ words per minute. Familiar with, or can learn, _____ word processing software.

Work Standards: Sets high personal standards of performance. Not satisfied with average performance.

Job Application Form (2-03)

CONFIDENTIAL APPLICATION FOR EMPLOYMENT

For Office Use Only
Hired _____
Dept _____
Starting Date _____
Salary $ _____

(Please print)

Date _____

Name (in full) _____

Address (in full) _____

Phone _____ Soc. Sec. # _____

Position applied for _____

Are you a citizen of the United States? ___Yes ___No

If you are not a citizen of this country, what is your status? (Do you have work papers?)

_____

Are you a veteran? ___Yes ___No

EDUCATION

Please record your education below

	Name of school/Location	Did you graduate?
High school	_____	_____
Bus./Trade	_____	_____
College/Univ	_____	_____
Graduate/Professional	_____	_____

PREVIOUS EMPLOYMENT AND REFERENCES

(Give in chronological order beginning with most recent position)

	Present or last employer	Previously employed by	Previously employed by
Name of firm	_____	_____	_____
Address	_____	_____	_____
	_____	_____	_____
Name of supervisor	_____	_____	_____
Nature of business	_____	_____	_____
Dates of employment	_____	_____	_____
Position(s) held	_____	_____	_____
Ending salary	_____	_____	_____
Reason for leaving	_____	_____	_____

Job Application Form (2-03) *continued*

Personal references—Please give the names and addresses of two persons to whom you are not related and by whom you have not been employed.

Name _____

Address _____

Name _____

Address _____

Who recommended you to us? (Person or agency) _____
_____

Summarize special skills and qualifications acquired from employment or other experience.
_____
_____
_____

I certify that answers given herein are true and complete to the best of my knowledge.

I authorize you to make such investigations and inquiries of my personal, employment, financial or medical history and other related matters as may be necessary in arriving at an employment decision. I hereby release employers, schools or persons from all liability in responding to inquiries in connection with my application.

In the event of employment, I understand that false or misleading information given in my application or interview(s) may result in discharge. I understand, also, that I am required to abide by all rules and regulations of the Company.

Signature of applicant_____ Date _____

**JOB APPLICATION DISCLAIMER
AND ACKNOWLEDGEMENT**

I certify that the information contained in this application is correct to the best of my knowledge. I understand that to falsify information is grounds for refusing to hire me, or for discharge should I be hired.

I authorize any of the persons and organizations listed on this application to give you any and all information concerning my previous employment, education and qualifications for employment. I also authorize you to request and receive such information.

In consideration for my employment, I agree to conform to the rules and regulations of the company. I acknowledge that rules may be changed, withdrawn, added or interpreted at any time, at the company's sole option and without prior notice to me.

I also acknowledge that my employment may be terminated, or any offer or acceptance of employment withdrawn, at any time, with or without cause, and with or without prior notice at the option of the company or myself. I understand that no representative of the company has any authority to enter into any agreement for employment for any specified period of time or to promise any other personnel action, either before or after I accept employment, or to guarantee any benefits or terms or conditions of employment or to make any other agreement which is contrary to this agreement.

I have read and understand this agreement.

Signature _____ Date _____

APPLICATION UPDATE

Thank you for your continued interest in our company. Please complete the following information to reactivate your application for an additional thirty days. Update your application only for an available position for which you feel qualified. Should you indicate a position that is not available or for which you do not qualify, your application cannot be considered.

Full name _____

Social Security Number _____

Home Telephone Number _____

Date of Previous Application _____

Position applying for _____

Information to be added _____

_____

_____

_____

_____

_____

_____   _____

Signature   Date

TELEPHONE REFERENCE CHECKLIST

Name of applicant _____

Position applied for _____

Person contacted _____

Telephone # _____

Title _____   Company _____

Address _____

_____ has applied for a position with us.

Would you please verify the following information:

• Dates of employment: From _____ To _____

• What was the nature of his or her position?

_____
_____
_____

• Did he or she have any supervisory responsibilities?

_____
_____
_____

• How would you evaluate his or her work?

_____
_____
_____

• Did this person progress in the job?

_____
_____
_____

• What were his or her strong points?

_____
_____
_____

• Were there any limitations?

_____
_____
_____

• Would you please comment on his or her:

dependability _____
_____
_____

attendance _____
_____
_____

ability to accept responsibility _____
_____
_____

amount of supervision needed _____
_____
_____

ability to get along with others _____
_____
_____

potential for advancement _____
_____
_____

• Why did he or she leave your company?
_____
_____
_____

• Would you confirm a salary level of $ _____

                      Yes _____ No _____

• Would you re-employ this person?
_____

• Any other comments about this person
_____
_____
_____

Date: _____ Reference checker: _____

EMPLOYMENT REFERENCE RESPONSE FORM

Name of employee: _____

Dates of service: _____/_____ to _____/_____

Position at termination: _____

Reason for termination: _____

NOTE: This company has adopted a policy of supplying brief, standardized reports in response to all employment reference requests. This report is used for all employees. The lack of any further information should not be interpreted as either a favorable or unfavorable reference.

Submitted by: _____   Title: _____

Date: _____   Company: _____

Company Name
Address
City, State Zip

**AUTHORIZATION FOR RELEASE
OF PRIOR EMPLOYMENT INFORMATION**

I have made an application for employment with Acme Corporation. Information regarding my employment with your organization follows:

Dates From: _____ To: _____
Position: _____

I authorize you to furnish Acme Corporation with any information you may have concerning my employment with your organization. I release you from any liability for damages for this information.

_____   _____   _____
              Signature   Date   Social Security Number

===

Any information furnished relative to the application of the above individual will be treated with strictest confidence. An applicant will not be eliminated or selected on the basis of a single reference. Please complete the employment reference section on the reverse side of this letter. A self-addressed, stamped envelope is enclosed for your convenience.

Thank you.

ACME CORPORATION

1. Date of hire _____ Date of termination _____
   Beginning salary _____ Ending salary _____
   Beginning position _____
   Ending position _____

2. Reason for termination _____
   _____
   _____
   _____

3. Please rate the applicant in the following areas:

	Not Satis-factory	Below Average	Satis-factory	Above Average	Excellent
Accuracy	_____	_____	_____	_____	_____
Volume of work	_____	_____	_____	_____	_____
Attendance	_____	_____	_____	_____	_____
Punctuality	_____	_____	_____	_____	_____
Cooperation with supervisors	_____	_____	_____	_____	_____
Cooperation with co-workers	_____	_____	_____	_____	_____
Time taken to learn new jobs	_____	_____	_____	_____	_____
Willingness to assume greater responsibility	_____	_____	_____	_____	_____
Ability to work under pressure	_____	_____	_____	_____	_____
Overall evaluation of job performance	_____	_____	_____	_____	_____

4. Would you reemploy?_____ If not, please explain _____
_____
_____

Signature _____ Title _____ Date _____

Company Name
Address
City, State Zip

REQUEST FOR COLLEGE TRANSCRIPT

I am applying for employment with Acme Corporation. This letter authorizes you to release a copy of my transcript. My graduation date was:_____.

If a transcript is not available, please provide the following information:

Date of graduation:_____

Grade point average:_____

Rank in class:_____

Enclosed is a self-addressed envelope for your convenience. Thank you for your cooperation.

_____
Name on Transcript

_____
Signature

_____
Social Security Number

APPLICANT RATING FORM

CANDIDATE: _____

POSITION: _____

DEPARTMENT: _____

Please circle the appropriate rating.

Rating Scale:
    5: Exceptional   2: Less than fully qualified
    4: Better than average qualifications   1: Unacceptable
    3: Fully qualified   0: Not observed

Background	5	4	3	2	1	0
Attention to Detail	5	4	3	2	1	0
Cooperation	5	4	3	2	1	0
Impact	5	4	3	2	1	0
Initiative	5	4	3	2	1	0
Integrity	5	4	3	2	1	0
Interpersonal Skills	5	4	3	2	1	0
Learning Ability	5	4	3	2	1	0
Stress Tolerance	5	4	3	2	1	0
Verbal Communication	5	4	3	2	1	0

Overall Impression:
_____ Exceptional   _____ Strong   _____ Capable
_____ Weak   _____ Very Weak

Recommendations:
_____ Hire
_____ Reject
_____ Refer for _____ position

Signed:

_____   _____
          Interviewer   Date

Company Name
Address
City, State Zip

Date

Mr. Philip Combs
456 Baxter Ave.
Portland, OR 97221

Dear Mr. Combs:

This will confirm the job offer we made when you were in our office yesterday. We are pleased to offer you the position of Office Manager in our headquarters office. The salary will be $34,000 per year, payable semi-monthly. A pamphlet outlining our benefits package is enclosed.

In addition, we will pay your relocation expenses to our city except for any lease commitments you may now have on your apartment. This offer is subject to your passing our company physical examination.

We understand that you will let us know your decision no later than two weeks from this date and will be able to start work two weeks after that.

We look forward to having you join our organization and are confident that this will result in a mutually advantageous relationship.

Sincerely,

Andrew Johnson
Vice President, Administration

AJ:slc

Applicant Rejection Letter (2-12)

Company Name
Address
City, State Zip

Date

Mr. John Santos
815 Archer Place
Atlanta, GA 30901

Dear Mr. Santos:

It was not an easy decision for us but, after careful deliberation, we felt that another candidate for the Office Manager's position was closer to our job specifications.

This is in no way a reflection on the quality of your background or your character. All the people in our company who interviewed you were impressed. Your experience is certainly excellent.

We wish you the best of luck in your career. With the strengths you have, you are sure to be an asset to many companies. We sincerely regret it couldn't be with ours.

Sincerely,

Andrew Johnson
Vice President, Administration

AJ:slc

ORIENTATION CHECKLIST FOR NEW EMPLOYEES

_____ Names and duties of fellow department members.

_____ Completion of necessary forms for payroll, personnel records, insurance coverage, etc.

_____ The section, group or department's major responsibilities and how they relate to the organization as a whole.

_____ Working hours, shift assignments, breaks, holidays and overtime policies, parking.

_____ Location of lockers, rest rooms, cafeteria, elevators, exits, stairs, fire extinguishers.

_____ What to do in case of illness, absenteeism or lateness.

_____ Pay policies, including when paid, in cash, check or direct deposit.

_____ Details of job duties.

_____ Whom to see for information or help with problems.

_____ Dress code, safety requirements and responsibility for tools and supplies.

_____ Performance expected during probationary period.

CONFIDENTIALITY AGREEMENT

When you begin employment with this company you will have access to information that the company considers confidential. This includes proprietary information, trade secrets and intellectual property to which the company holds rights.

The purpose of this agreement is to remind you of this obligation and to put it into force. We also wish to remind you about the types of information of which you will be aware as a result of your employment with the company and of the fact that the company considers this information to be confidential. The types of information you must not disclose are:

[List types of information]

You may already have been advised of your obligations in this regard. This letter is intended to help you understand the nature of your obligation and that it is a continuing one. It is not intended to cast any doubt whatsoever on your integrity or reliability.
If you have any questions prior to signing this document, please contact [name].

Employee signature _____   Date _____

NEW HIRE PERSONNEL DATA SHEET

Employee Social Security Number _____

Name _____
| Last | First | Middle |

Address _____

City _____ State _____ Zip _____

Pay frequency _____ Pay code _____ Annual salary _____

Employment date _____ Employment code _____ Cost center _____

Sex ____ Marital status _____ Birth date _____ Home phone _____

Driver's license: State _____ No. _____ Exp. date _____

Spouse's Name _____
| Last | First | Middle |

Children

    Name _____ Sex _____ Birth date _____

    Name _____ Sex _____ Birth date _____

    Name _____ Sex _____ Birth date _____

Education

    High school _____ Number of Years _____ Degree (Yes/No) _____

    College _____ Number of Years _____ Degree (Yes/No) _____

    Post-graduate _____ Number of Years _____ Degree (Yes/No) _____

Emergency Notification

    Name _____ Relationship _____

    Telephone number _____

    Address _____

    City _____ State _____ Zip _____

MILITARY SERVICE: Branch_____ Rank_____ Discharge date _____

PERSONNEL FILE CHECKLIST

_____ Employment application

_____ Formal job offer letter and employee acknowledgement

_____ Social Security number

_____ Verification of citizenship or legal employment status including copy of Form I-9

_____ Federal, state and local tax withholding forms as applicable

_____ Insurance forms: health, group life, disability, other

_____ Reports of physical examinations

_____ Applicable security records, such as bonding and fingerprint card

_____ Record of performance evaluations

_____ Retirement plan application

_____ Receipt for benefit plan options and record of elections

_____ Termination agreement and record of exit interview

NEW EMPLOYEE ACKNOWLEDGEMENT FORM

I. ORIENTATION MATERIALS
New employee packet
Employee guide & benefit
book

II. FORMS AND SIGNATURES
I-9 Form
Payroll procedures &
forms
New hire data sheet
Life insurance beneficiary
card
Supervisors checklist
W-4 form

III. BENEFITS

IV. POLICIES
Equal Employment
Opportunity
Harassment
Training & Probation
Performance appraisals
Vacation/holidays
Sick pay
Leaves of absence
Attendance policy
Personal appearance
Drugs & alcohol
Conduct
Employee assistance
Disciplinary procedure
Career development

I hereby acknowledge that I have been informed of the above information. In addition, I have received my copy of the Employee Handbook which outlines my privileges and obligations as an employee. I will familiarize myself with the information contained in this Handbook.

The information in the Employee Handbook is subject to change as situations warrant. I understand policy changes may supercede, modify or eliminate the policies in this Handbook. Changes in policies will be communicated to me by my supervisor or through official notices on bulletin boards. I accept responsibility for keeping informed of these changes.

The Employee Handbook does not, and is not intended to create any express or implied contractual rights. I understand my employment can be terminated at will and at any time at the option of either the company or myself.

_____   _____
Signature of employee   Date

_____   _____
Human Resources Representative   Date

**PART TIME EMPLOYEE
LETTER OF UNDERSTANDING**

I,_____, accept employment with [company name] in the Part Time Program. I understand my employment is subject to the following:

This Letter of Understanding is not an employment contract. My employment is for an unspecified period and is at will. My employment may be terminated at any time either by myself or [company name] for any reason and the terms of this Letter of Understanding may be changed at any time by [company name].

I am employed to work as a_____at [location] according to the attached schedule.

I further understand that my rate of pay is based on this schedule and location and that my rate of pay is as follows:

I will work my designated schedule and will receive $____ per hour for those hours.

In the event I should work any time in excess of this schedule, this Letter of Understanding and my rate of pay will be subject to revision.

I understand that the above rate of pay is a fixed rate and is subject to change in the event my designated schedule is changed.

I understand that I will not be eligible for regular performance pay increases. I further understand that the hourly pay may be adjusted from time to time at the company's discretion.

Additionally, I understand that I am subject to all other applicable employment practices not specifically excluded herein.

As a part time employee, I am eligible to participate in the following employee programs:

Company sponsored employee activities
Service awards
Leave of absence policy, but without pay

Other employee benefits, as well as all categories of "paid time off," are not available to part time employees.

In the event I should move from a part time to a full-time or benefit-eligible hourly position, I understand that I will have to satisfy any applicable service requirements for benefits beginning with the date of transfer to benefits eligible-status.

I hereby acknowledge that I have read and understand the above provisions.

_____   _____
              Signature   Date

HOURLY EMPLOYEE INFORMATION SHEET

An hourly employee is defined as an employee whose regular work schedule is less than 40 hours per week and who is not designated as part-time.

As an hourly employee, your pay is based on the number of hours worked each week. The Payroll Department must have your time card to determine the number of hours worked and to calculate your pay. Please turn your time card in to your supervisor in a timely manner.

For Full Time Employees Going to an Hourly Status

The Payroll Department must now have your time card in order to determine your pay. A period of time, not necessary for full time employees, must be allowed for Payroll to receive and process the time cards for part-time and hourly employees. If you change from full time to hourly, that change may result in a transitional pay period where no pay is received or the amount paid is less than normal, due to some hours being paid in advance of your final full time pay period. Keep in mind that this may affect any automatic payments that may be deducted from your pay. Please contact the Payroll Department to determine how this will affect you.

Hourly Employee Benefits Information
For Employees Working 20 Hours Per Week or More

Hourly employees who are regularly scheduled to work 20 hours per week or more are eligible for most employee benefits and programs after completing the applicable service requirements.

Compensation for holidays and sick leave will be based on the hours you are normally scheduled to work on the day you are absent and will be determined by the supervisor. The computation of vacation and sick leave accruals will be based on the number of hours paid in each calendar quarter, excluding overtime. Accruals may vary from quarter to quarter depending on the actual number of hours paid. The rate of accrual is based on the percentage of the full time rate. If the number of hours paid falls below 260 in any calendar quarter, you are not entitled to sick and vacation accruals the following quarter.

Hourly employees working 20 hours per week or more are eligible for all employee benefits and programs except the following: administrative leave, shift differential, perfect attendance day and college reimbursements.

If your regular work schedule changes to less than 20 hours per week, please refer to the section below.

For Employees Working Less Than 20 Hours Per Week

Hourly employees who work less than 20 hours per week are not eligible for employee benefits, with the exception of the following after completing the required amount of continuous service: Retirement plan, profit sharing plan, employee stock purchase plan.

They are also eligible to participate in the following employee programs: Company sponsored employee activities, service awards, and leaves of absence without pay.

An employee moving from a position with a schedule of 20 hours per week or more to a position of less than 20 hours per week will be paid all of his or her accrued vacation, if he or she has completed one year or more of service. Any sick leave which has accrued will be dissolved.

REHIRE FORM

In order for us to keep our files as current as possible, please complete the following:

Personal Information:

Name _____   Home phone _____

Address _____

Social Security number _____   Work phone _____

Current employer _____

Previous Employment Information: Original hire date _____

Department _____   Return date _____

Position title _____   Position number _____

Salary _____   Review date _____

Emergency Information:

Name _____   Phone _____

Address _____

Relationship _____

To the best of my knowledge the above information is correct.

_____   _____
Signature   Date

Building a Job Description Program 3

What is a job description?

A job description is a concise statement of the duties, responsibilities, authorities, relationships and environment built into a job. The description outlines the requirements for performing the work, its frequency and scope. It is based on the nature of the work and *not* on the individual currently performing it.

Why are job description programs needed?

To manage effectively, managers must be able to identify the work that needs to be performed, then delegate it to others and control its progress and accomplishments. This requires definitions of the various tasks, duties, responsibilities and relationships of all members of the work group. In addition, the way any organization operates can be improved by using job descriptions for assigning responsibility, delegating authority and identifying individual or collective duties.

A number of symptoms usually lead management to point out the need for a job description program. They include:

- inadequate, inequitable or inconsistent pay practices
- complaints from employees that they don't know what work is required of them
- frequent conflicts and misunderstandings about who is supposed to do what
- overlapping responsibilities and authority which result in duplication of effort
- selection and hiring of people who are not qualified for their jobs
- inadequate or poor training which shows up in poor productivity and low quality
- delays in production of goods or services.

Good job descriptions help in compensating, selecting and hiring of personnel, design of jobs, performance appraisals and manpower planning.

What are the benefits of job descriptions?

Job descriptions are used to compare one job to another and to rank them. This kind of analysis allows managers to evaluate jobs for compensation purposes and wage and salary administration, and assures consistency in setting pay rates among individual workers and groups of employees.

Properly drawn job descriptions can help in the recruitment, selection and hiring of new workers, supervisors, managers and technical personnel because they spell out the exact qualifications, education, skills, and experience candidates need in order to be successful on the job. They help direct the questions interviewers will ask job applicants by focusing only on relevant facts. In addition, job descriptions help growing companies plan future manpower needs by comparing current requirements with those jobs and skills expected to be important in the future.

Training and development are also administered with the help of job descriptions. Qualifications of current job holders can be compared to the ideal ones described, and appropriate training given to fill the gaps.

In the same way, job descriptions help define performance standards. Measuring employee performance against objective standards should be the basis for periodic formal appraisals of their efforts.

Job descriptions can also be instrumental in planning or changing workflow patterns. Workflow design shows what should be done, the steps between input and output. Job descriptions can be used to help construct flow diagrams which, in turn, may uncover tasks needed to be done that have been overlooked in describing certain jobs.

What kind of information should be included in a job description?

Experts agree that the style, content and form for job descriptions should include:

- **Job title, organizational unit, accountability.** These items identify the job and give it its unique characteristics.
- **Job summary.** This defines work to be performed. Two job descriptions with the same title and same level of pay may have differing duties, responsibilities, accountabilities and relationships.
- **Duties and responsibilities.** This part of the job description describes the tasks to be performed.
- **Skill and educational requirements.** Describe the skills needed, educational requirements, special training and amount of experience needed.

- **Interrelationships.** This specifies the relationships between the job and other jobs in the organization and outside.
- **Working conditions.** Describe any dangerous or unusual conditions, whether travel is required and how much, and unusual hours.
- **Needed attributes.** The qualities, aptitude and temperament required for the job.
- **Prepared by, approved by, and date.** These are important when questions arise and for keeping the description up to date.

Examples are provided at the end of the chapter for a Job Description Format (3-01) as well as a typical Job Description (3-02).

What is the best way to gain employee cooperation when starting a job description program?

Top management must support the program and that support must be visible. Key executives must clearly communicate the need for a job description program and what they expect from managers and supervisors. The chief executive officer or other top executive should issue a policy statement to everyone who will be involved.

Such communication should include these key elements:

- the primary reasons for establishing the program
- the individual or group who will be responsible for its development
- the units of the company which are covered by the program
- procedure for reviewing various drafts of the job descriptions.

Other steps to obtain maximum cooperation can include:

- delegating to one executive the responsibility for communicating program details to operating managers
- starting with a pilot program in one unit of the company to spot and correct program deficiencies
- holding meetings with managers and supervisors to answer questions, uncover conflicts, clarify goals and evaluate suggestions from participants.

How does the description writer collect information for a job description?

The description writer gets information about a particular job through analysis. The writer looks at information related to the job, not to its holder, in four main areas:

1. Title, reporting responsibility, accountability, location.

2. Essential tasks, duties and responsibilities. What is being performed, *how* it is performed, and its *purpose*.

3. What skills, knowledge and individual abilities are required of the job holder to provide an acceptable level of performance.

4. The working conditions, especially if they are unusual. This takes into account the physical surroundings of a job, such as noise, dirt or hazards. It can also mean the social atmosphere, which indicates to what degree the worker is isolated from or involved with other people.

What are the techniques of job analysis?

Job analysts use one or more of four methods to obtain information about jobs:

1. Interviews. Using a checklist to guide discussions, the analyst discusses details of the work with one or more job incumbents. From his notes he compiles the job description, or works with a job description writer on this task. He does not need to interview all holders of a particular job — a representative sample is enough.

2. Job observation. The analyst takes notes while observing several incumbents as they perform their duties.

3. Job questionnaires. Job holders complete a comprehensive questionnaire and return it to the supervisor or analyst. When management decides not to involve employees in preparation of their own descriptions, the questionnaire is completed by the supervisor rather than by the employee.

4. Employee logs. Management asks employee to keep a log of tasks and activities over a specified period of time. It is less useful for supervisory and managerial positions, sales jobs, and for professional and creative types of work.

A Job Analysis Worksheet (3-03) that can be used by the job analyst is found at the end of the chapter.

How does the job analyst determine the interrelationships of the job?

The best way is to make an outline or organizational chart of the company, department or unit which shows the positions and relationships of the jobs he is analyzing. These diagrams or charts help the job analyst do his job. He will eventually incorporate the details in the job descriptions for each position.

How does the job analyst conduct job interviews?

The job analyst (or description writer) should start the interview by explaining the purpose of the interview, how it will be conducted and how the information will be used. The job holder should be encouraged to speak and given plenty of time to answer or to demonstrate a particular point.

Before completing the interview, the employee should be given a chance to ask questions or amplify any of his or her answers. Note-taking should be kept to a minimum during the interview since it may be distracting or even threatening to the interviewee. When the interview is over, the job analyst can then complete an interview checklist in greater detail. The Interview Form for Job Analysis (3-04), found at the end of the chapter, can be used as a guide to conducting job analysis interviews.

How are job analysis questionnaires prepared?

When preparing job questionnaires, the preparer should try to include information that is primarily concerned with the job and not with the person who is currently holding it. It is often difficult to separate the characteristics of the incumbents from their job specifications.

The job questionnaire should come with clear instructions on how it should be filled out, and include an explanation of its purpose and what will be done with the data. The manager responsible for distributing the questionnaire should go over the instructions with employees and answer any questions.

An Employee Job Analysis Questionnaire (3-05) is found at the end of the chapter.

What guides do writers of job descriptions need?

The person who administers the job description program should try for uniformity of style even though a number of different individuals may be involved in preparing descriptions. To assure uniformity, he or she should prepare guides for the three major job levels. Guides for preparing job descriptions for hourly workers (3-06), supervisors (3-07) and managers (3-08) are located at the end of the chapter. In addition, a Job Requirements Glossary (3-09) is also shown.

JOB DESCRIPTION FORMAT

JOB TITLE

ORGANIZATIONAL UNIT
Division, department, location, section, etc.

ACCOUNTABILITY
Title of person to which this job reports.

JOB SUMMARY
A short statement outlining the purpose of this job; its supervisory, technical or administrative scope.

DUTIES AND RESPONSIBILITIES
Statements outlining particular duties, tasks, or responsibilities. They should identify the most predominant and significant duties.

SKILL AND EDUCATIONAL REQUIREMENTS
A description of the skills required, educational background, training and amount of experience.

INTER-RELATIONSHIPS
A statement describing the relationships of the job with internal and external groups.

WORKING CONDITIONS
A description of any unusual conditions, if travel is required, unusual hours, etc.

NEEDED ATTRIBUTES
Describe personal qualities, interests, aptitudes and temperament that the applicant should have.

Prepared by: _____

Approved by: _____ Date: _____

JOB DESCRIPTION FOR ADMINISTRATIVE ASSISTANT

JOB TITLE: Administrative Assistant

DEPARTMENT: Marketing

ACCOUNTABILITY: Reports to Marketing Manager

JOB SUMMARY
Performs wide variety of duties, some of a confidential nature, including administrative and clerical functions.

DUTIES AND RESPONSIBILITIES
Specific duties include:
- Taking and transcribing dictation.
- Scheduling appointments.
- Greeting visitors and screening telephone calls.
- Preparing reports, maintaining confidence when required.
- Observing and implementing established policies and procedures.
- Word processing and preparing spreadsheet data.

SKILLS AND EDUCATIONAL REQUIREMENTS
Ability to communicate effectively both verbally and in writing. Thorough knowledge of IBM PC, including WordPerfect and Excel software. Typing speed of 60 words per minute and dictation at 100 words per minute. Graduate of secretarial school or junior college with a minimum of two years of experience in secretarial or administrative position.

INTER-RELATIONSHIPS
Contact with all levels of personnel within company and with clients and vendors.

WORKING CONDITIONS
Overtime required occasionally, plus travel to conventions and client meetings throughout the country.

NEEDED ATTRIBUTES
Aptitudes: Verbal ability, ability to make simple calculations, ability to organize.
Temperament: Ability to perform a variety of tasks, often changing assignments on short notice.
Interests: Public contact, communication of plans and ideas.

Prepared by: _____

Approved by: _____ Date: _____

JOB ANALYSIS WORKSHEET

1. Job Identification
   (a) Name of organizational unit _____
   (b) Current title of job _____
   (c) Location _____
   (d) Reporting relationship _____

2. Work performed
   (a) Specific, frequently performed tasks _____
   _____

   (b) Responsibilities _____
   _____
   _____

   (c) Supervisory scope _____
   _____

   (d) Interaction _____
   _____

   (e) Who gives direction _____
   _____

   (f) Which tasks are supervised _____
   _____

   (g) Which tasks are not supervised _____
   _____

   (h) How is quality checked _____
   _____

3. Physical conditions
   (a) Conditions surrounding the work area _____
   _____

   (b) What are hours worked _____

   (c) Rest periods _____
   _____

   (d) Environmental conditions _____
   _____

4. Skills required
   (a) Mental _____
   _____

   (b) Manual _____
   _____

   (c) Interpersonal _____
   _____

5. Knowledge required
   (a) How are skills acquired (school, special courses, experience, training)
   _____
   _____
   _____
   _____

6. Special requirements (describe)
   (a) Travel _____
   (b) Isolation _____
   (c) Night work _____
   (d) Long hours _____
   (e) Other _____

7. Accountability (describe)
   (a) For equipment _____
   (b) Profit margins _____
   (c) Expenditure _____
   (d) Information _____
   (e) Outside relations _____
   (f) Other _____

INTERVIEW FORM FOR JOB ANALYSIS

A. 1. Interviewer _____
    2. Date _____
    3. Person interviewed _____

B. 1. Present job title _____
    2. Suggested job title _____
    3. Immediate superior _____
    4. Job title of immediate superior _____
    5. Department _____
    6. Job location _____
    7. Number of employees on this job _____

C. 1. Describe the most important duties that the employee or employees on this job perform daily. If important duties are performed at less frequent intervals, describe and give the frequency of performance.

     _____
     _____
     _____
     _____
     _____

    2. Describe the secondary duties that an employee on this job performs at periodic intervals, such as weekly, monthly, quarterly, etc., and state the frequency of performance.

     _____
     _____
     _____
     _____
     _____

D. 1. Describe equipment for office machine operations.

     _____
     _____

    2. Describe factory or shop machines and equipment.

     _____
     _____

E. 1. Describe the working conditions.

     _____
     _____

F. 1. Describe the formal education or its equivalent considered to be the minimum required for satisfactory performance of this job.

_____

_____

_____

2. Specify the prior special training or education necessary before an employee is assigned to this job or training necessary immediately after assignment.

_____

_____

_____

3. Describe any job experience required and indicate the number of weeks, months, or years needed to obtain such experience and state whether in this organization or elsewhere.

_____

_____

_____

G. 1. Describe the proximity, extent and closeness of supervision received by an employee on this job. To what degree does the immediate supervisor outline methods to be followed, results to be accomplished, check work progress, handle exceptional cases, check job performance?

_____

_____

_____

2. Describe the kind of supervision the employee or employees on this job give to other employees. What is the degree of accountability for results in terms of methods, work accomplished, and personnel?

_____

_____

_____

3. How many employees are supervised directly? _____

Indirectly? _____

H. 1. Responsibility for accuracy and seriousness of error. What is the seriousness of error on this job? Do errors affect the work of employee making mistake, others in the same department, other departments, persons outside the organization?

_____

_____

_____

I. 1. Responsibility for confidential data. State the type of confidential data handled, whether personnel, salaries, policy, business secrets, etc.

_____

_____

_____

J. 1. Responsibility for money or things of monetary value. State the type of responsibility and the approximate amount of money employee must safeguard.

_____

_____

_____

K. 1. Describe the kind of personal contacts made by employee as he/she performs job. Is contact with persons in the department, in other departments, outside the organization? Importance of contacts to organization should be described.

_____

_____

_____

L. 1. Describe the complexity of the job. What is the degree of independent action permitted the employee? What decisions is employee permitted to make?

_____

_____

_____

M. 1. Describe the type and amount of dexterity or motor skill required in the performance of the job. Indicate job duties where dexterity is required.

_____

_____

_____

N. 1. Describe the degree of repetitive detail required of the employee. Determine the possibility for the experience of boredom on the job.

_____

_____

_____

O. 1. List any unusual physical requirements of this job: vision, strength, etc.

_____

_____

_____

EMPLOYEE JOB ANALYSIS QUESTIONNAIRE

EMPLOYEE NAME _____

DATE _____

POSITION TITLE _____

DEPARTMENT _____

SUPERVISOR _____

EXPLANATION

Job Analysis is the process of determining and reporting pertinent information relating to the nature of a specific job. It is the determination of tasks which comprise the job, together with skills, knowledge, responsibilities, etc. required for successful performance and which differentiate the job from all others. The data will be used to prepare a job description. Please ask your supervisor or the job analyst for an explanation of the uses of job descriptions and for clarification of any questions you may have.

PROCEDURE

EMPLOYEE: Complete entries above and Section I. Describe in detail the most important duties that you perform. List the job duties in clear, concise sentences. Indicate the frequency (day, week, month) and amount of time spent performing these job duties. Be certain that you provide sufficient information about each duty to enable persons unfamiliar with your work to understand what the duty entails. Questions should be directed to your supervisor.

SUPERVISOR: Complete Section II.

SECTION I

1. Duty (what) _____
   Procedure (how) _____
   _____
   Reason for duty (why) _____
   _____
   Frequency_____and Percentage_____estimate of time spent performing duty.

2. Duty (what) _____
   Procedure (how) _____
   _____
   Reason for duty (why) _____
   _____
   Frequency_____and Percentage_____estimate of time spent performing duty.

3. Duty (what) _____
   Procedure (how) _____
   _____
   Reason for duty (why) _____
   _____
   Frequency_____and Percentage_____estimate of time spent performing duty.

4. Duty (what) _____
   Procedure (how) _____
   _____
   Reason for duty (why) _____
   _____
   Frequency_____and Percentage_____estimate of time spent performing duty.

5. Duty (what) _____
   Procedure (how) _____
   _____
   Reason for duty (why) _____
   _____
   Frequency_____and Percentage_____estimate of time spent performing duty.

6. Duty (what) _____
   Procedure (how) _____
   _____
   Reason for duty (why) _____
   _____
   Frequency_____and Percentage_____estimate of time spent performing duty.

What machines/equipment are you required to use on your job? How much time per day or week is spent using each machine/equipment listed?

Machine/Equipment | Time in Use (Specify daily or weekly)

_____ | _____
_____ | _____
_____ | _____
_____ | _____

What do you consider the most important task(s) you perform?

_____
_____
_____
_____

Describe the working conditions which may cause a feeling of pressure or discomfort. Consider environment, distractions and interference which might make completion of task(s) difficult:

_____
_____
_____
_____

Describe the personal contacts you are required to make to perform the job.

Who (Title?) _____   Reason _____

Who (Title?) _____   Reason _____

Who (Title?) _____   Reason _____

Signature   _____
                          Employee

SECTION II

Employee section reviewed and approved by _____
Immediate Supervisor

Comments: _____
_____
_____
_____
_____
_____
_____
_____
_____

Errors which may occur in performance of this job are:
(Check one)

_____ easily detected in normal routine of checking results.
Give example: _____
_____

_____ not detected until they have caused other departments considerable
inconvenience.
Give example: _____
_____

_____ not detected until they have caused considerable inconvenience to a
customer.
Give example: _____
_____

Describe responsibility of the occupant of this position for work of other employees.
(Check one)

_____ No responsibility for work of others. May show other employees how to
perform a task or assist in indoctrination of new employees.

_____ Guides and instructs other employees, assigning, checking, and maintaining
the flow of work.

PREPARATION GUIDE FOR HOURLY WORKER JOB DESCRIPTIONS

PURPOSE (Job summary)

The first item in this section is the line authority involved. This should then be followed by a two or three sentence summary of the basic responsibilities or purpose of the job. This section should read as follows: "Under the direction (or supervision) of _____ (the position exercising direct authority), is responsible for (two or three sentence summary)." Further elaboration should appear in the Responsibilities section.

RESPONSIBILITIES (Duties)

Duties should be listed in their approximate order of importance. In preparing the Responsibilities, observe the following techniques:

1. Use brief and to-the-point statements.

2. Begin each sentence with an action verb.

3. Use the present tense.

4. Avoid verbs which do not specifically indicate the action involved. "Handles mail" is better expressed as "sorts mail" or "distributes mail."

5. Describe those duties which differentiate this job from other similar jobs.

6. Do not attempt to set down every detail of the job. Give only as much information as is necessary to define clearly what levels of skills, responsibility and knowledge are required.

7. Include examples of any unusual duties, which occur only at certain intervals— monthly, quarterly, etc.—or as the occasion arises.

To be sure that the description accurately reflects the duties and responsibilities of the position, ask yourself these questions:

1. What is the general purpose of the job?

2. What are usual day-to-day duties performed (those of a recurring nature)?

3. What are other duties that occur at irregular intervals but that are of a recurring nature?

4. Will examples of non-recurring duties clarify the description?

5. From whom (state title) is supervision received on a particular duty, if other than the employee's immediate supervisor?

6. What are the titles of individuals who normally would receive supervision from the person who holds this job?

7. To what extent do employees in this job plan their own activities?

8. What responsibility will there be for company funds involved in any of the duties?

9. What office machines or equipment are operated in the performance of these duties?

10. What records are maintained by persons in this job and what action is taken in record-keeping?

11. What are the usual contacts made in this job? a.) Within the company? b.) Outside the company?

PREPARATION GUIDE FOR SUPERVISORY DESCRIPTION

Content of Description

SECTION I: PURPOSE OF JOB

Summarizes all of the duties listed under Section III. One or two sentences will usually explain the overall function of the job.

Example:
Determine on a continuing basis the manpower requirements to accomplish the expected workload by the use of published manpower standards. Plan, coordinate and regulate the development of personnel for the most effective and economical accomplishment of all phases of work within the service department.

SECTION II: PRINCIPAL FUNCTIONS OF JOB

List here, in order of importance, the major functions of the job.

SECTION III: DUTIES OF JOB

List in the order shown in Section II details of each function. Tell not only what is done but also how and why. Give an estimate of the time needed to perform each duty.

SECTION IV: REQUIREMENTS OF JOB

List the appropriate items from the Job Requirements Glossary.

SECTION V: WORKING CONDITIONS

List any unusual conditions such as noise, exposure to elements, hazardous working situations or travel.

PREPARATION GUIDE FOR MANAGEMENT JOB DESCRIPTIONS

Content of Description

SECTION I: BASIC FUNCTION

Summarize in three or four sentences the functions for which the position has been delegated responsibility and authority. State the overall objective of the position, what the position does, the reason for doing it and its intended result.

SECTION II: RESPONSIBILITIES

Outline in this section those duties which are performed personally by the individual holding the position. Duties which are supervised rather than personally performed are to be outlined under "Delegated Responsibilities."

A. Planning and policy responsibilities
   Planning: To devise and project a course of action.
   Policy: Broad objectives serving to direct the course of action toward the attainment of the company's goals. Policies should describe what the intended goal is.

B. Procedural responsibilities
   The manner or methods of proceeding in the direction outlined by policy. They provide the detailed "how" by which policy is carried out.

C. Other responsibilities
   List all other important functions which the person currently holding the position performs. These statements should begin with an "action" verb which denotes the type of responsibility or authority exercised. Each duty can usually be made complete by answering WHAT? HOW? WHO? and WHEN? and occasionally WHERE? and WHY?

D. Scope of responsibilities
   Indicate the area directly affected by the decisions required in this position, whether corporate, regional or local. One position may develop a policy which affects only a few employees, whereas another may develop a policy which affects all employees in the company.

SECTION III: DELEGATED RESPONSIBILITIES

This section lists the jobs that the person in the position directly supervises, and the "Basic Functions" for each of these jobs. Included are direct subordinates only (excluding clerical), and not areas of the organization over which the position exercises staff or functional supervision.

SECTION IV: SUPERVISION OF OTHERS

A. Administrative

This section should reveal the total number of employees reporting to the position for administrative as opposed to functional work direction. List the titles of all direct subordinates and indicate by classification the number of subordinate employees for whom each of the direct subordinates is responsible. Do not list an employee more than once.

B. Functional (Staff)

Some staff as well as line positions monitor or functionally supervise operations which report administratively to others. This includes monitoring policy and procedure performance by line personnel, providing advice and counsel to line personnel, etc. Describe briefly any assigned responsibilities which require the exercise of staff supervision including the type and approximate number of personnel who receive this supervision from the position being described.

SECTION V: INSIDE AND OUTSIDE RELATIONSHIPS

Describe internal and external contacts which are required by the assigned responsibilities of the position.

Include other positions in the department, those in other departments, in other locations and in other divisions. Outside the company, include vendors, clients, trade associations, etc.

SECTION VI: TRAVELING

Indicate if traveling is domestic or international and the number of days of each.

SECTION VII: SPECIAL QUALIFICATIONS

In describing any special qualifications such as formal training, kind of experience or particular abilities, give brief examples of why certain requirements are necessary. For example, if the job requires a degree in mathematics, briefly describe the need for such training.

JOB REQUIREMENTS GLOSSARY

Adaptability: Ability to perform a variety of tasks, often changing assignments on short notice.

Administration: Keeps other members of the organization informed of progress and problems. Monitors the progress and coordination of delegated assignments.

Analysis: Finds and uses relationships between data from different sources. Identifies research questions.

Attention to Detail: Accomplishes a task thoroughly with concern for all aspects, no matter how small.

Communication, Verbal: Expresses self clearly and effectively when talking with individuals and groups.

Communication, Written: Expresses ideas clearly in writing. Uses proper organization and grammar.

Control: Establishes techniques to effectively monitor and supervise the work of subordinates and the results of delegated assignments.

Cooperation: Works well with other people. Takes time to help co-workers, customers and others achieve their goals and assignments.

Decision-Making: Identifies problems, gathers data, develops and assesses alternative courses of actions. Makes timely decisions based on logical assumptions, using all available information.

Delegation: Assigns decision-making and other responsibilities to subordinates. Uses subordinates effectively.

Diagnostic Ability: Identifies likely causes of equipment problems through inspections, tests and observations.

Energy: Maintains a high level of activity.

Flexibility: Willing to modify plans and behavior when necessary to meet a goal.

Impact: Commands attention and respect. Shows an air of confidence.

Independence: Takes actions based on personal convictions. Does not rely solely on the opinions of others.

Information Retrieval: Develops a system that provides access to specific information. Shows ability to retrieve and deliver information.

Initiative: Actively tries to influence events to achieve goals. A self-starter, working well without close supervision. Tries to achieve goals beyond minimal levels of performance.

Integrity: Maintains the normal standards of ethics, conduct and organizational policies in job-related activities.

Interpersonal Relations: Maintains effective relationships with others. Uses tact. Is sensitive to feelings and needs of others.

Leadership: Guides subordinates in reaching goals. Uses appropriate methods and interpersonal styles.

Learning Ability: Has the ability and desire to quickly learn new job-related information.

Motivation: Activities on the job match personal interests and goals. Takes personal satisfaction in performance and accomplishments.

Organization: Can establish priorities and a course of action for handling multiple tasks.

Organizational Cooperation: Is familiar with the organization. Stays abreast of changing situations to identify problems and opportunities. Understands how activities and decisions will affect other parts of the organization.

Persuasiveness: Uses appropriate methods and styles of communication to gain acceptance of an idea, plan, activity or product.

Planning: Establishes courses of action for self or for others. Allocates resources and assigns personnel. Uses time efficiently. Is personally well-organized.

Presentation: Effectively prepares formal presentations of ideas and proposals. Effectively expresses self to groups and individuals.

Professionalism: Displays professional appearance and conduct. Makes a good impression on others.

Resilience: Maintains effectiveness in the face of disappointment or rejection.

Safety: Observes prescribed safety standards. Helps maintain safe conditions for self and others.

Stress Tolerance: Maintains stability under pressure or opposition.

Subordinate Development: Uses available training and development resources to improve subordinates' skills and abilities. Helps subordinates qualify for future job opportunities.

Technical Ability: Able to do necessary maintenance service on specified electrical, mechanical and other equipment.

Verbal Fact-Finding: Able to get information through verbal contacts with others.

Work Standards: Sets high personal standards of performance. Not satisfied with average performance.

Developing Successful Training Programs 4

What is "needs analysis?"

Needs analysis is a search for solutions to performance problems. Needs analysis not only identifies areas where training is needed in a company, but also helps determine exactly how training should be applied. For example, if employees feel that a computerized office system is going to eliminate their jobs, a training effort that just teaches them how to use new equipment is not going to succeed. Training must also be targeted at their concerns. They must be trained to understand and accept the new technology.

Needs analysis sets training priorities. It determines not only which problems are most pressing, but which can be most economically solved through training.

Where should needs analysis begin?

Experts agree that every successful needs analysis begins with an investigation of "optimals" and "actuals."

Optimals are the desired performance, what you and your managers determine is the right way to do the job. Actuals are what is happening now, how employees are actually performing.

Information about these factors forms the foundation of your needs analysis. It is impossible to set goals for training if you don't have a clear idea of the best, or optimal, performance you're aiming at. Understanding what employees already know and how they currently do their jobs is the key to devising ways to help them improve.

What are the most frequent causes of poor performance?

Usually they involve one or more of these factors:

1. Lack of skills. Either employees never knew how to do their jobs properly, or they forgot. If a former typist is not as productive after switching to a word processor, the problem could be that the person does not know how to use the new

system effectively. Fortunately, this is usually the type of problem most readily solved through training.

2. Environmental obstacles. Sometimes needs analysis will show that lack of skills is not the problem. Instead, it is poor workflow design, poor systems, poor plant or machine layout that undermines productivity.

3. Incentives. Needs analysis might reveal — by interviewing both workers and supervisors — problems that call for systematic changes, not training. For example, employees are not properly rewarded, or sloppy performers are not disciplined.

4. Motivation. Incentives are external factors affecting behavior. Motivation is internal. Therefore, needs analysis focuses on how employees feel about their jobs, their values, their confidence levels — information that helps devise training solutions.

What tools are used to conduct a needs analysis?

You can use one or more of the following tools:

- Existing data. Examine records of how well standards are being met in many areas, from performance appraisals to product quality to number of complaints.

- Interviews. Call supervisors on an informal basis and ask them what problems they're having. Speak in person to employees, customers, managers.

- Focus groups. Get together a small group of workers, supervisors, engineers, quality control people, for example, and have them share in a directed discussion of the area under study. Ask probing questions, then listen carefully while the participants discuss the matter. Note what problems and concerns come up, areas of agreement and disagreement, communication failures, conflicts, and feelings.

- Experts. Confer with engineers, designers and quality control experts, both within and outside the company, when attempting to pin down the optimals of performance.

- Best performers. Find out from your best workers how and why they are doing the job correctly. If they are more highly motivated or have found a way to streamline certain tasks, look for ways others can adopt the same methods.

- Surveys. Use surveys late in the research to pinpoint the focus you're getting from earlier research.

How can survey effectiveness be increased?

Here are some tips for increasing the effectiveness of surveys:

- Use forced-choice rather than open-ended questions for most items. That is, ask, "Which of these is the most common problem when interviewing clients: (a) a noisy office that makes it hard to hear; (b) customer rudeness; (c) not enough time." Don't ask, "What's your opinion of the interviewing process?" Base forced-choice questions on previous data (you have already determined from interviews, for example, the three reasons mentioned most frequently as causing interviewing problems).
- Don't begin by asking about solutions. For example, don't ask, "Would training help you do your job better?"
- As you narrow the focus, repeat questions, asking for the same information in different ways.
- Remember that because training is an interpersonal activity, feelings are important.
- Never start by questioning respondents about current skills. They will not cooperate if they feel the survey is a test.
- Have a reason for every question you ask. Know what you're looking for.
- Base questions on what you've already learned through interviews, talks with experts, examination of data.
- Survey the right number of people. Large samples are more costly and time-consuming to poll, but the resulting data is more reliable. Small surveys are easier, quicker and cheaper, but may not give you all the information you need.

What results can be expected from needs analysis?

Needs analysis should accomplish the following:

- Identify a specific training need.
- Outline optimals — the desired performance.
- Define actuals — the current state of employees' aptitudes.
- Discover employees' feelings about training.

- Elicit useful information from the best performing employees about their training needs.

What really drives the development of new training programs?

Corporate strategy dictates what employees need to know. Focus training programs only on those objectives which have direct application to corporate direction. Changes, strategies and growth usually lead to altered training needs. To keep them all tied together, keep up-to-date a Strategic Training Worksheet (4-01) similar to the one shown at the end of the chapter.

What pitfalls should be avoided when designing training systems?

Training efforts should always be shaped by needs analysis and corporate strategies. Follow these guidelines to avoid the most common training pitfalls:

1. Don't use training as a screening device. Training should challenge your employees, but not be a hurdle. The goal is for all trainees to succeed.
2. Don't try to cover large areas at once. People learn best when information is presented in small bits.
3. Don't confuse training with education. The purpose of training is strictly to produce a measurable improvement in productivity. Encourage your employees to continue their education — at their own expense and on their own time.
4. Provide short-term rewards. These can be monetary or simply the praise and encouragement of managers or trainers.
5. Set training priorities. Don't limit training to areas where the solutions are most obvious. Look at problems where the biggest gap between desired and actual performance exists — for the behavior that is the most common or most costly in terms of lost productivity — and seek solutions there. You cannot set up training systems to address all performance problems. Choose those that will be the most cost-effective.
6. Don't expect immediate results. While short-term training needs sometimes do arise, the training efforts of some companies consist of nothing but "quick fixes." Too often, this amounts to aimlessly throwing money at a problem, money that is usually wasted. Thorough needs analysis and systematic training design are the only cost-effective approaches to solving these problems.

Use the Training Design Checklist (4-02) shown later in the chapter to insure a systematic approach to designing your company's training programs.

Who should be responsible for administering training?

Responsibility for administering training should always be with line managers and supervisors. Training only works when the new skills are applied on the job. No training department can assure that this transfer will take place. The supervisor or manager has to be involved in the training process from beginning to end.

The staff training department's role is to support the line management's efforts. Some large companies rotate line supervisors into the training department on a temporary basis to carry out the training, but they still make line management responsible.

How can workers resistant to change be quickly retrained to handle new work methods?

A division of Goodyear Tire & Rubber Co. used the following retraining method when converting a bias tire plant to radial tires. Experienced workers were drawn from the ranks and made Program Development Instructors (PDIs). They were taught by corporate training staff how to write training programs and given a thorough view of the new tire-making operations at other Goodyear plants.

Course development and the actual instruction were reviewed by PDIs from other plants who monitored quality to check the outcome of the training. Continuous discussion and meetings were held with the PDIs to discuss experience and improvements. Once the changeover was complete, the PDIs went back to their regular jobs.

What are the most common training methods?

Although training needs will differ from company to company, the techniques used to carry out training are usually similar. Some of the most often-used techniques today include:

- On-the-job training
- Classroom instruction
- "Train the trainer" programs
- Video and computer-based training
- Skills practice techniques such as role-playing, modeling, and self-study

How can a company determine the best training techniques for its needs?

That depends on the training job. No one technique is ideal for all situations. Before deciding the best training technique, carefully weigh the following factors:

- Whom are you teaching? Sophisticated managers or new hires?

- What are you teaching? Specific skills? General skills like communication? Concepts like ethics?
- Where are trainees located? In a central location or scattered?
- How much time do you have?
- How many trainers do you have and how much can you spend?
- How motivated are your trainees? Can they train themselves on their own time? Or do they need a lot of disciplined instruction?

What are the advantages and disadvantages of on-the-job training?

On-the-job training (OJT) is the simplest and most basic form of training. You sit the employee down at the machine, show him how to run it, check up on him frequently at first, less often later. He receives direct experience and produces while he learns.

But OJT has costs. Supervisors have to spend time overseeing the training. The more trainees, the more time it takes as the supervisor goes from one to the other. Also, supervisors may not be especially skillful at delivering training.

A second cost is that of equipment. Trainees will never produce at the same rate as a trained worker, but will tie up the use of actual production machinery or facilities while being trained, and may inadvertently damage expensive equipment.

The great benefit of OJT is that it allows the trainees to experience the actual job conditions. A bank teller may learn certain skills in the classroom, but will have no experience in handling the pressure and conflicting demands of operating during a Friday afternoon rush in the bank.

When should OJT be used?

Use on-the-job training when:

- The number of trainees is small
- Training is best conducted under real work conditions
- You need to use the actual equipment in production
- You have good supervisors for training and they have the time
- Other employees can be used to teach their skills to others.

When should OJT be avoided?

Avoid on-the-job training when:

- You must train large numbers of employees quickly
- You can't risk errors by untrained employees
- The skills need not be learned under working conditions
- You can't take supervisors off the job to do training.

When should classroom training be used?

Classroom training should be used when you need more balance in the information you want to get across. With OJT, the trainee might get one or two things repeated over and over but miss the chance to really learn other important facets of the job.

In classrooms, the trainer can focus more strongly on the specific skills that trainees need to acquire. He or she has more control and can train a number of individuals at one time.

What methods are used in classroom training?

Classrooms offer wide choices of methods:

- Lectures — good for conveying a lot of information to a large group. Lacks employee participation.
- Case studies — prompts discussion from the trainees, especially when the case poses common, on-the-job problems.
- Lecture-discussion — actively draws trainees into discussing the material presented.
- Demonstration — the trainer illustrates what he or she is talking about through his or her own actions.
- Role playing — trainers take parts and demonstrate by playing their assigned roles. Trainees can also role play for practice.
- Panel discussions — managers or supervisors are brought in to discuss various aspects of the material being offered.
- Videos — when professionally done, videos or movies provide well-planned, consistent and interesting presentations.

Who should conduct classroom training?

While it is true that professional training personnel, either in-house or outside, are most skilled at presenting information, it is often more cost-effective to develop line personnel as trainers. When you train your own trainers, you help them develop new skills, and eliminate the need to explain highly complex or technical material to people not familiar with the company.

What qualities should be looked for in potential trainers?

The checklist below gives many of the qualities you should seek in trainers:

_____ ability to communicate effectively

_____ thorough knowledge of the subject matter

_____ enthusiasm

_____ experienced on the job and with the company

_____ adaptable, open-minded

_____ patient

_____ articulate

_____ works well with others

_____ careful and quality conscious

_____ good team spirit

_____ sense of humor

_____ ready and willing to involve others

What fundamentals should new trainers learn?

Focus on these four factors in any train-the-trainer program:

1. Task analysis. The new trainer has to be able to break down a task into parts that can be easily conveyed in the classroom or other training situation.
2. Lesson plan preparation. The trainer learns to present material in logical progression, to cover the right amount of material, to review key points.
3. Presentation skills. Videotaped presentations are played back for the participants so that they can learn from their mistakes. They also receive valuable feedback from the others in the train-the-trainer program.
4. Audio-visuals. These are an important aspect of effective training. The new trainers learn the fundamentals of creating good learning aids.

When should videotapes be used as training tools?

The subject matter dictates the usefulness of video. A course on memo writing, for example, does not demand a video to support print materials. One on interviewing techniques, though, would be enhanced by showing a video of a mock interview followed by a discussion. Videos are appropriate for smaller groups, or for self-study viewing by individual trainees.

Try not to rely on the videos alone. You'll get better results if you combine the tape with a workbook or text, or incorporate both into classroom instruction.

What are the uses of computer-based training?

Computer-based training (CBT) falls into three general categories:

1) Computer skills training. This includes tutorials and drills that teach the user how to operate the computer and to make the most use of applications software.

2) Management skills training. These programs provide practice in "soft" skills such as problem-solving and sales.
3) Simulations. These programs recreate an environment. A medical diagnosis simulator can reproduce a body of information, react to the trainee's queries and grade his response.

When is computer-based training the proper training tool?

Here is a checklist to help you decide whether computer-based training would be a feasible and useful part of your training efforts. Use CBT when:

_____ You need to deliver standardized content to a large group of trainees.

_____ Employees can complete drills on previously learned material.

_____ Trainees are prepared to absorb computer training, i.e., they have the necessary keyboard skills.

_____ You want to teach computer-related skills, such as statistical quality control systems, or computerized inventory management.

_____ Trainees need to work at their own pace.

_____ Trainees need frequent refresher sessions.

_____ You need to meet unscheduled training demands, such as when an individual manager is promoted and needs to acquire certain skills immediately.

What should be considered when buying training services?

Many products and services offered by outside trainers could supplement your training. In some instances, they could provide the core of certain programs.

You must, however, use care in buying from outside vendors. Cost and hidden charges are factors. So is the quality of the training to be provided.

A vital factor is how well the particular training services fit the needs you've identified to meet your corporate goals and strategies.

Use the Training Vendor Evaluation Sheet (4-03) at the end of the chapter to insure that you buy only those products and services which fit your needs. This worksheet can also be used to evaluate the training services after they are given.

How are training skills best transferred to the job?

Assuring that employees use the skills they acquire during training when they return to the job is the essence of training. The goal of training is performance improvement. If trained employees show no measurable improvement in their performance, your training effort and spending have been wasted. Therefore, transfer is not only essential to training success, it must be an integral part of the training process.

The immediate supervisor of the employee receiving the training is the key element in the successful transfer of the skills learned to the job.

Supervisors assure transfers in four ways:

1. By providing a model for the trained skill. Training gives employees the techniques; following the supervisor's example shows them how to apply the techniques.

2. By on-the-job coaching. The supervisors discuss how the skills are used and can demonstrate them again, if necessary.

3. By positive reinforcement. Supervisors must actively encourage and praise the newly trained person as he or she practices the skill.

4. By removing obstacles in the workplace. The supervisor makes sure the employee has the proper tools to get the job done.

How can trainees be encouraged to transfer their new skills to the job?

Give the trainee job aids. These are any materials that help a person perform better. An operational manual for a machine is a job aid. So is a checklist of things to do in a certain order. Others include templates, instruction labels on a machine, diagrams, tables, flowcharts, maps, etc. The key to designing effective job aids is to keep them as simple as possible.

You can also provide trainees with action plans to get them thinking about applications while the new skills and knowledge are fresh in their minds. The Trainee Evaluation Form (4-04) located at the end of the chapter illustrates a trainee action plan form that can be adapted for your own use.

How is training evaluated?

Companies can use these measures to evaluate their training:

1. Members of a training staff take a cross-section view of training by auditing courses, facilities, costs, skills transfer, etc. The audit is meant to aid trainers, not to criticize their efforts.

2. Managers and supervisors are surveyed to find out if they are satisfied with training results.

3. Focus groups of supervisors and trainees are formed to discuss the results, problems and techniques of the training effort.

4. Trainees are asked to complete questionnaires on the training.
5. In-depth analyses of specific courses are performed to discover the long-term results.

What items should an evaluation questionnaire include?

It should include a rating of the instructor on:

- Presentation techniques
- Technical knowledge
- Preparedness
- Encouragement of trainee participation
- Pace of the instruction
- Time allowance for questions

The questionnaire should also ask the trainees to rate themselves on how confident they feel about their new skills and how well they think they will be able to apply the skills to their jobs.

A Trainer Evaluation Form (4-05) for supervisors, located at the end of this chapter, will help evaluate training programs.

Why is supervisory input especially useful in developing new employee training?

Supervisors can tell you what their people need to know in order to quickly become productive on the job. Use the Position Training Evaluation Form (4-06) at the end of the chapter to get your own supervisors actively involved in the planning stages of new training programs.

Besides OJT and classroom instruction, what other training methods can be used?

Other methods you can use include:

- Assign a mentor — Make a manager or experienced employee responsible for the new employee's initial training and orientation.
- Use a team approach — Form teams and make one team member responsible for training.
- Rotate jobs — Move employees from one job to another during the first few months to maximize their skills.
- Shadowing — This is a form of apprenticeship where the new employee is under the close watch and supervision of an experienced employee or supervisor.
- Immediate immersion in the job — A form of learning by

doing. Okay to use except where errors have big negative or dangerous consequences.

- Internship — Usually employed for individuals who are still in school, interning is a part-time occupation that can lead to full-time positions after schooling is complete.

What are the guidelines for teaching computer literacy?

The best methods for teaching computer skills are to use the computers as the delivery system. That sometimes requires the development of software for large computers, though some packaged training programs are available. For personal computers, many packaged programs are available.

Keep in mind these guidelines:

1. Training should be machine specific. Teach employees the skills needed for your computers and other data processing equipment.
2. The content of the training should be related to your particular job requirements, not just general computer skills.
3. Learn the needs of all departments so that training is standardized throughout the company.
4. Make the training hands-on. Concentrate on giving trainees plenty of time for practice on the equipment, rather than long lectures by instructors.
5. Create job-related work samples which use the same documents and procedures that the employee will find on the job.
6. As much as possible avoid using computer jargon which your trainees do not understand. They are not technicians. Define all terms and make sure everyone can understand them.

What steps should be taken for supervisory training?

Follow these steps:

- Conduct a supervisory needs analysis.
- Set clear objectives: Decide what your supervisors need to know, decide what your supervisors already know, determine which skills can be acquired through training.
- Devise a curriculum.
- Decide on techniques.
- Establish a training agenda.
- Conduct the training.
- Evaluate the training.

To help gather information for needs analysis, ask supervisors to fill out the form Supervisor Training Needs Survey (4-07) at the end of this chapter.

Once your needs analysis is completed, enlist the help of department heads to shape an effective training program. Adapt the Supervisor Training Questionnaire (4-08) to guide your planning efforts.

How can a management training curriculum be developed for maximum effect?

The program for managers must be based on careful needs analysis. It should be flexible enough to meet the individual needs of managers, while giving all the managers the type of training your company needs to meet its strategic goals.

Divide management training and development into these nine areas. Refer to them as you organize your own program.

1. Assessment — a regular review of what managers need, where their strengths and weaknesses lie, and how training can help.
2. Developmental assignments — job rotation or movement from one department or division to another. Provides wide on-the-job experience.
3. Developmental projects or tasks — within a position a manager may work on a special project in order to gain experience and skills.
4. One-on-one counseling — to take advantage of the benefits of productive relationships.
5. Internal courses — originated by company training staff and customized for company needs.
6. External courses — short seminars or packaged programs that meet particular needs.
7. MBA-type programs — broader external thinking, usually conducted at a university.
8. Shadowing — on-the-job training involving learning from an experienced manager.
9. Self-development — focusing on such areas as assertiveness training and time management, which have direct applications on the job.

Should educational assistance programs be part of the overall training program?

Absolutely. The educational assistance will more than make up for the cost of such a program if it is monitored properly. Forms for an Educational Assistance Reimbursement Program (4-09) and Pre-enrollment College Reimbursement Request (4-10) are located at the end of the chapter.

STRATEGIC TRAINING WORKSHEET

1. List the major changes you've experienced during the last three years in the following areas.

   Markets and competition: _____

   _____

   _____

   New products: _____

   _____

   _____

   Sales growth: _____

   _____

   _____

   Technology: _____

   _____

   _____

2. List the training you expect to arise in these areas as a result of changes you forecast for the next three years.

   _____

   _____

   _____

   _____

3. How well do your current training programs meet these needs?

   _____ Completely _____ Somewhat _____ Not at all

4. Rank the top three training objectives as dictated by your company's strategy:

   1. _____

   2. _____

   3. _____

5. List your current training efforts and state the strategic need that each one fills. Are these needs still valid?

   Program: _____

   Strategic need: _____

   Still valid? (Yes/No) _____

Program: _____
Strategic need: _____
Still valid? (Yes/No) _____

Program: _____
Strategic need: _____
Still valid? (Yes/No) _____

6. What is the most important thing your employees are not learning that they need to know (e.g., computer literacy, sales skills, technical skills, etc.)?

_____
_____
_____

7. Which training program is costing you the most to teach employees skills that are helpful to know, but that are not essential to your defined strategic goals?

_____
_____
_____

TRAINING DESIGN CHECKLIST

TRAINING NEEDS

1. Have you identified specific performance discrepancies for which your employees need training? _____
2. Does the training you envision relate to current or new work duties? _____
3. Is training needed to prepare current employees for promotion? _____
4. Do accidents or other incidents point to training needs? _____
5. Do morale and attitude problems indicate a need for more training? _____
6. Do you need an orientation training program for new hires? _____
7. List all other major potential training needs:

_____

_____

_____

TRAINING SITUATIONS

8. Can the job be broken down into steps for training purposes? _____
9. Are there standards of quality which trainees can be taught? _____
10. Are there skills and techniques which trainees must learn? _____
11. Are there safety practices which must be taught? _____
12. Are there materials handling techniques that must be taught? _____
13. Have you determined the best way for trainees to handle equipment? _____
14. Are there performance standards that employees must meet? _____
15. Will information on your products help employees to do a better job? _____
16. Will the employees need instruction about departments other than their own? _____

TRAINING TECHNIQUES

17. Can you train on-the-job so that employees can produce while they learn? _____
18. Should you have classroom training conducted by a paid instructor? _____
19. Will a combination of on-the-job and classroom training work best? _____
20. Does the subject matter call for lectures? _____
21. Should the instructor follow up with discussion sessions? _____
22. Does the subject matter lend itself to demonstrations? _____
23. Can operating problems be simulated in the classroom? _____
24. Can the instructor direct trainees while they perform on the job? _____
25. Will a manual of instruction — including job instruction sheets— be used? _____
26. Will trainees be given an outline of the training program? _____
27. Can outside textbooks and other printed materials be used? _____
28. If the training lends itself to the use of motion pictures, film strips, slides, or videotapes, are they available? _____
29. Do you have drawings or photographs of the machinery, equipment or products which could be enlarged and used? _____

30. Do you have miniatures or models of the machinery and equipment which can be used to demonstrate the operation? _____

TRAINING LOGISTICS

31. If the training cannot be conducted on the production floor, do you have a conference room or a lunch room in which it can be conducted? _____
32. Should the training be conducted off the premises, in a nearby school, restaurant, hotel or motel? _____
33. Will the instructor have the necessary tools, such as a blackboard, lectern, film projector, and a microphone (if needed)? _____
34. Will there be sufficient seating and writing surfaces (if needed) for trainees? _____
35. Should the training be conducted during working hours? _____
36. Should the sessions be held after working hours? _____
37. Will the instruction cover a predetermined period of time (e.g., 2 weeks)? _____
38. Do you have enough instructors? _____
39. Do you have a personnel manager who has the time and ability to do the instructing? _____
40. Can your supervisors or department heads handle the instructing? _____
41. Should a skilled employee be used as the instructor? _____
42. Will you have to train the instructor? _____
43. Is there a qualified outside instructor available for employment on a part-time basis? _____

WHO WILL BE TRAINED

44. Should the training of new employees be a condition of employment? _____
45. Are there present employees who need training? _____
46. Should training be a condition for promotion? _____
47. Will employees be permitted to volunteer for training? _____

THE COST OF TRAINING:

48. Should you charge the program for the space, machines and materials used? _____
49. Will the wages of the trainees be included? _____
50. If the instructor is an employee, will his or her pay be included in the cost? _____
51. Will the time you and others spend in preparing and administering the program be part of the cost? _____
52. What is the estimated total cost of the program? _____

Notes:
_____
_____
_____
_____
_____

TRAINING VENDOR EVALUATION SHEET

Vendor name _____

Address _____

Contact _____ Phone _____

Training need _____

Affected department/division _____

Number of trainees _____ Approximate budget _____

Time span of training _____

Training objectives

_____ Skills _____ Motivation _____ Information

_____ Other _____

Detailed statement of training goal

_____

_____

Type of vendor(s) being considered

_____ Lecture	_____ Programmed instruction
_____ Seminar	_____ Experiential learning
_____ Packaged course	_____ Audio-visual material
_____ Customized course	_____ Computer-based instruction
_____ Needs analysis	_____ Training facility
_____ Other _____	

Reason for selecting outside source (time/cost/expertise/etc.)

_____

Vendor program/material previewed by

_____ Date _____

Vendor interviewed by

_____ Date _____

Selection criteria

1. Vendor uses appropriate language/terms   _____ Yes _____ No
2. Vendor willing to adapt
   to company environment and needs   _____ Yes _____ No
3. Vendor willing to modify program/materials   _____ Yes _____ No
4. Customized material will be company specific   _____ Yes _____ No
5. Vendor has good knowledge of target audience   _____ Yes _____ No
6. Vendor will give discount   _____ Yes _____ No
7. Vendor will base price on objective
   measure of results accomplished   _____ Yes _____ No

Speaker in presentation
   Name and title _____
   Area of expertise _____

Presentation rating (1 to 5, with 5 the highest)
_____ Interesting   _____ Clear
_____ Covered intended material _____ Handled questions well
_____ Memorable   _____ Related to trainees
_____ Presented concepts well _____ Class participation
_____ Chance to practice   _____ Adequate summary
_____ Good pacing   _____ Appropriate visuals
_____ Professional appearance _____ Class discussion

Vendor references
_____
_____
_____

Years vendor in business _____

Overall recommendation _____
_____
_____
_____

Completed by _____ Date _____

TRAINEE EVALUATION FORM

Employee _____ Date _____

List the three most important concepts that you have learned in this training session:
1. _____
2. _____
3. _____

Think of a situation on your first day back on the job in which you will be likely to make use of something you've learned in this training session. Describe the situation:
_____
_____
_____

How will what you've learned help you to perform better in this situation?
_____
_____
_____

Think of two more situations during the first two weeks back on the job in which you will use skills you've learned:
1. _____
2. _____

How will you perform better in these situations as a result of your training?
1. _____
2. _____

Of what you've learned in this session, which skill or knowledge will be the most useful in the long run?
1. _____
2. _____

List three ways in which your overall performance will be improved as a result of what you've learned:
1. _____
2. _____
3. _____

TRAINER EVALUATION FORM

Name of Program _____ Trainer _____

1. Did this training program achieve its objectives?
   _____ Yes _____ No If not, why not? _____
   _____
   _____

2. Were these objectives valid in relation to on-the-job needs?
   _____ Yes _____ No If not, why not? _____
   _____
   _____

3. Were the results obtained worthwhile in relation to the cost of the training?
   _____ Yes _____ No If not, why not? _____
   _____
   _____

4. Could the same results have been obtained through another means at a lower cost?
   _____ Yes _____ No How? _____
   _____
   _____

5. Did trainees learn the skills or information that were taught in the course?
   _____ Yes _____ No If not, why not? _____
   _____
   _____

6. Did trainees apply the skills or information on the job?
   _____ Yes _____ No If not, why not? _____
   _____
   _____

7. Did the application of the skills lead to improved results on the job?
   _____ Yes _____ No
   If yes, in what ways? _____
   _____
   If not, why not? _____
   _____

8. How could this program be changed to make it more effective?
   _____
   _____
   _____

9. How could the work environment be changed so that this training would yield more results on the job?

_____

_____

_____

10. How does this training contribute to the strategic goals of the company?

_____

_____

_____

POSITION TRAINING EVALUATION FORM

(Note to supervisors: Complete a separate form for each position you oversee)

Position _____

Reports to _____

Principal duties _____

_____

Average length of time a worker stays in this job:

_____ less than 1 year _____ 1 to 5 years _____ more than 5 years

List the three main skills the person needs to do this job well:

1. _____

2. _____

3. _____

List two additional skills that are useful in this position:

1. _____

2. _____

How was the current holder of this job trained (check all that apply)?

_____ on the job by supervisor _____ on the job by incumbent

_____ classroom _____ self study

_____ field experience _____ previous job experience

_____ seminars _____ academic training

_____ job rotation _____ by a mentor

Was this training satisfactory?

_____ Yes _____ No

If not, how could it have been improved?

_____

_____

_____

What are the most common problems encountered on the job?

_____

_____

_____

Could these problems be solved by better training?

_____ Yes _____ No

How? _____

_____

In what ways could training be improved?

_____ Longer, more thorough training

_____ More job experience sooner

_____ Job aids to back up learned skills (e.g., lists of steps, diagrams)

_____ More classroom instruction

_____ Orientation in company policies and procedures

_____ More skills practice

_____ Better use of visual aids

_____ More modeling

_____ Wider view of company operations

_____ Use of mentor to guide early job experience

_____ Use of role playing

_____ More self study

_____ Greater emphasis on employee motivation

_____ Other (explain) _____

_____

_____

_____

_____

Submitted by _____ Date _____

SUPERVISOR TRAINING NEEDS SURVEY

From the list below of supervisor skills and duties, select the letters of those which fit the following categories:

Which three do you use most
frequently on a daily basis?   1) _____   2) _____   3) _____

Which three consume the largest
proportion of your total work time?   1) _____   2) _____   3) _____

Which three contribute most to
your effectiveness on the job?   1) _____   2) _____   3) _____

Which three do you feel
the most competent in?   1) _____   2) _____   3) _____

Which three do you find
the most difficult?   1) _____   2) _____   3) _____

Which three contribute most
frequently to conflicts with
your subordinates?   1) _____   2) _____   3) _____

Which three do you feel least
confident about?   1) _____   2) _____   3) _____

A. Delegation of tasks
B. Discipline
C. Training
D. Running meetings
E. Communicating with subordinates
F. Motivating subordinates
G. Performance appraisals
H. Interviewing
I. Setting goals and objectives
J. Managing my time
K. Coaching subordinates
L. Administrative duties
M. Long-range planning
N. Short-range planning
O. Scheduling

P. Handling conflict
Q. Team building
R. Problem solving
S. Writing reports/memos
T. Dealing with company
   support staff
U. Interpreting
   policies/procedures
V. Dealing with
   technical problems
W. Union issues/labor
   relations
X. Budget and cost
   matters
Y. Quality problems &
   issues

List three additional problems that you frequently encounter on the job:

1. _____
2. _____
3. _____

Describe in a few sentences your view of the ideal supervisor:

_____
_____
_____
_____
_____

In what ways do you feel you could be a better supervisor?

_____
_____
_____
_____
_____

Submitted by _____ Date _____

**SUPERVISOR TRAINING QUESTIONNAIRE—
FOR TRAINING DIRECTOR**

Rank your top five supervisor training needs for:

New Supervisors   Experienced supervisors

1. _____   1. _____
2. _____   2. _____
3. _____   3. _____
4. _____   4. _____
5. _____   5. _____

List current or projected supervisor training programs that relate to:

Human relations skills (communication, conflict resolution, motivation, etc.)

_____
_____
_____

Administrative skills (report writing, budgeting, meetings, planning, etc.)

_____
_____
_____

Other skills (decision making, technical training, union relations, time management, etc.)

_____
_____
_____

List the three problems that are having the most effect on supervisor productivity (poor coaching, ineffective delegation of tasks, etc.).

1. _____
2. _____
3. _____

List possible non-training remedies for the above problems (more detailed policy manuals, redesigned procedures, etc.).

1. _____
2. _____
3. _____

List three possible training remedies for the above problems (a seminar on coaching, a delegation self-study module, etc.).

1. _____
2. _____
3. _____

List any important changes that your supervisors will have to deal with over the next two years (new human relations policies, administrative changes, etc.).

_____

_____

_____

What training implications do these changes have (need for training in participative management techniques, course in report writing, etc.)?

_____

_____

_____

What specific training programs are you considering to meet these future needs?

_____

_____

_____

Have you considered purchasing supervisor training programs from vendors?
_____Yes   _____No If not, why not? _____

_____

List the three most effective vendor programs you have reviewed and the rating for each:

1. Title/Vendor _____
      Rating (1 = least effective; 10 = most effective)
         1   2   3   4   5   6   7   8   9   10

2. Title/Vendor _____
         1   2   3   4   5   6   7   8   9   10

3. Title/Vendor _____
         1   2   3   4   5   6   7   8   9   10

Write a brief description of your supervisor training program as you see it evolving over the next two years.

_____

_____

_____

_____

Submitted by: _____ Date: _____

EDUCATIONAL ASSISTANCE REIMBURSEMENT PROGRAM

Thank you for contacting the Training Department about the educational assistance program. Listed below are some of the most frequently asked questions about the program. Please take a few minutes to look them over. If you have any additional questions, please call the Training Department.

Am I eligible for reimbursement?

For any local accredited universities, you must complete one year of full-time employment prior to the starting date of class to be eligible for reimbursement.

What courses can I be reimbursed for?

Only degree credit courses required for a business related degree are considered eligible for reimbursement. Non-degree courses that are job related will be considered for reimbursement on a case-by-case basis. All courses must be taken outside of an employee's regularly scheduled work day. A minimum grade of "C" must be achieved to receive reimbursement.

How much money is available to me?

The company will reimburse full-time employees up to $1,000.00 per calendar year (January 1 through December 31) for approved courses. Reimbursement can include both tuition and book expense.

Is the reimbursement taxable?

Reimbursement for courses which are directly related to your present job will not be taxable. All other reimbursements will be considered taxable.

How do I get reimbursed?

First make sure the course you're taking is approved for reimbursement. To receive approval, fill out the reimbursement form available from the Training Department. This form should be filled out and returned before the starting date of the class. The next step is to save your receipts for tuition and book expense.

At completion of the course, send photocopies of the receipts with a copy of your grade to the Training Department. All grades must be received within 60 days of completion of the course to receive reimbursement.

PRE-ENROLLMENT COLLEGE REIMBURSEMENT REQUEST

Name _____ Social Security # _____

Department _____ Position _____ Phone _____

Class _____ Day(s) _____ Time(s) _____

Starting date of class (Mo/Day/Yr) _____

Tuition _____ Book costs _____ Total cost _____

College or university _____ Degree pursued _____

How does this course relate to your present job responsibilities?

_____

_____

_____

What other finiancial aid, if any, will you be receiving?

_____

_____

_____

Employee's signature _____ Date _____

Department manager's
signature of approval _____ Date _____

Upon approval of this request, please forward a copy of the class schedule and your receipts to the Training Department.

==

For Training Department use:

Approved _____   Denied _____

Comments: _____

_____

Amount reimbursed _____ Date _____

Amount available _____ Through _____

Getting Results Through Performance Appraisal 5

What are the objectives of a good performance appraisal system?

When selecting an appraisal system for your company, your first concern should be to set up a system that is as fair as possible. The criteria against which you judge an employee must be clearly related to the demands of the job. The process must be as objective as you can make it. In general, objectivity in performance appraisal is possible only when following a fundamental rule: Judge the work, not the person.

An objective evaluation system will help your company to:

- Eliminate the uneven standards that can vary from manager to manager. For example, one manager may prize employees who are flexible and cooperative, and rank them very highly. Another manager might not consider "people skills" important at all.

- Remove the temptation to judge employees by their personalities. When every manager ranks employees by the same specific standards, appraisals can focus on qualities that are related to job performance, and not on whether a manager likes or dislikes an employee.

- Motivate employees with appraisals. Employees know that appraisals form the basis of many important promotion and salary decisions. When employees believe they are judged fairly, they will respect the system and view appraisal as a way to improve their performance.

- Create the most productive work force possible. Using appraisal standards that are objective and measurable insures that managers recognize and reward employees for skills that further the goals and profits of the company.

What kinds of appraisal methods are available?

There are several basic ways to appraise employees. Some of the most popular include:

- The rating scale system, in which the employee is given a numerical score for each item on a list of job-related performance characteristics. The characteristics are based on job requirements.
- The behavior scale, which assigns a number value to job-related behavior, such as whether their daily work habits are consistent or how well they respond to deadline pressure.
- The essay appraisal, which uses a narrative style.
- The ranking system, which assigns employees to points along a standard distribution curve or compares individual employees to each other to obtain a ranked list.
- Reporting of critical incidents. Here the employee's performance is noted in specific situations which illustrate how well that employee performs.
- Appraisal as part of a management by objectives program. After stating the job's objectives, it is determined how successful the individual was in reaching them.

These classifications are primarily for purposes of discussion. In practice, most appraisal systems are combinations or variations of these basic types.

When are rating scales the best appraisal method?

The key to success with a rating scale is to select the right characteristics with which to evaluate an employee and a scale with which to rate them.

Many companies start by establishing a scale of 1 to 5, such as:

1. Exceptional
2. Above average
3. Average
4. Needs improvement
5. Unsatisfactory

They then rate each employee according to that scale for commonly-used factors like quality and quantity of work, cooperation, initiative, planning and leadership abilities, etc.

A rating scale system works best when objective factors such as days late for work or the number of items produced are measured. This can't always be done, however. If you try too hard to establish a strictly quantitative system, you run the risk of one of these two problems—or both:

- Judging only those characteristics that are easy to measure quantitatively. You easily could overlook important but intangible assets, such as a worker's problem solving ability.
- Making a subjective judgment look objective by using numbers.

The numbers should be used as a basis for judgment, not as a substitute for it. The rating system's real purpose is not to attach a number to everything but to establish rational standards for an employee's performance.

What are the advantages and disadvantages of the "critical incidents" method?

Under this method, a running record is maintained of incidents in which the employee performs either well or poorly. "Critical" in this system doesn't refer to a crisis; it refers to events in an employee's work life that serve as examples of that person's job performance.

To some extent, a supervisor does this anyway, taking note of how well employees handle certain situations. The critical incident appraisal method simply formalizes this process and puts the observations in writing. A typical Critical Incidents Appraisal Form (5-01) is found at the end of the chapter.

A critical incident log might note, for example, that on a certain date the employee kept a high-priority job on schedule by going to extra lengths to obtain a necessary report. Another entry might note a time the employee was guilty of an outburst of bad temper.

Other possible entries in an employee's log could include:

- Important assignments the employee has carried out, and how well he or she performed them.
- Incidents in which the employee showed leadership.
- Incidents that illustrate the employee's working relationships with other workers.
- Incidents in which the employee either showed, or failed to show initiative and judgment.
- Examples of performance that were either above or below the expected standards.
- Incidents that show how well the employee has acquired new skills or developed in other ways.

The strength of this method is that judgments can be based on the employee's actual performance with specific on-the-job incidents. In addition, employees interested in getting ahead in the organization can keep their own critical incident report in preparation for their appraisal interviews.

The main weakness of this technique is that it requires a lot of time and paperwork. More important, it depends greatly on the selection of the incidents for the log. A supervisor who dislikes an employee will naturally tend to focus on incidents that reflect the employee's shortcomings. The log may not reflect an accurate overall picture.

How does the "management-by-objectives" approach fit with performance appraisals?

Management-by-objectives is the well-known technique of setting goals, then judging how well they are met. Performance appraisal is a major part of that process. The supervisor and the employee establish stated objectives the employee should reach by the end of the rating period. Then the appraisal becomes a simple matter of deciding how well the employee met those goals.

The key to this method's success is to clearly define the goals, and then accompany each one with specific standards that measure success.

The major advantage of the MBO system is that it offers a structured form of guidance. Employees know in advance exactly what is expected of them. They also know they will be judged by their accomplishments.

An effective plan requires that the supervisor and the employee agree on the proper objectives. Both must have the time to discuss and negotiate these goals. There also must be a provision to modify goals that clearly become impossible to meet.

What factors should be considered when evaluating an appraisal form?

Whether reviewing another company's form or trying to develop one of your own, ask yourself the following questions:

- Is it easy to understand and to administer?
- Does the form ask for information directly related to the tasks and responsibilities of the job?
- Does it require appraisers to give examples of the employee's performance, both good and bad?
- Can the form be adapted to other departments' needs and situations? Forms for sales people are not the same as those for engineers, foremen or marketing people.
- Is the form comprehensive so that performance on the total job can be described?
- Are criteria defined so all appraisers assess the same factors?
- Does the form encourage consistency?
- Are any legal requirements considered?

The Performance Appraisal (5-02) shown at the end of the chapter focuses on specifics but still allows the appraiser freedom of judgment.

Who should appraise employee performance?

Appraisals usually are conducted by someone higher in the organizational structure than the person being appraised. The supervisor usually controls the rewards and punishments that can be administered, and is in the best position to observe a subordinate's behavior and judge the relevance of that behavior to job objectives and organizational goals. But there are other sources of performance appraisals that are sometimes used including the following:

Self-appraisal—Employees first complete an appraisal form and then discuss their assessments with their managers. Companies using this method have found that subordinates are generally less defensive when discussions are based on self-appraisal, and self-ratings more often result in superior on-the-job performance than do traditional appraisals.

Peer appraisal—People working together as equals know one another well and usually understand the scope of the job. Studies have shown peer appraisal to be a reliable judge of performance even though friendships, animosities and prejudices can be problems.

Subordinate appraisals—This method has had mixed reviews but seems to have advantages when used as a basis for team building. The superior is provided with a summary of anonymous ratings and also a comparison of his rating by subordinates to the ratings of the other supervisors.

Appraisals by outsiders—At assessment centers, the participants are observed by line managers two or more organization levels above the participants. They rate the employees based on their performance in simulated business situations, in discussion groups and during case study discussions.

How can a company choose an appraisal method that's most appropriate for it?

As a general rule, detailed checklists like the rating scale are good choices for office employees, production workers and others where performance traits are easy to measure. Professional, creative workers and others whose personal talent and skill are important, probably are best evaluated by the essay method or some other less structured technique. And even before it was known by its initials, MBO was a standard method for judging sales performance.

Look for the right blend to fit your organization. If you need objective standards for a rating scale, MBO techniques can help provide them. A ranking technique can help determine if the standards are appropriate for your work force. If the proposed standard falls well above or below the group's average performance, take another look. An essay can help explain what you can't readily reduce to numbers. The types of goals used in an MBO system are best applied to executives and department heads. For lower-level employees, a rating scale is probably most appropriate.

What do employees expect from performance appraisals?

To improve their skills employees need to know what responsibilities have been assigned to their jobs, what future goals they are expected to meet, how their performance is going to be measured, what it takes to get an outstanding rating, and what their superiors' goals are. Most employees want to do a good job. They need someone to help them answer the question — How can I do my job better? — in a constructive, supportive way.

Should appraisals be used primarily to correct poor performance?

No. Corrective criticism is only a small part of a good appraisal. Coming to an agreement on goals and outlining courses of action between a superior and subordinate are also important. In any appraisal, criticism is useful only after the goals are clearly defined and realistic ways to reach them have been discussed first.

What are the five basic steps of performance appraisal?

The appraisal process progresses as follows:

Step 1— The individual discusses his or her job and job description with the supervisor and they agree on the content of the job and the relative importance of the major duties and activities.

Step 2— Performance targets are established for each responsibility for the coming period.

Step 3— The supervisor and employee meet to discuss the targets and to reach agreement on them.

Step 4— Checkpoints are established for the evaluation of progress toward goals and the methods of measuring progress.

Step 5— The supervisor and employee meet at the end of the period to discuss results.

How are goals and standards used in appraisals?

Executives and managers are usually judged by their success in meeting stated goals. Lower-level employees are usually appraised on how well they meet certain performance standards.

Keep in mind that the goals and standards are not just criteria for making judgments. They are also incentives for the employee to succeed.

The first step in setting these criteria is to look at the company's overall goals and those of the particular group. Then decide on what must be expected of the individual so the group can meet its objectives.

The employee's role at this stage is critical to the success of the appraisal program. The employee draws up a list of performance goals for his job, usually for a period of six months. This list of goals embodies his plans in all of the major areas of his job. The goals he selects should be challenging, representing improvements over his previous accomplishments. They should be realistic and attainable within the time frame selected.

Whenever possible, goal statements should be accompanied by a specific date for completion and include the standard of performance to be reached. Thus, "to increase sales" is sufficient as a goal statement, while "to increase sales 10 percent by December 31" is a workable target. The Performance Appraisal Interview Report (5-03), found at the end of this chapter, can be used to record and keep track of agreed-upon goals.

Start with the job description. Take the job tasks and develop a list of goals which will accomplish these tasks. Keep in mind that the goals must be related to the job, able to be observed, and able to be measured in some way. The Summary of Departmental Goals (5-04) will help in establishing such goals. It is found at the end of the chapter.

How should managers prepare for the appraisal interview?

The appraisal form is a checklist for the items to be covered during the interview. The employee should review a blank form in advance of the interview, too.

Before the interview takes place, the supervisor should fill out the form. It is now a "report card" on the employee. The supervisor should be prepared to explain his judgments. There should be a private place for the interview without interruptions. Rather than having a desk between the supervisor and the person being appraised, two chairs, set side by side, at a table, will be more likely to encourage discussion.

A good way to start is for the supervisor to ask the employee how well he or she thinks they have met expectations. Then the supervisor should go over the appraisal, item by item. Any serious disagreements over items should be discussed. The appraised person should have plenty of time for comment, explanations, opinions and questions. If there are mitigating circumstances, they should be taken into account when the final evaluation is made.

The most successful appraisal interviews occur when the employee does 90 percent of the talking and the appraiser 10 percent. When that ratio occurs, the employee is likely to be accepting his or her shortcomings and making sincere plans to improve. The Performance Appraisal Interview Checklist (5-05) located at the end of this chapter, should be used as a general review before the appraisal is scheduled.

What is the purpose of "feedback" in performance appraisals?

Feedback is defined as the way of telling an employee whether or not he is on target regarding a goal he is trying to achieve. Its purpose is to reinforce or correct the employee's behavior.

How should corrective feedback be offered in the appraisal interview?

Corrective feedback can be made more effective by giving it some structure. The interview might follow this format:

1. State the context. Lets the employee know the supervisor is concerned and why.
2. Acknowledge the employee's effort. If the employee has been working hard to meet a standard, acknowledge the effort. Cite some specific example to show that the employee can definitely meet the goal.
3. Describe the behavior that has the supervisor concerned. Give specific instances of the employee's behavior.
4. Describe the effect of that behavior. Make the employee aware of the consequences. Heighten the employee's sense of responsibility.
5. State the standard. The employee needs a clear picture of what is expected. Even if the standard has been set earlier, state it again.
6. Ask for reasons and explanations. Be careful not to phrase this as a "why haven't you?" type of challenge. Give the employee a chance to describe why he or she acted as they did.
7. Ask the employee to suggest solutions. Be ready, though, to suggest solutions if the employee doesn't offer an acceptable response.
8. Decide together on a plan of action.

What is the best way to give negative feedback?

The following techniques soften the criticism, but still get the point across:

1. Make the message very clear. Confusion and misunderstandings can result if words are too vague, or can be misconstrued.
2. Be specific. Use actual examples of behavior or performance problems. Give employees a chance to explain their actions when they don't immediately recognize where they've fallen short.
3. Reassure employees that the comments are directed only at the part of their behavior that needs improvement, and not at them personally.
4. Restate the performance standards the employee is expected to meet.

How can feedback techniques be improved?

Feedback is most likely to be effective if it is:

- Related to mutually agreed upon goals and standards.

- Primarily objective, with subjective assessments playing a very minor role.
- Related to overt and identifiable behavior and incidents which both superior and subordinate are able to observe.
- Given close enough to the incident to permit the subordinate to see the connection.
- Well balanced between positives and negatives.
- Related only to activities over which the subordinate has control.
- Not threatening to the appraised person's self-esteem.

Should performance appraisals and salary reviews be conducted at the same time?

Many organizations do combine performance appraisals with salary reviews. Most consultants and professionals in the field, however, agree that salary considerations should be separate from performance evaluations.

While it is true that ultimately the results of appraisals will appear in paychecks, human resource experts believe that, during the appraisal session, feedback on performance gets better results than money discussions.

It is feedback that helps accomplish the goals of appraisals — improved performance and morale, identification of training needs, resolution of uncovered problems, opportunities for employees to discuss their jobs and careers with their bosses. Those objectives should take precedence and the results can be seriously diluted by discussions of salary during the performance evaluation. Salary reviews are better held at a different time.

How are appraisals used in promotion decisions?

Some companies make good use of performance appraisals as instruments of counseling and career development. To make this a part of an appraisal program, employees and manager are asked to complete an Employee Career Interest and Qualifications Form (5-06) and Employee Career Development Form (5-07).

The first form enables employees to express their career interests and tell how they hope to develop them. Then the employee's immediate superior completes the second form and discusses it with a reviewing manager to prepare for a counselling interview. The interview should focus on the employee's personal career goals and on the next steps to be taken to achieve them.

What preparations should be made before introducing a new performance appraisal program?

Before inaugurating a new program, many companies test its validity and acceptability in one department, perhaps the human resources area. Such tests give managers in that department useful experience when they must explain the system to other managers and answer questions once the system is fully implemented.

The wholehearted support and enthusiasm of top management is also important. The president of the company should support the program with memos and discussion in management meetings. Recognition from top management is essential for the success of any performance appraisal program.

What should be done to maintain a company's appraisal program?

The steps to make an appraisal system a standard procedure for the firm are:

1. Make sure that all managers are rewarded for their participation and support.
2. While it may be started within a small segment of the organization, try to get it working across the whole company within a reasonable time. That helps the appraisal philosophy take root, grow quickly and become a positive force.
3. Install the system in departments where it will be adopted most easily. Once it becomes accepted there, move on to more complex or resistant groups.
4. Review the system each quarter with top executives in operations and human resources/personnel.
5. Appoint an individual or corporate department to schedule, coordinate and promote the system on a company wide basis.
6. Hold workshops and seminars regularly to reinforce the importance of appraisal and help managers with interviewing skills.

How should the performance appraisal system be reviewed?

Focus on critical aspects — goal setting, feedback and employee participation. Here are guidelines for review:

- Do employees know well in advance of the actual interview what subjects will be discussed?
- Do employees receive a copy of the appraisal form and a copy of last year's review? Both the supervisor and the employee should be well prepared.
- Are the appraisers creating an open, supportive atmosphere at the beginning of the appraisal interviews?
- Are appraisal discussions focused on identifying problems that prevent the employee from performing in the best way?

- Are discussions encouraged that focus on solutions — ways obstacles to good performance can be overcome?
- Are specific solutions suggested and agreed to by both appraiser and employee?
- Are specific goals set for the next review period?
- Are criticisms of past performance kept to a minimum?
- When criticisms are needed, are discussions focused on performance problems and not on personalities?
- Are follow-up dates for progress review set prior to the end of the interview?
- When a reduction in grade, suspension or termination is being contemplated, is the employee given in writing a description of the unacceptable performance? Is this step taken after counseling, a verbal warning and a written warning about the unacceptable work behavior?
- Are employees given adequate time to respond to items that comes up in the appraisal interview?

What appraisal records should be kept?

Appraisals should be documented. Include the job description, the completed appraisal form and any notes made by the supervisor during or after the interview.

Keep a statement of the goals and standards the employee is expected to meet. This may already be a part of the appraisal form.

It is also useful to have an appraisal summary record. This is a sheet for each employee which lists the following data: employee name, date of appraisal, appraiser's name, brief summary of results, comments. The summary allows the supervisor to note progress, or lack of it, as time passes by.

Why should supervisors and managers be trained in performance appraisals?

Training helps supervisors and managers use uniform methods of appraisal throughout the organization. Training also reduces biases, promotes accuracy and stimulates participation in the system.

Effective performance appraisal training almost always involves modeling and role playing. There's no standard method for conducting a performance appraisal interview because each employee is unique. Supervisors and managers will learn best by observing "model" interviews and by receiving feedback.

To uncover training needs of managers, use the Manager's Performance Appraisal Training Survey (5-08). To help plan the training, use the Performance Appraisal Training Form (5-09). Both forms are shown at the end of the chapter.

The Exit Performance Appraisal (5-10) can be used during the exit interview of each employee as the final evaluation of the success of the performance appraisal/training process. It is found at the end of the chapter.

CRITICAL INCIDENTS APPRAISAL FORM

INSTRUCTIONS: Appraise the employee on both daily job activities and the handling of special projects and non-routine situations.

Date: _____

Incident:

_____

_____

_____

Employee's action:

_____

_____

_____

Expected performance:

_____

_____

_____

Supervisor's appraisal:

_____

_____

_____

Supervisor's signature _____

PERFORMANCE APPRAISAL

Name _____ Date _____

Job Title _____

JOB RESPONSIBILITIES
List the employee's four major responsibilities and rate the employee on each one,
giving examples of performance that most accurately describe your rating.

	Needs Improvement	Satisfactory	Very Good	Excellent
(1) _____	_____	_____	_____	_____
Examples: _____				
_____				
_____				
_____				
(2) _____	_____	_____	_____	_____
Examples: _____				
_____				
_____				
_____				
(3) _____	_____	_____	_____	_____
Examples: _____				
_____				
_____				
_____				
(4) _____	_____	_____	_____	_____
Examples: _____				
_____				
_____				
_____				

MANAGES THE JOB

	Needs Improvement	Satisfactory	Very Good	Excellent
Recognizes problems	_____	_____	_____	_____
Analyzes causes of problems	_____	_____	_____	_____
Generates alternative approaches	_____	_____	_____	_____
Sets realistic goals	_____	_____	_____	_____
Establishes work priorities	_____	_____	_____	_____
Organizes people and materials to reach goals	_____	_____	_____	_____
Handles pressure	_____	_____	_____	_____
Evaluates results	_____	_____	_____	_____
Other: _____	_____	_____	_____	_____

Examples of MANAGES THE JOB that describe your ratings:

_____
_____
_____

GETS THE JOB DONE

	Needs Improvement	Satisfactory	Very Good	Excellent
Follows through	_____	_____	_____	_____
Meets deadlines	_____	_____	_____	_____
Achieves balance between work quality and quantity	_____	_____	_____	_____
Takes responsibility for actions	_____	_____	_____	_____
Other: _____	_____	_____	_____	_____

Examples of GETS THE JOB DONE that describe your ratings:

_____
_____
_____

ATTITUDE ON THE JOB

	Needs Improve-ment	Satis-factory	Very Good	Excel-lent
Cooperates with others	_____	_____	_____	_____
Takes criticism well	_____	_____	_____	_____
Has a positive outlook	_____	_____	_____	_____
Tries to do the best job possible	_____	_____	_____	_____

Examples of ATTITUDE ON THE JOB that describe your ratings:

_____
_____
_____

STRENGTHS AND ACCOMPLISHMENTS
Identify the three most significant strengths or job accomplishments:

_____
_____
_____

COMMENTS ON AREAS REQUIRING DEVELOPMENT
Identify three areas where this employee needs to improve:

_____
_____
_____

PERFORMANCE ASSESSMENT
Overall Performance Assessment (check one)
( ) Needs Improvement   ( ) Satisfactory   ( ) Very Good   ( ) Excellent
Previous assessment _____ Date _____
Previous assessment by _____
If there is a change in assessment, state the major reason for the change:

_____
_____
_____

EMPLOYEE COMMENTS (USE ADDITIONAL PAPER IF NECESSARY)

_____
_____
_____

Supervisor's Signature _____ Date _____

Employee's Signature _____ Date _____

PERFORMANCE APPRAISAL INTERVIEW REPORT

Employee _____   Department _____

Appraised by _____   Appraisal period _____

Date _____

GOAL	PERFORMANCE STANDARD	RESULTS	COMMENTS
_____	_____	_____	_____
_____	_____	_____	_____
_____	_____	_____	_____
_____	_____	_____	_____
_____	_____	_____	_____
_____	_____	_____	_____
_____	_____	_____	_____
_____	_____	_____	_____
_____	_____	_____	_____
_____	_____	_____	_____
_____	_____	_____	_____
_____	_____	_____	_____

Manager's recommendations:

_____

_____

_____

_____

Manager's signature _____   Date _____

Employee's signature _____   Date _____

Summary of Departmental Goals (5-04)

SUMMARY OF DEPARTMENTAL GOALS

Department: _____   Manager: _____

Period: _____

GOAL	PERFORMANCE STANDARD	RESPONSIBLE EMPLOYEE	TO BE MET BY (DATE)
_____	_____	_____	_____
_____	_____	_____	_____
_____	_____	_____	_____
_____	_____	_____	_____
_____	_____	_____	_____
_____	_____	_____	_____
_____	_____	_____	_____
_____	_____	_____	_____
_____	_____	_____	_____
_____	_____	_____	_____
_____	_____	_____	_____
_____	_____	_____	_____
_____	_____	_____	_____
_____	_____	_____	_____
_____	_____	_____	_____
_____	_____	_____	_____
_____	_____	_____	_____
_____	_____	_____	_____
_____	_____	_____	_____
_____	_____	_____	_____
_____	_____	_____	_____

PERFORMANCE APPRAISAL INTERVIEW CHECKLIST

BEFORE THE DISCUSSION
1. Schedule the discussion and give the employee a copy of the completed appraisal forms at least one week in advance. If this is the employee's first appraisal, sit down with him/her and explain the form and procedure.
2. Review the employee's results over the past six months. a) Think of specific examples that will help the employee. b) Develop alternatives for improving and correcting problem areas.
3. Are the agreed-upon goals for the next 6-12 months clearly understandable and specific? a) Include criteria and measures for success. b) Include significant interaction needed to get the job done. c) Think of specific types of assistance needed such as resources, information, advice/consultation.
4. Plan for the meeting. a) Develop a tentative sequence, such as results, goals and development plans. b) Try to anticipate problem areas and alternatives for handling these. c) Make the room comfortable and try to eliminate potential interruptions.

DURING THE DISCUSSION
1. Develop a non-defensive, problem-solving "we" (not "you vs. me") climate.
2. Use feedback in a constructive, developmental way.
3. Avoid arguments which can quickly develop into stalemates. If deadlocks occur, talk about the feedback from your point of view and what you see as the consequences for continuing the current behavior or approach.
4. Be flexible when you can.
5. Frequently check for clear understanding of what is being discussed.

AFTER THE DISCUSSION
1. The employee prepares a summary of the discussion, especially the commitments, as a final check on clarity of understanding. Both the employee and the supervisor keep a copy.
2. Both the employee and the supervisor should discuss any changes in the goals.
3. Feedback and performance discussion should continue on a regular basis and as specific issues arise. Do not wait more than a week or two after the formal discussion to give feedback or discuss issues. Timeliness is very important.

EMPLOYEE CAREER INTEREST AND QUALIFICATIONS FORM

Name _____

1. CAREER INTERESTS (Show your specific preferences and alternatives including position title plus desired timing.)
   A. Within one year _____
   _____
   _____

   B. Longer range (within five years) _____
   _____
   _____

2. QUALIFICATIONS
   A. Technical, managerial, interpersonal qualifications
   _____
   _____
   _____

   B. Areas in which you feel you need further development
   _____
   _____
   _____

3. DEVELOPMENT ACTIONS AND PLANS
   A. Actions taken in last 12-18 months to enhance skills, knowledge, experience, etc.
   _____
   _____
   _____

   B. Plans
   _____
   _____
   _____

Signed _____
Date forwarded to manager _____

EMPLOYEE CAREER DEVELOPMENT FORM

(to be filled out by supervisor)

Name of employee_____

1. ACCOMPLISHMENTS AND QUALIFICATIONS
   A. Accomplishments (Based on most recent performance appraisal, summarize accomplishments against goals during the last year—indicate overall trend.)

   _____
   _____
   _____

   B. Qualifications
      Strengths

   _____
   _____
   _____

   C. Development needs

   _____
   _____
   _____

2. DEVELOPMENT AND CAREER RECOMMENDATIONS
   A. Development recommendations (Specify development plans for the next 12 months which are responsive to identified needs.)

   _____
   _____
   _____

   B. Recommended next assignment

   _____
   _____
   _____

   C. Career route and goals (How realistic are the individual's career goals and are they compatible with your views? Specifiy long-range development needs and recommendations for future positions.)

   _____
   _____
   _____

Completed by _____ Date _____

Date discussed with reviewing manager _____

Date discussed with employee _____

MANAGER'S PERFORMANCE APPRAISAL TRAINING SURVEY

Name _____ Date _____

Title _____

Department _____

How many people report to you directly? _____

What are their titles/jobs? _____

_____

_____

How often do you currently review your subordinates' performance?

_____ at least quarterly   _____ as necessary

_____ twice a year   _____ in conjunction with

_____ yearly   salary review only

_____ less than once a year

Do you fully understand corporate performance review policy and procedures?

____ Yes ____ No

What aspects do you feel uncomfortable with?

_____

_____

_____

Which aspects create the most conflict between you and your subordinates?

_____

_____

_____

Which aspects do you feel are ineffective or need to be changed?

_____

_____

_____

What three specific changes would make our performance evaluation process more effective?

1. _____

2. _____

3. _____

Which of the following training techniques have been or would be the most valuable for increasing your skill at performance appraisal?

_____ Lecture by in-house expert	_____	Lecture by outside
_____ Video tape/film		expert
_____ Role playing with video	_____	Role playing
_____ One-on-one training	_____	Modeling
_____ Written material		tape feedback
_____ Audio tapes	_____	Programmed learning
_____ Discussions	_____	Demonstrations

In what ways could your subordinates be better prepared to attend performance review sessions?

_____

_____

_____

What one thing do you need more experience at in order to conduct better performance appraisals?

_____

_____

_____

PERFORMANCE APPRAISAL TRAINING FORM

Schedule of performance appraisal introduction/review

Department   Date   Trainer
_____   _____   _____
_____   _____   _____
_____   _____   _____
_____   _____   _____

Briefly describe each facet of the training program

1. Manager input _____
   _____
   _____

2. Presentation of performance appraisal concepts/overview
   _____
   _____

3. Explanation of performance appraisal form _____
   _____
   _____

4. Modeling/demonstration _____
   _____
   _____

5. Role playing _____
   _____
   _____

6. Discussion/question and answer session _____
   _____
   _____

7. Follow-up _____
   _____
   _____

Time required for training _____

Check the aspects of performance appraisal which need to be covered most carefully

_____	Written material	_____	Demonstrations
_____	Preparation	_____	Creating an effective setting
_____	Job definition	_____	Performance criteria
_____	Handling conflict	_____	Listening skills
_____	Positive feedback	_____	Negative feedback
_____	Goal setting	_____	Planning
_____	Other _____		

Describe the most common difficulty managers encounter in the performance appraisal process

_____

_____

_____

What specific type of training will help overcome this difficulty?

_____

_____

_____

Are managers passing on performance appraisal skills to their subordinates?

_____ Yes _____ No

If not, how can training help them to do so? _____

_____

_____

_____

EXIT PERFORMANCE APPRAISAL

Submit all supporting documents including the letter of resignation to the Human Resources Department prior to:

_____ Termination _____ Transfer _____ Leave

Name _____ Position Number/Title _____

Department _____

Date of Hire _____ Last day of work _____

1. State the reason for termination, transfer or leave.
   Check and explain. __ Voluntary __ Non-voluntary

   _____
   _____
   _____

2. Evaluate the quality and quantity of work produced by the employee.

   _____
   _____
   _____

3. Comment on the employee's behavior in relating to fellow employees and supervisors.

   _____
   _____
   _____

4. If termination, is replacement needed?
   _____ Yes _____ No   Date _____

OVERALL ASSESSMENT OF PERFORMANCE

Unsatis-factory Performance	Perfor-mance Needs to Improve	Fully Meets Require-ments	Consis-tently Exceeds Require-meets	Distin-quished Perfor-mance
1	2	3	4	5

Supervisor's explanation of rating:

_____
_____
_____

Supervisor _____ Date _____

Manager _____ Date _____

Evaluating and Improving Employee Attitudes 6

What is the best way to systematically gather information about employee attitudes?

An employee attitude survey is the most efficient way. It is comprehensive, allows management to gather information on a wide range of topics and enables management to research a large number of employees in a relatively short period of time. It provides standardization by asking the same questions, in the same way, of all participants. Surveys are an anonymous and confidential way for employees to express their opinions and for management to gain valuable insights.

How can the data acquired from attitude surveys be used most effectively?

The data acquired from employee surveys can be used for finding the effects of short-range organizational changes, for identifying problems that require immediate attention, and for long-range planning to increase both organizational and individual effectiveness.

Traditionally, attitude surveys have been used to identify job satisfaction or dissatisfaction and to measure morale so that something can be done about those factors. Recently, attitude surveys have taken on new importance as management development and decision-making tools. Also, views expressed by employees are used to create a smoother-running organization through better communications and better human relations.

What concerns do companies usually have about introducing attitude surveys and what can be done to alleviate them?

Management concerns usually fall into the following categories:

- Will a survey raise employee expectations, which may be difficult to fulfill? Employee expectations can be brought to realistic levels by planning effective communications before, during and after the survey. Focus employee communications on what the survey can and cannot do.

- Will employees be open and honest in responding to the survey? They'll respond openly and honestly if they believe their responses will be treated confidentially, and that the survey will be of value. Insure confidentiality throughout.
- What if the survey identifies issues that management hadn't anticipated? That result can be the survey's real value. Communicate with employees on those issues you're not now ready to tackle. Then use the data to plan how to tackle them.
- What if employees feel that the survey results will be used against them? Make a point that attitude surveys are not performance evaluations. Communicate to everyone that results of the surveys will be used to improve company results as well as individual working conditions.
- What if the survey only tells you what you already know? It is unlikely that a survey won't give you new insights. It may provide confirmation of things already known, but that can be valuable when documented.

What are the important stages of the attitude survey process?

There are seven important stages:

1. Planning
2. Design
3. Administration
4. Analysis and reporting
5. Data interpretation
6. Problem solving and action planning
7. Employee communications

How does a company get the commitment of line managers to the introduction of employee attitude surveys?

The best way to gain the commitment of your entire management team and reduce resistance is to:

1. Involve the line managers in the survey planning process from the start.
2. Acknowledge and address managers' needs and concerns regarding the survey.
3. Keep managers fully informed throughout the survey process.

How is a survey committee set up and who should be represented?

The makeup of the committee depends on the size of the organization and the scope of the survey. The survey committee should have representation from those members of the organization who will benefit from the survey, those who will have primary responsibility for carrying it out, and those who will be implementing the strategies that arise from it.

The committee should have no more than 10 to 12 members. Choose a chairman to keep the project going, to monitor assignments and to serve as the survey spokesperson to the organization. A coordinator should be appointed by the committee members. The coordinator will attend to the day-to-day details. Often, coordinators are members of the company personnel department.

How should the objectives of attitude surveys be defined?

To be successful, an attitude survey requires well-defined objectives. When you specify your information needs, what is to be collected and its purpose, you help insure that both management and workers will have realistic expectations regarding the survey effort.

To define the survey's purpose, the survey committee members should begin by listing their objectives. Top management should be represented. The survey committee should also interview managers for their information needs and expectations.

Once the manager interviews are completed, they should be summarized for the survey committee. The committee should then specify the survey's objectives.

Keep these points in mind when delineating objectives:

1. Be as specific as possible. Write objectives so that each one has a single purpose.
2. Use action verbs that describe measurable or observable behavior. Action verbs include "to measure," and "to increase." Avoid using weaker, non-specific verbs such as "to enhance," "to promote," and "to understand." They are subject to too many interpretations.

How should the results of a survey be followed up?

The value of attitude surveys comes from using the results to identify weaknesses in the organization plan, deciding on actions to address those weaknesses, and bringing about changes to improve efficiency and effectiveness.

Survey follow-up can be handled by individual managers, by work groups, a quality circle or management team, or by specialists within the company.

Who should be responsible for survey follow-up?

One individual who can be made responsible is a "local" manager. He or she is best able to plan actions for the key issues identified in the survey. The local manager may also involve employees in a team problem-solving approach.

Management teams are best able to address issues that cut across individual departments, such as work flow issues, intergroup relationships and areas that deal with organization structure and decision-making.

Issues relating to specific policies or programs, such as pay, training, benefit or career development, are best handled by specialists within the company.

What kinds of questions should be used in an attitude survey?

To give an idea of the types of questions that might be included in an attitude survey, use the Employee Attitude Survey (6-01) shown at the end of this chapter.

What are the most important factors to be considered in group interviews?

You don't need to include all employees in group interviews. It's important, though, to receive input from representatives of key employee groups and different management levels.

Keep these factors in mind:

- Composition. Each group should be composed of people from similar functions and levels. Do not mix workers with supervisors, or office staff with production personnel.
- Size. Make the group between seven and 12 people. That size gives everyone a chance to participate and still provides a variety of perspectives.
- Setting. Use a comfortable setting away from distractions. Don't use a public area such as a cafeteria or employee lounge. Seat members in a circle to encourage discussion.
- Length. Provide at least an hour for the interview. This should allow enough time to cover three areas — job satisfaction, productivity and quality —without getting bogged down.
- Leaders. Have two people conduct the group interview. One facilitates the discussion and keeps it on track while the other takes notes on employee responses. Both leaders remain neutral and should not contribute or evaluate ideas.

What are the ground rules for participants in group interviews?

Follow these rules:

1. Give everyone the right to be heard without interruption or criticism.

2. Don't allow personal attacks on anyone. Keep the discussion work-centered, not personality-centered.
3. Focus on issues of concern to many — not just one or two.
4. Keep a balanced perspective. Make it clear to the group that management is interested in both positive and negative aspects of the workplace.

What kinds of information should be discussed at group interviews?

The Group Attitude Interview Questions form (6-02) located at the end of this chapter will help develop group interviews for employees and managers.

What are the most common response scales that are used in surveys?

Most attitude surveys use five-point, balanced response scales that provide two positive, one neutral and two negative response options. In addition, a "no opinion" option is often provided.

The most common attitude survey response scales are agreement and satisfaction scales:

__ Strongly agree	__ Very satisfied
__ Agree	__ Satisfied
__ Uncertain	__ Uncertain
__ Disagree	__ Dissatisfied
__ Strongly disagree	__ Very dissatisfied
__ No opinion	__ No opinion

A performance rating scale may be used to evaluate management performance and company programs:

__ Very good
__ Good
__ Fair
__ Poor
__ Very poor
__ No opinion

A frequency scale may be used to measure productivity and quality issues:

__ Almost always
__ Very often
__ Half the time

___ Seldom

___ Almost never

___ No opinion

When is it best to schedule attitude surveys?

The best time to schedule an employee attitude survey is when employees will have the time to complete the survey and when management will have the time to study and address the results.

Keep in mind these times when you should *not* schedule surveys:

1. At peak production times. Work pressures divert both employees and management from thoughtfully answering survey questions.
2. Holiday and vacation periods. Avoid periods when many of your employees may be away.
3. Times of labor unrest. You won't get the cooperation of outside officials, and employees will question your motives.
4. Periods of management or structural changes. During these changes, both employee and management may be heavily influenced by uncertainty and fears about their job security. The main exception to this general rule occurs when a key objective of the attitude survey is to gather data about the possible effects of an organizational change or to measure reactions to recent changes.

How does a company decide on the scope and size of the survey?

Your survey objective will give you a general idea of the employee groups you want to survey.

As to scope, there are three basic sampling strategies:

1. A census of the entire organization
2. A sample of the entire organization
3. A census of certain organizational groups

In an organization of fewer than 100 employees, the entire organization can be surveyed at one time.

The main advantages of surveying only a sample of employees are logistical and economic. It may be difficult to survey all employees when they are scattered widely. In a large company, cost is a consideration.

When considering the size of a sample survey, you can use what's known as a "confidence level" which takes into account the accuracy of surveying only a small sample of employees. The Statistical Sample Size Table (6-03) found at the end of the chapter will help you select the size commensurate with various confidence levels. The column on the left refers to the employee population. The other columns give the percent you want your results to fall within. The numbers in those columns tell you how many employees to survey.

What are the most common statistical techniques for tabulating data?

The most common are percent distributions, means, and standard deviations.

Percent distributions indicate the percent of employees who answered each of the available response options for each survey item.

Example item: "My job makes good use of my skills and abilities."

Response Options	Number of Employees	Percent Distribution
1. Strongly disagree	14	3%
2. Disagree	92	20%
3. Uncertain	73	15%
4. Agree	158	34%
5. Strongly agree	128	28%
6. No opinion	0	0%
Total	465	100%

Percentage distributions result in a large number of statistics. Management often wants to summarize survey results with a single number. A mean score can accomplish this. There are three steps to calculating the mean score:

1. Determine the value of each response. The value is the number of employees selecting a response option multiplied by the numerical value of that option.

Example: "My job makes good use of my skills and abilities."

	Response Option	Numerical Value		Number of Employees		Value
1	Strongly disagree	1	x	14	=	14
2.	Disagree	2	x	92	=	184
3.	Uncertain	3	x	73	=	219
4.	Agree	4	x	158	=	632
5.	Strongly agree	5	x	128	=	640
6.	No opinion	0	x	0	=	0
	Total			465		1689

2. Add up the values of their responses:
   $14 + 184 + 219 + 632 + 640 + 0 = 1689$

3. Divide the sum of the values by the number of employees responding to the survey:

   1689 divided by 465 = 3.6 mean score.

Mean scores measure the similarity in employee responses, but they do not indicate how responses vary. The standard deviation measures this variance in responses. The larger the standard deviation, the more dispersed the employee response to the item. The standard deviation indicates the interval where 68% of the responses fall. For example:

	Item 1	Item 2
Mean score	3.0	3.0
Standard deviation	0.7	1.5

Both items have a mean score of 3.0, indicating that, overall, employees were neutral in their response to both items. The standard deviations, however, indicate that employee attitudes toward Item 1 were more similar than attitudes toward Item 2.

In response to Item 1, 68% of the ratings fell between 2.3 and 3.7 (3.0 plus and minus 0.7). In response to Item 2, however employees were more varied in their opinions. That is, 68% of the responses fell between 1.5 and 4.5 (3.0 plus and minus 1.5).

What information should the administrator of the survey cover when distributing the survey?

Survey administrators should provide consistent instructions to all employees. They should answer all questions regarding the survey process.

Administrators should be provided with a sample script so they can communicate a standard set of instructions. Use the Attitude Survey Script (6-04) at the end of the chapter as a model for administrators in your company.

How can a high response to a mail survey be assured?

Take these steps to get high response to mail surveys:

1. Advance communication. Let employees know about the survey before you send it to them in the mail.
2. Cover letter. Send a short cover letter with the survey questionnaire. Have the letter assure participants that the survey replies are confidential and give them a telephone number which they can call to ask questions.
3. Marking instructions. Be sure you've given clear instructions for completing the survey. They should be easy to follow, with a short example on how to enter the responses, and should be short enough to fit on one page.
4. Reminder card. Send out a postcard reminding all surveyed

employees to complete and return the questionnaire. Send the card one week after you've mailed the survey.

5. Return envelope. Provide a postage-paid return envelope for employees to use to return their survey forms.

After survey data is gathered, how is the survey analysis planned?

If possible, conduct the survey analysis in stages. Begin with a descriptive summary of the overall company results. This identifies companywide strengths and concerns and serves as a standard against which to compare the results for departments, divisions or other sub-units of the company. Give these results to your top management team, since it has the authority to plan actions that are companywide in scope.

The second step in the analysis plan is to analyze the results for major sub-units of the organization. You can also analyze groups in different job classifications. As different groups in the organization begin to interpret and plan actions based on survey results, they may ask for survey data for smaller groups. You can plan to offer that at a later date.

What ways can be used to report the results of employee attitude surveys?

Reports of attitude survey results can be organized in many ways, including these:

- Item ranking from most favorable to least favorable items
- Percent distributions of employees' responses
- Trend data
- Relating data to a norm
- Demographic information

How are survey items organized?

Survey items should be organized into topic areas such as job satisfaction, training and development, work group, working conditions, productivity/quality, management support, pay and benefits, etc.

Start by listing the survey items in their appropriate topic areas on the data interpretation worksheet.

How are responses interpreted as favorable or unfavorable?

The most common response scales are five-point, balanced scales. Take the two items on each scale that are "favorable" to management and add them together to determine the total of favorable responses. Take the two items that are "unfavorable" to management and add them together for the unfavorable responses. Then enter these numbers on the data interpretation worksheet in the appropriate columns.

Why are employees sometimes "neutral" on certain items on an attitude survey?

There are several reasons. They may be uncomfortable responding favorably, especially on items which ask them to evaluate their superiors such as "I trust my manager." They may not have enough information to evaluate situations or issues outside their experience, such as "Top management is aware of the problems on my level in the organization."

At times employees have mixed feelings, especially about items that are too general, such as "Overall, how good a job do you feel is being done by your manager?"

If a "not applicable" response option is not included in the scale, employees may select the neutral response. For example, an item such as "I have been properly trained in the safe operation of the tools/machinery I use" may not be relevant to professional office staff.

Employees may be withholding judgment on an issue and thus select the neutral response. For instance, new employees may not yet have an opinion on "How satisfied are you with the way things are run around here?" because they aren't yet sure. Even veteran employees may be uncertain after an organizational change.

What points must be kept in mind when developing trend data from successive surveys?

You do not, of course, have data to develop trends from the first attitude survey. For successive surveys, keep these points in mind to develop trend data:

1. Be sure to word survey items identically from year to year. Even small changes in wording may affect results.

2. Always measure survey items on the same response scale. Changes or additions to the scale such as "no opinion" or "don't know" can influence response distributions dramatically.

3. Pay attention to the changes in the composition of the survey group, such as a substantial increase in new hires.

4. Pay attention to the size of the surveyed groups. For a large group of 1,000, for example, a change of 63 percent to 61 percent may be statistically significant. Such a change for a group of 10 may not be meaningful.

5. As you continue to survey over the years, smaller increases or declines may become more meaningful if they are part of a larger trend.

What does it mean to compare norm differences?

Companies often compare the results of one work group in the company to others.

One group may represent the norm for other groups, and if it does, surveys of that group may make surveys of other groups in the company unnecessary.

When you use normative data, though, follow these guidelines:

- Make sure the data come from comparable sources. Data should represent responses from the same or similar industries (when comparing to external norm bases), job families, locations, etc. Comparing responses from production workers in a rural location to programmers in an urban location won't be meaningful.
- Collect data in a comparable way. Make sure that item wordings and response scales are the same.
- Make sure the size of groups are about the same.
- Note any meaningful norm differences in the appropriate column of the data interpretation worksheet.

How are " strengths" and "concerns" issues determined from the survey data?

Using the Data Interpretation Worksheet (6-05), found at the end of this chapter, classify survey items into "strengths," "concerns," and "borderline" issues. These classifications help management decide priorities for your action plans based on survey results.

The following criteria will help classify the results, but you must also use your own best judgments.

STRENGTHS

- Items with more than 50 percent favorable responses and less than 30 percent unfavorable responses.

CONCERNS

- Items with less than 50 percent favorable responses and more than 30 percent unfavorable responses.
- Items showing a meaningful drop in satisfaction over time.
- Items significantly below the favorable rating of a comparable norm group.

BORDERLINE ISSUES

- Items with a high percent of neutral responses or items with an even split across the favorable/unfavorable/neutral categories.
- Items that are peripheral to the functioning of the group.

Classify the items for each topic area and note them with an "S," "C," or "B" in the appropriate column of the data interpretation worksheet.

Who should be assigned to do the interpretation of surveys?

Because interpreting survey results can be highly complex, you may want to include a group of managers from other areas; or, you may assign certain topic areas to members of the management team.

For example, you may assign a representative from benefits to interpret pay and benefits items; a management team to interpret strategy items. You may also decide to bring all these groups together to share their interpretations.

The group can explore issues of strengths and concerns and begin to set priorities for action plan solutions.

What must be done to make an employee attitude survey serve a true problem-solver?

A feedback process which allows management to use the survey information to improve conditions in the organization must be established.

Successful feedback systems have these components:

1. Top management must develop action plans based on the survey data and share survey results with managers and employees.
2. Direct attention to future improvements, not to assigning blame for past mistakes.
3. Identify resource specialists in the company who will help managers in interpretation and action planning. These are usually human resource and organizational development specialists.
4. Monitor progress of the action plans and recognize improvements.

What steps should be taken to follow up on a survey?

Survey follow-up begins with a presentation of the survey results. This should include both presentations by top management to executives and then to managers, supervisors and employees.

Issues should then be defined in terms of:

- Who has the problem?
- When does the problem occur?
- What is the effect of the problem on organizational goals?
- Why does the problem occur?

Because surveys normally identify several issues, priorities in addressing them should be set. Once a problem has been identified and targeted, the next step is to generate, evaluate and select solutions.

Formal, written action plans should be developed to deal with the problems. The plans will spell out the exact action to be taken and the time span for each action. Action plans also communicate needs and requirements to top management for gaining approval.

An important part of the follow-up process is monitoring progress and the effects of the actions. It is critical that employees be informed of the actions planned as well as the survey results. Publish them in company newsletters and magazines, through memos and meetings.

What are the best survey follow-up strategies?

Three common follow-up strategies are through management teams, organizational specialists, and local managers. Examples of each—Forms 6-06, 6-07 and 6-08— are shown at the end of the chapter.

How should survey follow-up and feedback be planned?

There is no one best way to plan your survey follow-up and feedback. Conditions vary widely from one company to another. The variations make it even more important, though, to make your plans concrete.

An Attitude Survey Follow-up Strategy Worksheet (6-09), located at the end of the chapter, should be used by managers assigned to the follow-up task so that effective plans and timetables can be set.

What are the most common ways of sharing survey results?

There are many methods of sharing survey results. One or more of the following may be used:

1. Share the complete survey report with executives and managers. After they have time to read the report, have a meeting to discuss it.

2. Some organizations prepare videotapes. A high-level executive outlines the survey results on the video. An advantage of this method is that everyone receives the same interpretation of the survey.

3. Perhaps the most common method is an oral presentation, supplemented by slides, overhead transparencies or other visual aids. The presentation should be organized to help the audience see patterns in the data. Displays should be kept simple and limited in number, with the key results emphasized in the presentation.

What should be covered in a meeting to present survey results?

Be sure to outline the objectives of the meeting, the steps in the survey process and the ground rules for participation.

Explain why the survey was conducted, who was involved in planning and designing the survey, how many employees were surveyed, what is to be covered at the meeting, and management's commitment to follow up on the problems uncovered. Explain, too, who are the members of the surveyed group and what methods of comparison will be used.

Keep in mind that participation from the individuals at the meeting should be encouraged. So, ground rules should include the following:

- Everyone should feel free to participate and to be heard without interruption.
- Aim for understanding first, and focus on possible solutions later in the process.
- Discuss strengths as well as concerns.
- Avoid personal attacks; issues must be work-centered.
- Focus on solving problems for the future, not on assigning blame for the past.

Finally, outline the procedure for planning actions in response to the survey results.

What are usually the most sensitive issues from the survey to be discussed and how should they be handled?

The most sensitive issues are the ones that refer to individuals, their job performance, and their roles in the organization. These may include such topics as management styles, leadership abilities and company policies and procedures. Management must show that it is sincerely interested in understanding these issues, and express concern and willingness to listen.

Other sensitive topic areas include problems between individuals or groups, problems with company policies, and individual concerns, some of which may be unrelated to the survey.

How can solutions be generated for the problem areas revealed by an employee attitude survey?

Solutions are usually generated in a group setting. One proven technique is brainstorming. For that technique, emphasize these guidelines:

1. No idea is too out-of-the-ordinary to be suggested.
2. Ideas are not to be evaluated at this time.
3. Others' ideas are not to be criticized. It's best to build on them.
4. Generate as many ideas as possible.

Organized Quality Circles, if you have them, are also good generators of solutions. In separate meetings, have the groups begin to evaluate the ideas for solutions. The

Attitude Survey Solution Evaluation Form (6-10) shown at the end of the chapter, will help guide groups or individuals in evaluating solutions.

How are action plans made to get the necessary organizational changes underway?

Employee attitude surveys won't change an organization. Changes occur when information is used to plan and implement changes. Plans must be put into writing. Include the following key facts:

- Problem summary
- Goals
- Proposed actions
- Responsible parties
- Time frames
- Tracking procedures.

An action plan should be written up by a manager for all issues within his control. Other issues should be referred to individuals who can plan the actions for issues in their control. The Action Planning Form (6-11) at the end of the chapter will help put an action plan in writing.

What information must always be included when communicating survey results to employees?

There are two important pieces of information that should be included:

1. A summary of the survey results, including the strengths and concerns identified by the survey.
2. A summary of management actions taken in response to survey results.

How should survey efforts be reinforced?

Organizational change takes time. Remind employees from time to time of the connection between survey results and changes in management practices, programs and policies — or they may think nothing has happened as a result of the survey.

Whenever implementing a change, inform employees of the connection between the survey and the management action to make the change. Report on progress of action plans throughout the year, since many changes take a year — or even more — to take place.

EMPLOYEE ATTITUDE SURVEY

(Circle one number for each question)

	Strongly Disagree	Disagree	Uncertain	Agree	Strongly Agree	No Opinion
TRAINING AND DEVELOPMENT						
1. I am given a real opportunity to improve my skills in this company.	1	2	3	4	5	0
2. I am satisfied with on-the-job training I received for my present job.	1	2	3	4	5	0
3. I am satisfied with opportunities to get a better job with this company.	1	2	3	4	5	0
4. I am satisfied with the progress I'm making in my career.	1	2	3	4	5	0
WORK GROUP						
5. Things run smoothly in my work group.	1	2	3	4	5	0
6. The work load is divided fairly among the people in my work group.	1	2	3	4	5	0
7. The people I work with cooperate to get the work done.	1	2	3	4	5	0
8. My work group has enough people to get the work done.	1	2	3	4	5	0
9. Morale is high in my work group.	1	2	3	4	5	0

	Strongly Disagree	Disagree	Uncertain	Agree	Strongly Agree	No Opinion
WORKING CONDITIONS						
How satisfied are you with...						
10. The physical working conditions - heating, lighting, ventilation?	1	2	3	4	5	0
11. The attention paid to safety in the workplace?	1	2	3	4	5	0
12. The equipment you use to perform your job?	1	2	3	4	5	0

PRODUCTIVITY/WORK QUALITY

How frequently is each of the following conditions a road block to you in getting work done in your current job?

How often...	Almost Always	Very Often	Half the Time	Seldom	Almost Never	No Opinion
13. Do you have trouble getting the information you need to do your job well?	1	2	3	4	5	0
14. Are you given deadlines that are unreasonable?	1	2	3	4	5	0
15. Does meeting a deadline get higher priority than providing quality products or services?	1	2	3	4	5	0
16. Does keeping costs down get higher priority than providing quality products or services?	1	2	3	4	5	0
17. Does your work group have problems doing the work because of another group?	1	2	3	4	5	0
18. Do you have trouble getting the materials or equipment you need to do your job?	1	2	3	4	5	0

MANAGEMENT SUPPORT

Your manager is the person primarily responsible for giving you work direction and evaluating your performance. Supervisors and foremen are managers. The following questions are about your current manager, even if you have been reporting to that person for only a short time.

	Strongly Disagree	Disagree	Uncertain	Agree	Strongly Agree	No Opinion
19. I trust my supervisor.	1	2	3	4	5	0
20. My manager is fair toward me.	1	2	3	4	5	0
21. My manager makes it clear what I am expected to do.	1	2	3	4	5	0
22. My manager gives me useful feedback on how well I'm doing my job.	1	2	3	4	5	0
23. My manager listens to my ideas.	1	2	3	4	5	0
24. My manager keeps me informed of upcoming changes that affect my job.	1	2	3	4	5	0

ATTITUDE GROUP INTERVIEW QUESTIONS

JOB SATISFACTION

1. We are interested in finding out what factors are important in determining job satisfaction. What do you like best about your job?

_____

_____

_____

(Probe for information on the following topics:
the job itself, supervision, working conditions, employee programs.)

2. What things make you most dissatisfied with your job?

_____

_____

_____

PRODUCTIVITY

1. What things get in the way of doing your job efficiently?

_____

_____

_____

(Probe for information on the following factors:
procedural barriers, resources, manpower, training, lack of information.)

2. Have there been any recent changes that have helped you become more productive in your job?

_____

_____

_____

WORK QUALITY

1. What factors contribute to the quality of the product or service you provide?

_____

_____

2. What things prevent you from providing as high quality a product or service as you would like?

_____

_____

_____

(Probe for information on the following factors:
material and equipment specifications, cost and time considerations.)

STATISTICAL SAMPLE SIZE TABLE

POPULATION SIZE Column A	Column B +/-1%	CONFIDENCE LEVEL Column C +/-3%	Column D +/-5%	Column E +/-10%
10	10	9	9	7
20	19	17	16	12
30	29	25	22	16
40	38	32	28	19
50	46	39	33	22
60	55	46	38	25
70	64	52	43	27
80	72	58	47	29
90	81	64	51	31
100	89	70	55	32
120	106	81	63	35
140	122	92	70	37
160	138	102	76	39
180	153	111	82	41
200	169	121	87	43
250	207	142	99	46
300	244	162	110	48
350	279	180	119	50
400	314	196	127	52
450	348	212	134	53
500	382	226	141	54
600	446	253	152	56
700	509	276	161	58
800	569	298	169	59
900	627	317	176	60
1000	683	334	182	60
1500	941	403	203	63
2000	1169	451	216	64
3000	1560	516	231	65
4000	1888	557	240	66
5000	2169	586	245	66
10,000	3163	657	257	67
50,000	5387	730	268	68

1. First choose the population size (Column A) representing the total size of the group you are researching.
2. Then read to the right to choose the sample size from Columns B through E that will give you the confidence level you seek. Most researchers will be satisfied with a +/- 5% confidence level (Column D).
3. For example, if surveying a company with 100 employees, a sampling of 55 will yield a confidence level of +/- 5%, indicating that under exactly the same conditions, the results produced would be no more than +/- 5% from those received.

ATTITUDE SURVEY SCRIPT

KEY POINTS	SCRIPT
Purpose of survey	This survey is designed to capture your opinions on what it is like to work for (company name). Your honest opinions are important because you are in the best position to know what aspects of your job are important and how they influence your attitudes about your work and your company.
Confidentiality	Your answers will be completely confidential. Do not sign your name on your survey. Results will be reported only in groups to protect your privacy. No individual responses will be identified through the survey. After the surveys are scored and transcribed, they will be destroyed.
Follow-up plans	Management will receive a report on the survey results and will meet to discuss the results and plan actions in response to the survey.
Employee communications	There will be companywide communications on the survey results and planned actions by (date).
Opinion statements	There are (number) opinion statements that make up the core of the Employee Attitude Survey. Read each statement and mark the response that best describes your opinion.
Demographic items	Certain questions ask you to identify characteristics of your job or yourself. This information will be used only to identify critical employee groups and will not be used to identify individual responses.
Written comments	The final section of the survey provides space for you to write your comments. We encourage you to do so.
Marking instructions	Select only one answer for each survey question. Mark your answer by circling the number that best represents your views. A "No Opinion" option has been provided for you. Use this option only if you feel you do not have enough information to answer the question. If you decide to change an answer, please erase it completely.
Not a test	Let me emphasize that this survey is not a test. There are no right or wrong answers. We want your candid opinions, whether they are positive or negative.
Return envelope	When you've finished your survey, please seal it in the return envelope and place it in the collection box.

DATA INTERPRETATION WORKSHEET

Topic Area: SUPERVISORY RELATIONSHIPS	Percent Favorable	Percent Unfavorable	Percent Neutral	Strength/ Borderline/ Concern
1. Overall, how good a job do you think is being done by your manager?	65	14	21	S
2. My manager is fair toward me.	63	25	12	S
3. My manager is available when I need to talk about my job.	43	31	26	C
4. My manager makes it clear what I am expected to do.	73	17	10	S
5. My manager gives me useful feedback on how well I'm doing my job.	46	39	15	C
6. The supervision I get from my manager helps me do a better job than I could do on my own.	37	29	34	B
7. My manager sees that I get recognition when I do a good job.	40	35	25	C
8. My manager shows favoritism toward certain employees.	49	27	24	B
9. My manager respects me as an individual.	69	13	18	S

ATTITUDE SURVEY FOLLOW-UP—
MANAGEMENT TEAM APPROACH

1. Presenting results. Survey results are summarized by survey specialists and reported to a 12 member executive committee.

2. Clarifying issues. Committee discusses survey results, clarifies issues and identifies information needs.

3. Setting priorities. Committee members individually review results and compile a list of the top strengths and concerns. Committee reconvenes to share their lists and to collectively prioritize issues.

4. Generating solutions. Committee brainstorms follow-up strategy and possible solutions for priority concerns.

5. Action planning. Committee members are assigned problem areas for follow-up.

6. Tracking. Committee meets monthly for next three months to report on progress.

7. Employee communications. Company president sends all employees a letter outlining survey results and planned actions.

ATTITUDE SURVEY FOLLOW-UP—
ORGANIZATIONAL SPECIALIST APPROACH

1. Presenting results. Organizational specialists interpret the survey results for each department and meet with the department manager to review the findings.

2. Clarifying issues. Organizational specialists lead clarification meetings with employees and department manager to clarify and discuss survey results.

3. Setting priorities. Issues within the department's control are identified and prioritized.

4. Generating solutions. Department manager and employees brainstorm possible solutions to problem areas. Organizational specialist and department manager meet to evaluate and select solutions.

5. Action planning. Organizational specialist drafts an action plan for department manager's approval. Action plans are presented to employees by department manager.

6. Tracking. Department manager meets with his superior every three months to review progress on action plans.

7. Employee communications. Employees are updated on progress of action plans at monthly department meetings.

**ATTITUDE SURVEY FOLLOW-UP—
LOCAL MANAGEMENT APPROACH**

1. Presenting results. Overall survey results are presented to employees by plant manager at special communication meeting. Individual department results are presented to employees by department managers.

2. Clarifying issues. Line managers clarify issues with employees at department meetings. Employees recommend solutions.

3. Setting priorities. Managers meet in teams to prioritize issues for functional areas.

4. Generating solutions. Managers merge their lists of employee recommendations, evaluate and select solutions.

5. Action planning. Action plans are drafted by managers and presented to plant manager for approval.

6. Tracking. Managers report on progress of action items in monthly staff meetings with plant manager.

7. Employee communications. Approved action plans are presented to employees by their managers. Managers report on progress of action items in monthly communication meetings with employees.

SURVEY FOLLOW-UP STRATEGY WORKSHEET

STEP	PLANNED ACTIVITIES	PARTICIPANTS/ RESPONSIBILITIES	TIME FRAME
Presenting Results			
Clarifying Issues			
Setting Priorities			
Generating Solutions			
Action Planning			
Tracking			
Employee Communications			

ATTITUDE SURVEY SOLUTION EVALUATION FORM

PROBLEM: _____

_____

_____

PROPOSED SOLUTION: _____

_____

_____

(For each criteria, indicate the impact of the proposed solution)

CRITERIA

1. Cost—Human resources _____

_____

_____

2. Cost—Capital expenditures _____

_____

_____

3. Time to implement _____

_____

_____

4. Side effects _____

_____

_____

5. Policies/procedures _____

_____

_____

6. Other _____ _____

_____

_____

7. Other _____ _____

_____

_____

Action Planning Form (6-11)

ACTION PLANNING FORM

Department/Committee: _____

Manager/Leader: _____ Date: _____

Problem Summary: _____
_____
_____

Goals: _____
_____
_____

Proposed Actions	Responsible Party	Time Frame	Tracking Procedures
1. _____ _____ _____	_____	_____	_____ _____
2. _____ _____ _____	_____	_____	_____ _____
3. _____ _____ _____	_____	_____	_____ _____
4. _____ _____ _____	_____	_____	_____ _____
5. _____ _____ _____	_____	_____	_____ _____
6. _____ _____ _____	_____	_____	_____ _____

Approved by: _____ Date: _____

Manpower Planning 7

What is manpower planning?

Manpower planning is an important development in human resources management. It has spread rapidly to nearly every size organization in almost every kind of business.

The primary function of manpower planning is to analyze and evaluate the human resources available in the organization, and to determine how to obtain the kinds of personnel needed to staff positions ranging from assembly line workers to chief executives. Smaller companies put manpower planning in the human resource or personnel department. Some of the largest corporations have established separate departments for this function.

What are the purposes of manpower planning?

Manpower planning aims to reduce waste in employing people, lessen uncertainty about current manpower levels and future needs, and eliminate mistakes in staffing.

Its purposes also include avoiding worker and skills shortages, stopping the profit-eroding effects of being over- or understaffed, preparing succession plans and shaping the optimum future work force by hiring the right managers, technical specialists and skilled workers in appropriate numbers.

What are the trends that impact manpower planning?

A manpower planner seeking to identify trends in human resource management should include the following variables:

1. The state of the economy. The larger the company's sphere of operations, the broader the spectrum of economic activity to consider.
2. Demographics. The age and sex groupings of the population and what may happen to them in the future.

3. Employee losses or turnover. How will retirements, deaths, promotions and resignations affect the current number of individuals employed at every level?
4. New skill requirements. What new skills will be needed due to new technology markets or products?
5. Obsolescence of current skills and its effects.
6. The status and direction of materials prices.
7. The availability of materials—can they be cut off by uncontrollable events?
8. Technological changes.
9. Social changes. What effects do upgrading of educational backgrounds have on the willingness of people to take menial or other types of lower level jobs?
10. Labor costs. In which direction and how far will they go? What are the alternatives?

How does a company organize for manpower planning?

While manpower planning does not require formation of an independent department in most companies, it does require a manager or executive responsible for studying trends and for identifying and calculating manpower requirements. The responsible person, who may have other duties in the company, must know company policy and be acquainted with its long-range objectives. He or she should understand what's involved in training and career development, and should be able to design career programs to improve basic capabilities, develop professional competence and teach new skills.

The manpower planner must organize in the following areas:

- Maintenance of a good data base of the organization's human resources.
- Acquisition, retention and career development of the company's high talent people, such as engineers, scientists, and key managers and executives.
- Supervision of the design of various training programs.
- Surveys of current economic and social conditions and their trends.

Where does the manpower planner fit into an organization?

Companies with fewer than 100 employees usually assign the manpower planning function as an additional duty to a specific executive, such as general manager, production manager or the personnel manager. Large companies employ a manpower-planning specialist and may create a separate department for the function.

The position of the planner is not as important as the qualifications of the individual. The task is advisory and investigative. Whoever runs the planning operation is a staff rather than line person and will not issue direct orders to other managers.

Where does manpower planning begin?

Manpower planning begins with a clear understanding of the current manpower situation in the company. The first step is an analysis of current manpower—numbers, skills and skill levels. The second is the creation of a skills inventory.

How do employment applications contribute to manpower planning?

Employment applications, when properly constructed, can help build a database for manpower planning. Research starts with employment applications. The more detailed the application, the more information the planner can gather.

From the employment application form, the manpower planner can compile certain information such as:

1. Number of secondary school graduates
2. Number of college graduates
3. Disciplines studied at colleges and types of degrees earned
4. Listings of prior work experiences
5. Listings of types of work desired

What information should be included in an inventory of skills currently available in a company?

A well-designed skills inventory includes much information not directly related to on-the-job skills and performance. Include many kinds of information for the start-up of manpower planning. Your organization may grow, shrink or have changing needs. It's easier to gather information at the beginning rather than to re-work it at a later date.

Include the following data in your skills inventory:

Name, address, telephone number	Date of birth
Current position	Skill level
Years (months) with company	Education
Marital status	Dependents and their ages
Salary history	Seminars and training completed
Disciplinary actions	Date of retirement
Future assignments (company planned)	Future assignments (employee preferences)
Willingness to relocate	Language abilities
Restrictions on assignments	Hobbies

| Published works | Patents obtained |
| Special qualifications | Unusual combinations of high-level skills |

For each group of employees, gather as much information in your skills inventory as possible. Some companies supplement the information gathered from the employment application by asking employees to fill out comprehensive personal history files after they've been on the job for awhile. Add new items as they seem necessary. Be sure to keep the inventory up-to-date as changes are made. And in all cases maintain only that information permitted by federal and state law.

What are the steps to develop human resource data for future manpower needs?

Organizing the data requires a certain amount of cross-filing and tabulating. In a small organization, this can be done manually, though a personal computer will serve to make organizing, updating and accessing data easier.

Large companies use their central data processing systems to store human resource data and write programs to accomplish tasks the manpower planner desires. Among the data processing capabilities the planner should have are abilities to sort data relating to the length of service, pay grade, educational level, disciplinary background, marital status, and number of dependents. Other classifications are possible, especially when the data is gathered and stored by computer. The Human Resources Data Sequence Checklist (7-01), shown at the end of the chapter, graphically depicts the data gathering and organization sequence.

How can occupational codes be developed to help organize and access employee information?

An occupational code, which is a numerical designation for each type of job, focuses on the qualities of each individual and permits planners to see at a glance not only the skills of each individual, but the level of competence and other data.

Most planners do not need the precise designations of an occupational code that the government has devised, though you can use such a system if available. Usually, a simple alphabetical list of skills will serve the purpose of listing individuals with the same qualifications under one heading.

For instance, a partial listing might look like this:

- Assembler, electrical
- Assembler, mechanical
- Machinist
- Mechanic, fork lift
- Operator, drill press
- Operator, milling machine

List the names of each person possessing a skill on the appropriate skill card, or store on a computer. List those with combinations of skills, too.

What are the effects of turnover on manpower planning?

Turnover creates unnecessary expense and reduces efficiency. Productivity drops. When a planner identifies high turnover in a specific department, the quality of training and supervision in that department should be looked into. As a part of the human resources function, the planner would contribute to the decision on what steps should be taken to remedy the turnover situation, such as training, pay and incentive improvements, and the like. The human resources manager would then go to management with the problem of turnover and make the combined recommendations.

It's also important to determine exactly why workers, supervisors or managers leave. Every departing employee should have an exit interview and your company should maintain a record of the reasons for leaving. You should ask individuals who quit to fill out an Exit Interview Attitude Survey (7-02) shown at the end of the chapter.

Plans to reduce turnover are an important part of a manpower planner's job. The success in the task of reducing turnover goes a long way to insuring that a company has the right number of persons with the right skills to fulfill the company's needs and make it a successful organization.

What uses do manpower planners make of turnover figures?

Planners use turnover figures to pinpoint departments where turnover is occurring and to discover its causes. For instance, the planner may find that poor supervision is an important cause of turnover. If so, he or she can take steps to have something done about the quality of supervision in the affected area.

Age is also a factor in turnover. Older employees tend to be more stable than young workers. Overqualified employees are very unstable and entry level workers are likely to quit soon after they are hired.

Among executives, a high turnover rate among the younger ones often indicates that something is wrong with the way the company manages its career advancements. Manpower planners should bring these matters to the attention of top management with recommendations for corrective actions.

How do changes such as automation and computerization affect manpower planning?

When planners examine company records, they should learn whether the introduction of new machines, methods or materials have altered the numbers of people with certain skills. Such information is important for forecasting future requirements.

If the introduction of a computer-controlled machine, for example, results in the elimination of machine operators, these skills should be eliminated from the inventory of needed skills. They should be replaced, of course, with those needed to run the computer-controlled machines and with specialists skilled in electronic maintenance.

As planners uncover such changes and trends, they can concentrate on the new skills needed and no longer consider those that are not. Turnover figures also affect training programs. The planner examines them to find out how well or poorly such programs are serving the company's objectives.

What is the role of the manpower planner in career planning?

The manpower planner usually has a distinct advantage over other managers and executives when it comes to career matters. It is essential for successful execution of the job that the planner be very clear and up-to-date about the organization's objectives.

The objective of career management from the company's viewpoint is to ensure the availability of qualified successors for every important position. Managers and supervisors want to get ahead, earn good salaries and gain new opportunities. Only rarely can these individuals clearly define what getting ahead means to them.

The planner, though, knows what sort of person should be in a specific job, or as a backup for a specific person. Through skillful career guidance, the planner has the leverage to encourage supervisors and managers to prepare for advancement.

How does the manpower planner prepare for forecasting future manpower requirements?

Practical manpower forecasting should generally be limited to five years or less. Society and technology change too rapidly to permit accurate forecasting for longer periods of time.

The planner begins by studying the company's operational plan in detail to determine its objectives regarding:

- Capital investment in buildings and new machinery
- Proposed changes in product design
- Proposed introductions of new products
- Changes in materials to be used
- Changes in sales volumes forecast

In addition to these major influences on future manpower requirements, the planner considers turnover rates, retirements, internal promotions, and effects of improved supervision. He or she must also consider the learning curve, that is, how long it takes for qualified personnel to reach full output after any changes have been made.

How does the manpower planner estimate the numbers of people and the skills the company will need?

Estimates of the company's economic activity, usually prepared in the marketing or budgeting area, form the basis for the planner's calculations. He or she first determines the relationship between how many and what kinds of people the company requires to produce the current volume of product.

There is not a linear relationship between increases in volume and manpower requirements. An increase of 50 percent in annual production will not necessarily require a 50 percent increase in managers. It might, though, require a 50 percent increase in entry-level workers, depending upon their productivity levels.

A Manpower Requirements Planning Form—Short Term (7-03), located at the end of the chapter, is used by planners to estimate the numbers of people and skills a company will need within the next year. The Manpower Requirements Planning Form—Long Term (7-04) is used for periods beyond one year. When using the worksheet, a planner discusses actual needs with various managers. He or she also gets input from top management. The planner enters on the worksheet a consensus, tempered by personal knowledge and experience, of everyone's best estimates.

Forecasting high-level personnel needs is directly related to the accuracy of the company's plans, particularly its long-range ones. The planner must make allowances for promotable individuals within the company, as well as the need to recruit managers from outside.

Requirements for high-level personnel do not appear as quickly as for production people. The business can grow substantially before it becomes necessary to create new areas which require managers or new divisions or groups headed by general managers. A planner must take these lags in the timing of personnel requirements into account.

What role does the manpower planner play in succession planning?

Every company should have a succession plan that identifies a qualified subordinate who is ready to replace each key manager or executive. While the planner has no authority to select successors, he or she should, with the help of top management, prepare a succession chart that does name subordinates who can step up when a superior departs.

A Succession Chart (7-05) is shown at the end of the chapter. Such charts should, of course, be kept strictly confidential. Advance publication is likely to demoralize managers who find themselves passed over.

The names above each job title are the incumbents. The names below the line are the prospective successors. A more complete chart would extend further to show the succession at more levels, especially in a large company. To be useful, the succession chart must be kept up-to-date.

How does manpower planning help cope with skill shortages?

Rapid advances in technology cause serious mismatches between the jobs that are available and the number of people with the necessary skills to fill those jobs. In addition, rising levels of education have brought with them rising expectations among employees at all levels. As a result, some workers will not accept training or positions that they believe are not beneficial to their careers.

By analyzing tasks, the manpower planner often finds that a company is not achieving maximum efficiency in its use of a certain type of talent. Some jobs are held by individuals who have more advanced skills or training than is needed. Sometimes the task can be done by a lower-level worker, rather than, say, a university educated employee. The planner should bring this situation to the attention of managers who have the authority to make the necessary changes and thus relieve what seems to be a skills shortage.

Another approach which the planner might use would be to redesign jobs. Reducing boredom and monotony, and increasing comfort, often increases productivity. As a result, positions for which skills are in short supply may not require more personnel, as more productive and skilled individuals produce more.

One company, faced with a shortage of skilled warehouse workers, built automated warehouses. That reduced the number of workers needed while increasing efficiency in the warehousing operation. Other options include finding machines that can do the work; breaking down skilled jobs into less skilled components; or modifying the product to eliminate the need for the skill that is in short supply.

What is involved in administrative control regarding a manpower program?

The planner must monitor the system on a continuing basis to ensure that it gets results. Your manpower planner will benefit from clearly expressed interest in the program from top management. Such recognition gains cooperation throughout the organization.

Whatever actions are taken in manpower planning that affect the skills or experiences of workers, office employees, supervisors or managers, must be recorded. All such data must be made part of each individual's personnel record. They must also be entered on the planner's skills inventory. Only when this is done can the planner know the nature and number of personnel and skills available.

Regular reports from department heads play a part in administering the manpower planning program. Information the manpower planner should receive on a regular basis includes:

- Absentee rate
- Turnover rate
- Hard-to-fill jobs
- Names of exceptional individuals and their skills
- Requests for training programs
- Individuals who have been trained in certain skills but are not working at the skill in which they are most proficient

Monitoring the program allows the manpower planner to compare what was planned with what is actually happening. Thus, monitoring provides an important form of administrative control.

Human Resources Data Sequence Checklist (7-01)

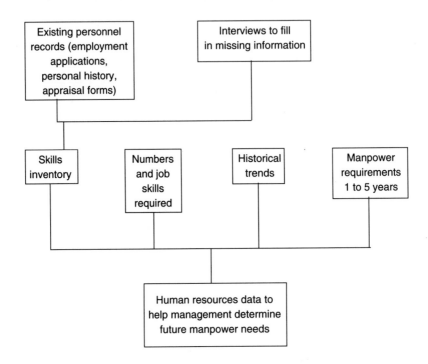

EXIT INTERVIEW ATTITUDE SURVEY

Please circle the response that best describes your feelings, using the key as follows:

1. Strongly agree
2. Agree
3. Neutral
4. Disagree
5. Strongly disagree

1. The work I was doing on the whole was approximately what I originally expected to be doing.	1	2	3	4	5
2. My superiors demanded a lot less of me than I thought they would.	1	2	3	4	5
3. I wanted more responsibility than the company gave me.	1	2	3	4	5
4. The people I worked with were interesting and stimulating.	1	2	3	4	5
5. Generally, my co-workers were friendly and supportive.	1	2	3	4	5
6. Overall, I was satisfied with the working conditions.	1	2	3	4	5
7. I had the necessary freedom to make my own decisions.	1	2	3	4	5
8. I would recommend the company to my friends as a good organization to work for.	1	2	3	4	5
9. There was too much pressure on the job.	1	2	3	4	5
10. I found my work load to be excessive.	1	2	3	4	5
11. I found my work to be interesting and challenging.	1	2	3	4	5
12. I was able to make good use of my skills and abilities.	1	2	3	4	5
13. I had ample opportunities for personal training and career development.	1	2	3	4	5
14. I had ample opportunities to advance within the company.	1	2	3	4	5

15. I knew that if I performed
well I would get ahead.   1   2   3   4   5

16. The company's performance
appraisal system accurately
reflected my strengths and
weaknesses.   1   2   3   4   5

17. In my division/department,
salary increases and promotions
are clearly linked with
performance.   1   2   3   4   5

18. I was satisfied with my salary.   1   2   3   4   5

19. I received adequate support
(materials, resources,
etc.) from the company.   1   2   3   4   5

20. I did not always find the company's
promotion policy a fair one.   1   2   3   4   5

21. I did not have easy access to my
supervisor/manager.   1   2   3   4   5

22. My supervisor/manager treated
me fairly.   1   2   3   4   5

23. My supervisor/manager supported
me adequately.   1   2   3   4   5

24. My supervisor/manager was generally
sensitive to my needs.   1   2   3   4   5

25. My supervisor/manager was open
and willing to aid me in planning
a career path.   1   2   3   4   5

26. My supervisor/manager let me know
when he/she was pleased with
my work.   1   2   3   4   5

27. My supervisor/manager made every
effort to be fair with me regarding
pay increases.   1   2   3   4   5

**MANPOWER REQUIREMENTS
PLANNING FORM—SHORT-TERM**

1. What are our two major labor requirements in the next year?

   _____

   _____

   _____

2. What skills are required? What level of skills?

   Skills required   Level of skills

   _____   _____

   _____   _____

   _____   _____

   _____   _____

3. What is the situation in regard to the supply of persons who have, or can quickly acquire, these skills?

   _____

   _____

   _____

   _____

   _____

4. What is likely to happen to wage rates, benefit costs, holiday time and employee attitudes during the next year?

   _____

   _____

   _____

   _____

   _____

5. What training capabilities are immediately available if needed?

   _____

   _____

   _____

6. Considering the sales and cash flow anticipated from future production and marketing estimates, can the company finance the costs associated with acquiring, training and compensating the total manpower requirements?

   _____

   _____

   _____

**MANPOWER REQUIREMENTS
PLANNING FORM—LONG-TERM**

(To calculate manpower requirements for periods of longer than one year)

Time Period From _____ To_____

Number of people required at end of time period   _____

Number employed now   _____

Loss of personnel
    Retirements   _____
    Deaths   _____
    Discharged   _____
    Quit   _____
    Promoted Out   _____
    Laid Off   _____

Total losses during time period   _____

Gains of personnel
    New hires (routine)   _____
    Promoted In   _____
    Training Graduates   _____

Additional personnel required   _____

Submitted by _____ Date _____

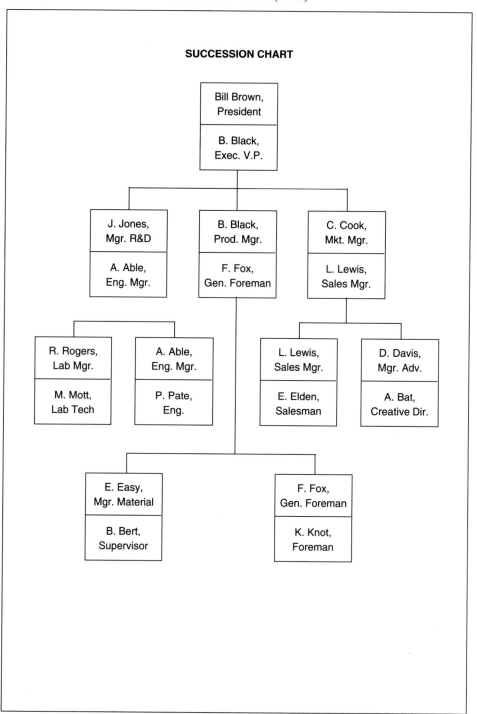

SUCCESSION CHART

Developing Successful Personnel Policies and Procedures 8

Why does a company need written personnel policies and procedures?

Written policies and procedures are an essential tool in the daily battle against the barrage of inquiries and complaints about pay procedures, promotion policies, vacation scheduling conflicts, turnover problems and grievance procedures—to name just a few.

Company policies set productive standards of conduct, create systems to deal with complaints, reduce faulty communications, and insure consistency in discipline, safety and work rules. Moreover, written policies help avoid charges of favoritism on the one hand and unfairness and discrimination on the other. Written policies and procedures help create and maintain a happier, more satisfied and more productive workforce.

How does a policy manual differ from an employee handbook?

A policy manual is used by managers and supervisors. It establishes how they are to implement the company's policies. An employee handbook, in contrast, is given to all employees. Its purpose is to provide employees with information about the company and its policies and to advise them of their benefits.

The policies in this chapter were written to be included in a policy manual. They can be easily modified for inclusion in an employee handbook by simply removing the sections meant only for supervisory personnel.

What policies are essential for running an organization effectively?

While there are no limits on the number of policy statements that can be put in a company policy, the following are essential and should be clearly and carefully worded:

1. Employee responsibilities — general
2. Compensation practices and pay schedules
3. Employee discipline
4. Grievances and appeals
5. Safety and health
6. Eligibility for paid holidays

7. Sick leave
8. Employee benefits programs
9. Termination of employment

Policies and forms covering these areas and others of interest to most companies are found at the end of the chapter.

What key information should be included in policies on employee responsibilities?

Policies on employee responsibilities should include the following items in detail:

1. Attendance and punctuality—exact work hours, what to do when late for work, absent, discipline for absenteeism and lateness.
2. Overtime availability—your company's policy on overtime and its expectations for employees' availability.
3. Performance review—the fact that reviews of performance by supervisors will be made; encouragement of employees to discuss their performance with supervisors at any time.
4. Safety—compliance with rules, and reports of violations.
5. Ethics and personal conduct—relationships with other workers and honesty.

Why is a written policy on compensation and pay policies essential?

Few managers or supervisors, and even fewer employees, are required to have an in-depth knowledge of compensation. You should require that your compensation and pay practices policy include these items:

1. Rate of pay before anything is deducted or extra pay is added
2. Extra pay — overtime, holiday pay, weekend premiums, shift differentials, cost of living allowances
3. Salary or wage ranges by grades
4. Effect on pay of promotions
5. Effect on pay of reassignments
6. Premium pay for working under unusual conditions
7. Merit pay — how earned
8. Incentive pay — how earned
9. Time and day of delivery of paychecks
10. Vacation paychecks
11. Advance paychecks

Why should companies issue policies on employee discipline?

In few areas of employee relations is a companywide policy so important as in employee discipline. Policies governing the handling of employee misconduct, lateness, absence, abuse of meal and break time, and failure to comply with company procedures are crucial to ensure consistency and fairness.

Penalties that employees may be subject to include:

1. Warnings
2. Oral or written reprimands
3. Suspension without pay
4. Reduction in position grade and salary
5. Termination of employment

As part of your written policies you should explain:

1. Responsibilities of supervisors to enforce discipline
2. How to implement discipline
3. Follow-up actions and record keeping

Should there be a provision for grievances?

Fair treatment of employees requires that you structure a grievance system to deal with employee complaints and to resolve problems.

The provision should cover these important points:

1. Steps in the formal filing procedure
2. Guidelines for grievance hearings
3. How to appeal a grievance

What points should be covered in a policy on safety and health?

Blame for injuries or health failures is often shifted to the company these days. Occasionally, legal actions will be taken against the company by injured or ill employees. Therefore, your policy should cover these points as a benefit for both the employee and the company:

1. Requirements for initial medical examinations
2. Responsibilities of employees to inform their supervisors of any health or disability condition that may affect the safe performance of the job
3. Location of safety rules posted around the plant or office
4. Responsibilities of supervisors to enforce safety rules
5. Reporting of on-the-job accident or illness
6. Safe operation of machinery and equipment
7. Safety equipment and protective clothing requirements

Why do all organizations need a policy on vacations?

Vacation time is not considered a benefit by employees. Rather, they consider it a right. Few rights are more important to the average employee, and many individuals will seek employment and accept job offers from the organization which has the most liberal policies on vacation.

To add to the problems of satisfying employees on their vacation rights, it's a subject that has so many twists and turns that you must have a clear and comprehensive written policy so that it can be easily explained to every employee and every job applicant. Be sure that your policy takes into account these crucial points:

- Computation of vacation days
- Pay for vacations not taken for terminated employees
- Whether vacation time can be carried over from year to year

How should sick leave be treated in the company policy manual?

You should state whether or not your company has a sick leave policy. Some companies do not. They treat each sickness on an ad hoc basis. If that is the case, you should say so in writing in your company policy manual. In effect, you're making a policy by saying you have "no policy."

A sick leave policy should cover the following items:

1. How the number of sick leave days earned is calculated
2. What provisions, if any, are made for pay for absences longer than those covered
3. What verification of illness is required
4. The procedure to be followed

How should a policy statement on an employee benefits program be handled?

Most companies plan the benefits programs administration through the Personnel or Human Resources Department. The "hidden paychecks" of items which employees now receive in addition to wages currently aggregates between 35 percent and 50 percent of base pay. It's vital, therefore, that eligibility requirements be covered in the Employee Benefits Handbook.

What are the elements of a termination of employment policy?

Few things cause more anxiety and trepidation among employers and employees alike than terminating employment. That is why it is absolutely essential that your policy in this regard be clear and comprehensive. When you prepare your policy on termination, be sure to cover the following points at a minimum:

1. Who is authorized to terminate employees?
2. Guidelines for discharge due to performance and for disciplinary terminations.
3. A description of the termination procedure.

POLICY MANUAL DEVELOPMENT GUIDE

I. YOUR WORKING ENVIRONMENT

    A. What are the prevailing legal requirements in your state?

    B. To what extent can you establish policies in the form of guiding principles and where must you establish firm rules?

    C. What subjects should you handle in an employee handbook and which should be treated in a separate policy manual?

II. THE GOALS OF YOUR PUBLICATION

    A. Present information on policies and practices.
        1. Organizational structure.
        2. Pay and benefits.
        3. New employee orientation.
        4. Employer services and activities.
    B. Set standards for performance and behavior.
        1. Work rules.
        2. Disciplinary procedures.
        3. Performance appraisal and career development.
    C. Build morale and team spirit.
        1. Create pride in the organization.
        2. Present a complete picture of the benefits your company provides.
    D. Answer routine questions.
    E. Meet legal and procedural requirements.

III. TOPICS TO CONSIDER

    A. Introduction to the company.
        1. Welcome letter from senior official.
        2. History and philosophy.
        3. Organization, divisions and departments.
        4. Products, services and philosophy.

B. General communication.
   1. Company publications, bulletin boards and other communication media.
   2. Ethical standards of your business.
   3. Conflicts of interest.
   4. Information to be treated in confidence.
   5. Working hours.
   6. Employee rights.
   7. Health and safety requirements.

C. Dispute resolution system.
   1. Handling grievances.
   2. Counseling services.

D. Hiring policies.
   1. Equal opportunity.
   2. Employee selection.
   3. Probationary periods.

E. The disciplinary program.
   1. Frequency and method.
   2. When exceptions are in order.

F. Performance appraisal.
   1. Frequency and method.
   2. How performance is measured.
   3. How the results affect retention, pay and promotion.

G. Discipline.
   1. Typical offenses and penalties.
   2. Normal steps in the process.
   3. Guidelines for exceptions.

H. Discharge procedures.
   1. Guidelines for decisions.
   2. Procedural steps.
   3. Security and confidential information.
   4. Outplacement services.

I. Work rules and standards.
   1. Hours, regular and overtime.
   2. Attendance standards and notification requirements.
   3. Vacations, sick leave and personal time off.
   4. Time clock rules; breaks and lunches.
   5. Smoking.
   6. Solicitation and visitors.
   7. Telephone use.
   8. Alcohol and drug policies.
   9. Security requirements.
   10. Travel expenses and their reporting.
   11. Care of company property.
   12. Waste control and prevention.
   13. Safety procedures and equipment.
   14. Dress and appearance.
   15. Outside employment.
   16. Sexual harassment.
   17. Tools.

J. Pay policies.
   1. Paydays and payroll periods.
   2. Salary administration.
   3. Payroll deductions.
   4. Overtime and shift premiums.

K. Benefits.
   1. Available benefits.
   2. Eligibility standards.

L. Other personnel policies.
   1. Jury duty.
   2. Leaves of absence.
   3. Sick leave.
   4. Employee classification.
   5. Referrals and references.
   6. Assignments and transfers.
   7. Layoffs and recalls.

POLICY ON ATTENDANCE AND PUNCTUALITY

GENERAL POLICY

All employees are expected to report to work at the time scheduled for their attendance as indicated below. Unexcused absences will result in disciplinary actions as indicated under the disciplinary section of this policy.

HOURLY EMPLOYEES

a. Normal shift schedules are:

First Shift: 7 a.m. to noon and 12:30 p.m. to 3 p.m.

Second Shift: 3 p.m. to 6 p.m. and 6:30 p.m. to 11 p.m.

Third Shift: 11 p.m. to 7 a.m. with a 30 minute lunch period at the supervisor's discretion.

b. Two rest periods of 15 minutes each may be scheduled at the supervisor's discretion.

c. All hourly employees must remain at their work stations until five minutes before the scheduled end of each shift. Employees may then clean up, clock out and leave the facility.

SALARIED EMPLOYEES

a. The normal work week is five eight-hour days, Monday through Friday. Department heads may schedule additional time when necessary to meet operating needs.

b. Each department will post a schedule of its normal working hours on a bulletin board within the department.

c. The normal lunch period is 30 minutes. In addition, employees are allowed two breaks of up to 15 minutes each during the working day.

WHEN LATE OR ABSENT

All employees are expected to arrive at their work stations at their scheduled times. When employees anticipate that they will be late or absent, they should telephone their immediate supervisor to report the circumstances, advising how late they may be or how many days they may be absent. The supervisor will notify Personnel and Payroll as to whether the lateness or absence is excused or unexcused and whether to pay or not pay.

Failure to request advance approval or to report absence or lateness will result in the absence being recorded as unexcused and subject to discipline.

DISCIPLINE

Absence is the failure to report for work or to remain at work as scheduled. It includes late arrivals and early departures as well as absence for an entire day.

An employee who fails to call in for three successive days to report an absence shall be considered to have voluntarily terminated employment with the company.

Employees with above average absenteeism, as calculated by Personnel, may be required to document the reasons, including providing a doctor's certificate. Upon returning to work from an unexcused absence, an employee must report to his supervisor and disclose the reasons for the absence. If the reason is not acceptable, the employee may be disciplined in accordance with the following schedule:

First unexcused absence — oral warning.

Second unexcused absence — written warning.

Third unexcused absence — 3-day suspension.

Fourth unexcused absence — 10-day suspension.

Fifth unexcused absence — discharge.

The same schedule applies to unexcused lateness.

POLICY ON HOLIDAYS

RECOGNIZED HOLIDAYS

The company provides time off with pay for these yearly holidays:

        a. New Year's Day

        b. Martin Luther King Day

        c. President's Day

        d. Memorial Day

        e. Independence Day

        f. Labor Day

        g. Thanksgiving Day

        h. Day after Thanksgiving

        i. Christmas Day

In addition, there is one floating holiday which will be announced at the beginning of each year.

HOLIDAY PAY

a. To be paid for a holiday, the employee must be present on the normally scheduled work days immediately before and after the holiday. Supervisors may make exceptions to this policy for valid reasons such as illnesses or vacations.

b. Holidays which fall on a Saturday are normally observed the preceding Friday. Holidays which fall on a Sunday are normally observed the succeeding Monday.

POLICY ON JURY DUTY

POLICY

1. When an employee is called for jury duty, that employee should be released for adequate time to fulfill his or her obligation.

2. During the period of jury service, the company will pay the difference between the employee's normal earnings and the amount received for jury service.

3. In return for the partial salary, the employee is expected to report to work when not called to court or when excused early.

4. This policy applies to jury duty only. It does not apply to other court appearances, such as in response to a subpoena. The employee should normally use personal days for this purpose.

PROCEDURE

Employee

1. Notify your supervisor as soon as possible after receiving a notice for jury service.

Supervisor

1. Determine the probable duration and scheduling of the jury service.

2. Inform the Personnel Department of the jury summons.

3. Arrange any necessary reassignments, rescheduling or use of temporary help to accommodate the juror's absence.

Personnel Department

1. Arrange for salary reimbursement as provided by this policy.

2. Maintain records of the individual's jury service.

Policy on Family and Medical Leave (8-05)

Note: This policy incorporates the major provisions of the Family and Medical Leave Act of 1993. You can use or modify these sample provisions to meet the requirements of the law in your area and the needs of your organization, either as a sample policy or an employee information sheet.

The law does not pre-empt state and local laws providing greater family leave rights. It does not modify or affect in any way any federal or state civil rights laws, including Title VII of the 1964 Civil Rights Act and the Americans with Disabilities Act. You should integrate this policy with your policies on other leaves, such as maternity, military, sick and personal.

A covered employer is one who employs 50 or more employees for each working day during each of 20 or more calendar workweeks in the current or preceding calendar year. An eligible employee is one who has been employed for at least 12 months by the employer and for at least 1,250 hours of service with that employer during the previous 12 months.

POLICY ON FAMILY AND MEDICAL LEAVE ACT OF 1993

The company will comply with all provisions of the Family and Medical Leave Act of 1993 by providing up to 12 weeks of leave for covered employees in any 12-month period due to:

- the birth of a child or the placement of a child for adoption or foster care;

- the employee's need to care for a family member (child, spouse or parent) with a serious health condition;

- the employee's own serious health condition which makes the employee unable to do his or her job.

In order to be eligible for FMLA leave, an employee must have worked 1,250 hours for a minimum of one year, and in a location where at least 50 employees are employed by the covered employer within 75 miles. Part-time employees are eligible if they meet these requirements.

Note: If there is any question about the coverage requirements, or the definition of a "serious health condition," Personnel will make the final determination after examining the employment records of the applicant and the medical evidence.

NOTICE REQUIREMENTS

The employee is expected to give the company 30 days advance notice, if practical, when applying for an FMLA leave. When the need for the leave is not foreseeable, an employee is expected to give notice as soon as possible, except in extraordinary circumstances.

The company will waive advance notice in the case of a medical emergency requiring leave, because of an employee's own serious health condition or to care for a family member with a serious health condition.

While the company will make every effort to provide FMLA leave for qualified employees, it is absolutely essential that proper notice be given. An employee who fails to give proper notice may be denied FMLA leave.

LEAVE EXCLUSIONS

FMLA leave will not be granted for voluntary or cosmetic treatments, such as orthodontia or acne, which are not medically necessary and are not considered serious health conditions. Minor illnesses that last only a few days and surgical procedures that do not involve hospitalization and require only a brief recovery period do not qualify under FMLA. Complications that arise out of these procedures may develop into a "serious health condition" that would qualify the employee for an FMLA leave.

MEDICAL CERTIFICATION

The company requires an employee to submit certification from a health care provider to substantiate that the leave is due to the serious health condition of the employee or the employee's immediate family member.

In most cases, the employee should furnish medical certification at the time the leave is requested or, in the case of an emergency, as soon as possible after the leave has started. For normal requirements, an employee is expected to provide medical certification within 15 days of making application for an FMLA leave.

If an employee fails to provide a medical certification within a reasonable time, the company has the right to deny the leave. If an employee who has taken a leave on an emergency basis fails to supply the medical certification within a reasonable time under the pertinent circumstances, his or her continuation of leave may be denied.

If the company doubts the validity of a medical certification, it may require the employee to obtain a second opinion at company expense. If the opinions of the employee's and the employer's designated health care providers differ, the company may require the employee to obtain certification from a third health care provider, again at company expense. This third opinion will be final and binding on both the company and the employee.

DETERMINING PAID OR UNPAID LEAVE

FMLA leave is unpaid. However, the company requires employees to substitute paid vacation, personal or family leave for all or part of any unpaid FMLA leave. **Example:** If an employee is entitled to three weeks paid vacation, he or she must count this total towards the 12-week entitlement.

CONTINUATION OF BENEFITS

Employees on FMLA leave are entitled to have health benefits maintained while on leave. The company's and the employee's share of health plan premiums will be paid in the same manner customarily used. The company will continue to pay its share of the health plan premiums throughout the leave, while the employee will be expected to pay according to a signed agreement, which will be executed prior to the leave.

The company will provide a 30-day grace period after the agreed upon date for payment within which the employee may make payment of the premium. If an employee does not make payment within the grace period, his or her health coverage may be terminated. All other benefits, such as group life insurance, disability insurance, sick leave, annual leave, educational benefits and pensions will remain in force throughout the FMLA leave.

RECOVERING PREMIUMS

The company will recover premiums it paid for maintaining group health plan coverage if the employee fails to return to work after the leave entitlement has expired, unless the reason the employee does not return to work is due to:

- The continuation, recurrence or onset of a serious health condition affecting the employee or an immediate family member.

- A sudden change in the employee's circumstances during leave.

- An employee on FMLA leave was laid off.

In the absence of any of these conditions, the company reserves the right to recover its share of health premiums by deducting the amount due from any sums owed to the employee in vacation pay, profit-sharing or a final paycheck.

An employee who does not return to work within 30 calendar days after the leave expires is considered to have failed to "return" to work under guidelines set by the FMLA.

DETERMINING THE LEAVE YEAR (OPTIONS)

The company will use a "rolling" method to determine the 12-month leave period. Each time an employee takes FMLA leave, the remaining leave entitlement would be any balance of the 12 weeks which has not been used during the period of the immediately preceding 12 months.

Example: If an employee used four weeks beginning Feb. 1, 1996, four weeks beginning June 1, 1996 and four weeks beginning Dec. 1, 1997, the employee would not be entitled to any additional leave until Feb. 1, 1997. However, on Feb. 1, 1997, the employee would be entitled to four weeks of leave; on June 1, the employee would be entitled to another four weeks, etc.

LEAVE RESTRICTIONS

An employee's entitlement to FMLA leave for birth or placement of a child expires 12 months after the birth or placement. A husband and wife working for the company are limited to a combined total of 12 workweeks during any 12-month period if leave is taken for birth or placement for adoption or foster care, or to care for a parent with a serious health condition.

This limitation does not apply to leave taken by either spouse to care for the other who is seriously ill and unable to work, to care for a child with a serious health condition, or for his or her own serious illness.

INTERMITTENT OR REDUCED LEAVE SCHEDULES

Under certain conditions, the company will allow employees to take intermittent leave or work on a reduced schedule. "Intermittent leave" is leave taken in separate blocks of time rather than one continuous period of time. It may range from an hour or more to several weeks. The company will allow intermittent leave to be taken on an occasional basis for medical appointments, or leave taken several days at a time spread over a period of months.

A "reduced leave schedule" is one that reduces the usual number of hours/days per workweek or hours per workday. It could include a schedule of a three-day week, or working only mornings or afternoons, to meet the employee's requirements.

The company does not set a limit on the size of an increment of leave for an intermittent or reduced leave schedule. This type of leave will not reduce the total amount of leave available to an employee. Only the time actually taken is charged against the employee's entitlement to 12 weeks of leave.

A reduced leave schedule or intermittent leave will usually be beneficial to both the company and the employee. Managers and supervisors are urged to recommend these alternatives when employees first apply for an FMLA leave.

EMPLOYEE TRANSFER

If an employee selects intermittent leave or a reduced work schedule, the company has the right to transfer him or her to a job that is more suitable to recurring periods of leave. There are two conditions for this transfer:

- The equivalent position must have equivalent pay and benefits, but it does not have to have equivalent duties.

- The employee must be qualified to perform the job.

The company reserves the right to make such a transfer, with or without the employee's permission.

An alternative position must meet the provisions of the Americans With Disabilities Act (ADA) if the employee meets the definition of disabled.

RESTORATION TO PRIOR POSITION

The company will restore an employee to the position he or she held when the leave began, or to an equivalent position, with equivalent benefits, pay and other terms and conditions of employment. An equivalent position will involve the same or substantially similar duties and responsibilities, and must include substantially equivalent skill, effort, responsibility and authority.

The employee is also entitled to be returned to the same shift or equivalent schedule, and will have the same opportunity for bonuses, profit-sharing and other non-discretionary payments.

If special qualifications are required for the position, and they have lapsed during the employee's leave, he or she will be given a reasonable opportunity to fulfill the requirements after returning to work.

If the employee's original work site has been closed or moved, and other employees were transferred to another work site, the employee will have the same rights for transfer as would have been available had the employee not taken leave.

REDUCTION-IN-FORCE

The company will not offer any special protection to employees who are on FMLA leave at the time of a layoff. Managers will make the same decisions that they would have made if the employees had not been on FMLA leave.

KEY EMPLOYEE DESIGNATION

The company has the right to deny restoration rights to individuals who qualify for the "key" employee exception requirements of the FMLA. A key employee must be among the highest paid 10% of all salaried and non-salaried employees.

In addition to the earnings test for the "key" employee designation, the company must prove that the leave would cause substantial and grievous economic injury to its operations. The company must also demonstrate that the employee's restoration to employment after taking leave would cause financial hardship.

Managers should not make "key" person designations without clearance from Personnel. If it is determined that an employee qualifies for the "key" person designation, he or she must be informed prior to the commencement of the leave or as soon as possible after it has started.

The company will continue to pay its share of health benefits for employees who have been identified as "key." No effort will be made to recover these premiums, even if reinstatement is denied.

COMMUNICATIONS DURING LEAVE

Managers will contact employees who are on family leave to check on their status and intention to return to work, but not more than once every 30 days. The company will request medical recertification for any of the following reasons.

1. The employee requests a leave extension.

2. Circumstances described by the original certification have changed significantly.

3. The employer receives information that casts doubt upon the continuing validity of the certification.

4. The employee is unable to return to work after FMLA leave because of the continuation, recurrence or onset of a serious health condition.

If at any point, the employee gives an unequivocal notice that he or she will not be returning from FMLA leave, the manager should request a written resignation. Situations change, and an employee might decide at a later date that he or she wishes to return. The company's obligation for restoration rights ends with a formal resignation. Personnel should be notified immediately, so that the company can stop paying its share of health care costs.

COBRA RIGHTS

FMLA does not constitute a qualifying event triggering continuation of health benefit provisions under the Consolidated Omnibus Budget Reconciliation Act (COBRA). If an employee resigns, for whatever reasons, during an FMLA leave, he or she would be eligible for COBRA coverage by paying his or her full share of health care costs, plus a 2% administrative charge. Employees who are terminated for gross misconduct will not be eligible for COBRA coverage.

RETURN TO WORK CERTIFICATION

The company will require a fitness-for-duty certification with regard to the particular health condition that was the cause of the employee's FMLA leave. All information obtained in a fitness-for-duty certification will be treated as a confidential medical record, stored in a locked cabinet apart from the location of personnel files. Only the following will have access to this information:

1. Supervisors and managers who must be informed about necessary restrictions on the work or duties of the employee and necessary accommodations.

2. First aid and safety personnel who must be informed if the disability might require emergency treatment or any specific procedures in the case of fire or other evacuations.

3. Government, state and insurance officials with a "need to know."

WHEN RESTORATION RIGHTS ARE DENIED

There are four reasons why employees may not be restored to their former positions at the end of an FMLA leave:

1. The individual cannot perform the essential functions of the job, with or without accommodation.

2. The individual would pose a significant risk to the safety of other employees.

3. The individual's job was eliminated or he or she was laid off because of business conditions.

4. The individual was identified as a "key" person and informed of this designation before or during the FMLA leave. His or her return to the job would represent an economic hardship for the company.

PROVISIONS FOR THE DISABLED

Not every individual who is unable to return to the job is protected by the ADA. Illnesses or injuries do not always cause physical or mental impairments severe enough to "substantially" limit a major life activity, the ADA definition of an individual with a disability. If the employee is unable to perform his or her former job or an equivalent position because of a disability, and has exhausted the FMLA entitlement, the Americans With Disabilities Act (ADA) may be triggered.

Employees who meet the definition of disabled will be offered every reasonable accommodation to return to their jobs or an equivalent position.

POLICY ON LEAVES OF ABSENCE

POLICY

The company will allow employees to take official leaves of absence, without pay, for reasons that are acceptable to the company. Leaves of absence are not intended for employees who are leaving their employment and do not intend to return to work.

DURATION

Leaves of absence are normally limited to a maximum of six months, although exceptions can be made if circumstances warrant. Duration will be one factor in deciding whether to grant the employee's request for a leave.

REQUIREMENTS AND CONDITIONS

a. Any non-probationary employee may request a leave of absence. The type of leave and its duration will be determined by the department head with the advice of the Personnel Department.

b. A leave of absence will not normally be granted to an employee with less than one year of service. This requirement can be waived in case of an emergency.

c. A leave of absence will not normally be granted to an employee who has vacation time available. The employee should exhaust all available vacation before taking a leave of absence.

d. A leave of absence will normally be without pay, but seniority and benefits will normally remain in effect for the duration of the leave.

CRITERIA FOR GRANTING LEAVES OF ABSENCE

a. The duration of the leave, with consideration to the purpose for which the leave is requested.

b. The department's ability to complete the employee's work during the leave period.

c. The employee's overall work record and value to the company.

PROCEDURE

Supervisor

a. On receiving a request for a leave of absence, help the employee, as needed, to prepare a Leave of Absence Request Form. Be sure the employee provides all pertinent information.

b. Determine whether the request and the duration of the leave will adversely affect operations. Determine how readily you can compensate for the absence.

c. Review the employee's overall work record and the reasons for the request.

d. Submit a recommendation to the Personnel Department.

PERSONNEL DEPARTMENT

a. Working with the supervisor, determine whether the leave of absence should be granted.

b. If the leave is approved, determine which benefits should be continued and how payment should be made while the employee is on leave.

POLICY ON MATERNITY LEAVES

POLICY

a. It is this company's policy to treat pregnancy, childbirth and related medical conditions as it would any other form of disability, including providing temporary disability pay and other employment benefits.

b. It is also this company's policy to comply with all applicable local, state and federal laws, in spirit as well as in specific detail. Should any provision of this policy be found to be inconsistent with an applicable legal requirement, the law shall prevail. All other provisions of this policy that are consistent with the law will remain in effect.

REQUIREMENTS AND PROCEDURES

a. A mother who observes the requirements of this policy is entitled to such leave as her physician may recommend, up to a maximum of 12 months. If she returns to work within 6 months she shall be guaranteed a return to her previous position. If she returns after 6 months and before 12 months she should be assigned to any vacant position she is qualified to perform.

b. The purpose of this policy is to provide for the medical and physical requirements of pregnancy, childbirth and related conditions. If there is any question whether a condition for which leave is sought is related to pregnancy and childbirth, the company may request verification from the mother's physician.

c. The leave will normally begin when the employee's physician states in writing that the mother is no longer able to work because of her condition, or on request of the employee's supervisor. Leave may be granted at an earlier date at the employee's request, but disability payments will not be made until the employee is certified as actually being unable to work.

d. The company at its discretion may change the work assignment of an expectant mother when it is necessary for her own safety and that of the child. Any such determination will be made in consultation with the employee's physician. Transfers for this reason will be made only if a suitable opening is available and there is no harm to the rights of other employees. Should no suitable assignment be available, the employee's supervisor may certify that she is no longer physically able to perform her present job, and the period of disability leave may begin.

e. Any woman who becomes pregnant should notify her supervisor as soon as possible after a physician confirms the pregnancy. Employees should be encouraged to report pregnancies as early as possible, to better accommodate planning for their absence and return.

f. A supervisor who receives such a notice should arrange with Personnel to counsel the employee on the benefits and requirements of this policy.

POLICY ON MILITARY LEAVES

POLICY

It is the policy of this company to grant military leave of absence as required by law and by the needs of employees who are members of the military service.

LONG-TERM TOURS OF DUTY

a. Any permanent full-time employee who enlists or is called to active military duty will be granted a military leave of absence. The duration of the leave shall be the term of the enlistment plus any additional time that may be required by the government. Reenlistment or any other voluntary extension of the tour of duty will cancel the leave of absence.

b. Any permanent full-time employee who has completed his or her probationary period at the time of enlistment and who is granted a military leave of absence is eligible for an additional compensatory payment at the beginning of the leave as follows:
   i. Two weeks of base pay if the prospective tour of duty is two years or less.
   ii. Four weeks of base pay if the prospective tour of duty is more than two years.
   iii. Probationary employees will receive two weeks of base pay regardless of the prospective tour of duty.

c. On return from military leave of absence, the employee will be reinstated as required by law, subject to these conditions:
   i. The employee must apply for reinstatement within the time required by law.
   ii. The employee must be physically qualified.
   iii. The employee must have a creditable military record, including completion of all required raining and full-time service and a discharge under honorable conditions.
If the employee's former job is not available, the company will provide a job of similar status and pay, as near as possible.

RESERVE AND NATIONAL GUARD DUTY

a. Any employee who is required to report for temporary tours of duty with Reserve or National Guard units should submit to his or her supervisor a request to be released for such duty. This request should be on the form prescribed by the U.S. Department of Labor (available at the Personnel office). The employee should also give the supervisor a copy of the orders assigning him or her to military duty.

b. Such leave will be granted if the company can make suitable arrangements to accommodate the employee's absence. If this cannot be done, the company will assist the employee in requesting an exemption from the military requirement.

c. A permanent full-time employee who has completed the probationary period will be paid the difference between his or her normal pay and military pay for up to 10 days per year. On returning from the tour of duty, the employee should give his or her supervisor a voucher or other evidence of the military pay earned. The supervisor should attach this document to a request that the employee's pay be adjusted according to this policy.

d. When employees are called to military duty under emergency conditions, adjustments and exceptions to this policy may be made as circumstances require.

POLICY ON SICK LEAVES

POLICY

The company will continue to pay the normal base pay of any employee who is absent due to illness, injury or disability that is not job-related. The maximum period of time for which this benefit will be continued will be determined according to the guidelines provided in this policy.

AUTHORIZATION

The payment of this benefit must be authorized by the employee's supervisor. The employee must report illnesses or other reasons for absence according to procedures established by the supervisor. No sick pay will be allowed until after the employee has properly made such a report.

GUIDELINES FOR THE DURATION OF BENEFITS

a. It is the company's policy to be flexible in granting sick leave benefits according to the individual employee's needs and circumstances. However, to provide some consistency, the allowable leave should not normally exceed these guidelines:

Continuous Service	Normal Maximum
Less than 2 years	10 days
2-3 years	20 days
3-4 years	30 days
4-5 years	40 days
5-10 years	50 days
10 years or longer	5 days for each year of continuous service

b. In cases where the absence exceeds these guidelines, the supervisor may recommend to the Personnel Department that the benefit be continued at either full or partial pay. Personnel will base its decision on the nature of the ailment and the employee's previous work and attendance record.

VERIFICATION

In connection with this policy, the company reserves the right to:

a. Verify the illness or disability through its own medical staff or by requiring that the employee furnish a statement from his or her own physician.

b. Deny pay when the illness or disability is a result of the employee's misconduct or when the employee sustains the injury while working for another employer, including self-employment.

c. Deny pay in any case where the employee has a record of excessive absences.

PROCEDURE

a. Each employee who is absent from work due to illness or disability must notify his or her immediate supervisor as soon as possible, according to procedures established within the employee's department. Failure to report can be cause for considering the absence to be unauthorized and without pay. Throughout the absence, the employee is responsible for keeping the supervisor informed of his or her progress.

b. Each supervisor is responsible for staying informed and keeping others informed of the employee's progress and for ordering verification in any case where the employee's statements might be in doubt.

c. On returning to work from a prolonged absence the employee may be asked to provide a report from his or her physician regarding any limits on physical activity and the likely duration of these limits.

POLICY ON TIME CARDS

Time cards will be furnished to each employee each week. Employees must record the times at which they begin and end work for the day. This will be done by punching time clocks in departments where these are installed. Employees in other departments must record their working hours manually.

No employee may record the time of any other employee or request that another employee record his or her time. Violators will be subject to disciplinary action under the Progressive Discipline policy.

Supervisors must keep all employees informed of their scheduled starting and stopping times. Any variations from normal working hours must be recorded on the employee's time card and initialed by the supervisor.

No employee may work more than 15 minutes before or after the scheduled work day without permission from the immediate supervisor.

Time cards should record the actual hours worked. Exceptions from normal hours must be initialed by the supervisor as noted above.

The normal breaks and lunch periods provided in the policy on Hours of Work need not be recorded. Exceptions to this standard schedule should be recorded and initialed by the supervisor.

POLICY ON TRANSFER AND RELOCATION

The company may ask certain employees to relocate to other facilities from time to time.

Employees who are relocated will be given assistance to minimize the disruption of their personal, social, educational and business lives. The following relocation benefits are provided:

1. 100% of the cost of moving all household goods and temporary living expenses.

2. Career counseling and employment search assistance for an employee's working spouse.

3. A relocation assistant who will be responsible for helping the employee and his or her family plan and conduct their move.

4. Home purchase and sale. The company's real estate department will be responsible for the job of purchasing and reselling a transferred employee's home. The employee's home should be purchased by the company at fair market value, and it should be sold as quickly as possible on the basis of a reasonable offer.

5. Mortgage subsidy program. The company will provide a mortgage subsidy for ___ years if an employee must accept a new mortgage at an interest rate higher than his or her old mortgage.

6. The company will provide a cost-of-living differential of no more than 15% based on the national cost-of-living figures set by the Department of Commerce. The differential will be determined by comparing the cost-of- living in a transferred employee's present Standard Metropolitan Statistical Area (SMSA) and the SMSA into which the employee moves. The percentage difference between the two provides a basis for the employee's cost-of-living increase.
If an employee transfers to a less expensive area, he or she will not be penalized.

7. Education subsidy. The company may provide a tuition subsidy for up to two of an employee's children if the employee must place them in private schools so they can receive the same quality education as they had at their previous schools.

8. Foreign transfers. The company recognizes the special difficulties faced by families transferred overseas. The company will pay the cost of storing household goods for the term of the overseas assignment and will assist in placing the employee's home with a real estate management firm if he or she chooses to rent it rather than sell.

POLICY ON VACATIONS

POLICY

Each employee is entitled to paid vacation as provided for by this policy. Each employee must take the full vacation entitlement during the calendar year in which it is accrued. Vacations cannot be carried over into a succeeding year.

VACATION RIGHTS

Employees will be entitled to vacations according to this schedule:

a. An employee who has completed less than six months of continuous service during a calendar year is not entitled to vacation for that year.

b. An employee who completes more than six months but less than two years of continuous service during a calendar year is entitled to one week paid vacation during that year. The vacation may not be taken until the employee has completed at least one year of continuous service.

c. An employee who completes two years or more of continuous service during a calendar year will be entitled to two weeks of paid vacation during that year.

d. An employee who completes five years or more of continuous service during a calendar year is entitled to three weeks of paid vacation.

e. An employee who completes 10 years or more of continuous service during a calendar year will be entitled to four weeks of paid vacation during that year.

HOLIDAYS DURING VACATION

If a paid holiday falls during an employee's vacation, the employee is entitled to an additional day off with pay, at a time mutually agreeable to the company and the employee.

VACATION RIGHTS FOR TERMINATED EMPLOYEES

a. An employee who leaves the company with less than one year of continuous service is entitled to no allowance for accrued vacation time.

b. An employee who leaves the company with one year or more of continuous service will receive the unused vacation pay to which he or she is entitled for that year, prorated to the date of termination.

c. The vacation pay provided by this section will not be granted to any employee who resigns without due notice.

d. The vacation pay for retiring or deceased employees will be paid as provided in this section.

VACATION SCHEDULING

a. Whenever possible, supervisors will schedule vacations to meet the wishes of employees, giving consideration to the needs of the department and the requests of other employees.

b. Supervisors will use seniority or some other equitable and acceptable means to resolve conflicts over vacation time.

c. Vacations may not be scheduled so they carry over from the end of one calendar year into the beginning of the next.

d. Unless it conflicts with other terms of this policy or with the department's needs, employees may take their allotted vacations at one or more times as long as each vacation period is at least one week long.

e. When needed for security or other reasons, supervisors may require that employees take at least two weeks of their vacation at one time.

POLICY ON ETHICS AND PERSONAL CONDUCT

POLICY

The company expects all employees to avoid activities that create conflicts of interest with their responsibilities to this company. Each employee has an obligation to refrain from activities which conflict or interfere with company operations or with others with whom the company does business.

Conflicts of interest include, but are not limited to:
1. Outside employment — such as with a competitor or supplier.
2. Outside business interests — such as those under Outside employment.
3. Gifts and entertainment — employees shall not accept gifts of more than nominal value from individuals or businesses which do or seek to do business with this company. This also includes travel, living or entertainment expenses.
4. Legal requirements — employees must not do anything in the conduct of business which would violate any local, state or federal law.
5. Fair competition — all employees will conduct themselves in a fair and ethical manner when dealing with customers and suppliers.
6. Speculation — employees must not speculate in materials, supplies or services produced or purchased by this company.
7. Political activities — employees are encouraged to vote. All support of political candidates must be on employees' own time, with no use of company facilities, and the employee must not represent him/herself as acting on behalf of the company.

COMPANY PROPERTY

No employee will remove company property without written permission from the supervisor responsible for the property in question. This includes, but is not limited to:
1. Materials, equipment and tools.
2. Property owned by the company or other employees.
3. Confidential literature including technical, sales and quality control documents.
4. Computer disks, tapes and other storage media.
5. Information identified as proprietary or a trade secret.

Removing or attempting to remove company property without permission can be grounds for disciplinary action.

PERSONAL CONDUCT

1. Employees must take no action or work in any manner that may cause injury to themselves or their fellow employees.
2. Employees must not do anything to interfere with other employees' abilities to get their own work out.
3. Employees must treat other employees with courtesy and respect. They should behave toward others as they would prefer that others behave toward them.
4. Fighting is absolutely prohibited, as is roughhousing and horseplay, and is subject to disciplinary action.
5. Abusive language and threatening gestures toward other employees will not be tolerated.
6. Gambling of any kind or bookmaking on company premises is prohibited.
7. Drinking alcoholic beverages on company premises is prohibited.
8. Posting or showing obscene drawings or photographs, or using sexually-oriented language is considered sexual harassment and will be dealt with under the company's sexual harassment policy.

POLICY ON SEXUAL HARASSMENT

POLICY

Sexual harassment of any kind will not be tolerated in this company. Sexual harassment is defined as a continuing pattern of unwelcome sexual advances, requests for sexual favors or physical contact of a sexual nature under any of these conditions:

1. When submission to the conduct involves a condition of the individual's employment, either stated or suggested.

2. The individual's submission or refusal is used, or might be used, as the basis of an employment decision which affects the individual.

3. The conduct unreasonably interferes with the individual's job performance or creates a work environment that is intimidating, hostile or offensive.

PROCEDURE

The Director of Personnel is responsible for managing all complaints of sexual harassment and for insuring that all complaints are investigated fully and fairly, regardless of the manner in which they are made or the individuals involved.

Employees are encouraged to take complaints of sexual harassment to their immediate supervisor or, if that supervisor in involved in the accusation, directly to the Director of Personnel. A female Personnel Department employee will be available should the complaining employee indicate such a preference.

INVESTIGATION

A management investigator designated by the president will thoroughly and fairly investigate every complaint, without bias or premature judgment. Such an investigation should include interviews with the complaining employee, the subject of the complaint, and co-workers and former employees who may have knowledge of the situation. The investigator should also conduct a thorough review of files and other tangible evidence, and should be given all necessary access privileges for this purpose. The investigator should make every reasonable attempt to rationally and objectively resolve any questions of credibility between the complaining and the accused employees.

DISCIPLINARY ACTION

The Director of Personnel will review every case, including the investigator's findings and the recommendations of counselors assigned to the case. The Director should insure that the complaint has been fully and impartially investigated. If the evidence shows a pattern of harassment as described in the general policy, the director should recommend appropriate disciplinary action against the offending employee. Further action should follow the established policies and procedures of the disciplinary system.

TRAINING

The Director of Personnel is responsible for insuring that all managers and supervisors are fully trained in their responsibilities under this policy. This training should include all details of this policy. It should also attempt to sensitize managers and supervisors to the full range of practices that might constitute sexual harassment and to build sensitivity to the feelings of employees.

POLICY ON DRESS

Each employee is expected to dress appropriately for the job. Supervisors are responsible for setting appropriate dress standards for their departments. In setting dress standards, supervisors should consider these factors:

1. The nature of the work.
2. Safety considerations, such as necessary precautions when working near machinery.
3. The nature of the employee's public contact, if any, and the normal expectations of outside parties with whom the employee will work.
4. The prevailing practices of other workers in similar jobs.
5. The preferences of higher management, including considerations of the type of image the company wishes to project.

When an employee's dress does not comply with established standards, the normal response should be to discuss the matter with the employee. If continued counseling fails to bring the desired response, the supervisor may initiate disciplinary action.

An employee who disagrees with a supervisor's judgment on matters of dress shall have recourse to the dispute resolution system. No disciplinary action shall be taken until that dispute resolution process has been completed.

POLICY ON TELEPHONE USE

1. The company maintains its telephone facilities for business purposes. It is recognized that some personal telephone calls are necessary. Employees are allowed to make reasonable numbers of personal calls. They should keep these as brief as possible to avoid interfering with their normal work or with business use of the telephones.

2. No personal toll calls should be made from company telephones. Use pay telephones for this purpose, or charge the call to your home telephone.

3. If a supervisor believes an employee is abusing this privilege, the matter should be processed under the disciplinary system with an informal warning as the first step.

4. These rules may be waived in case of an emergency.

POLICY ON HOUSEKEEPING

In the interest of safety, personal well-being and a pleasant working atmosphere, the company expects that all employees will keep their work areas clean and neat at all times. Supervisors may assign such clean-up duty as is necessary to meet the intent of this policy.

Neat working areas also help prevent waste. All employees are expected to take every reasonable step to avoid waste. Everything we use in this business costs money. The more we save in operating costs, the more resources the company has to improve its competitive position and to offer more and better-paying jobs.

POLICY ON DISCIPLINE

When any employee violates a company rule, the supervisor will follow this process:

First violation

Counsel the employee and issue a verbal warning. Make every effort to determine and resolve the cause of the problem. At the same time, state specifically that the employee is receiving a formal warning. Place a memo in the employee's file describing the incident and your actions.

Second violation

Hold a meeting with the employee at which you explain the nature of the offense and warn the employee that any repetition could lead to suspension or discharge. Offer to help the employee solve the problem. Issue a written warning of the offense, including a reference to the prior incident. Give one copy to the employee; place another in the employee's file.

Third violation

Place the employee on suspension without pay for three days. Notify the employee that after the suspension he or she will be on probation for 90 days. During that time the employee will receive extra attention and scrutiny whose main purpose will be to try to solve the employee's problems. Warn the employee, though, that even a single further offense is grounds for immediate discharge.

Fourth violation

Discharge the employee, observing the procedures in this manual for processing an involuntary termination.

An employee can be discharged at any time, without regard to the preceding steps, if he or she commits an offense for which immediate discharge is specified as a penalty or if, in the supervisor's judgment, the employee's continued presence would be contrary to the well-being of the company or any of its employees.

Every discharge must be approved by the Director of Personnel. If that approval is not granted immediately, the supervisor should suspend the employee pending a decision by the Director.

DISCIPLINARY OFFENSE DESCRIPTIONS

LEVEL 1

Corrective action is normally the proper response to offenses like these when they are isolated and not part of a continuing pattern:

1. Excessive absence or lateness.
2. Neglect of company property.
3. Unintentional violations of safety rules.
4. Excessive personal use of the telephone.
5. Use of abusive language.

Counsel the employee on the first offense, prepare a formal written warning on the second, suspend the employee or impose probation on the third offense and discharge for the fourth offense.

LEVEL 2

These offenses are more serious and must be dealt with firmly and immediately. Typical offenses in this group include:

1. Drug or alcohol abuse on the job.
2. Conduct which disrupts business activities.

A written warning is the normal response to a first offense. In the case of drug or alcohol abuse this should include a referral to an appropriate treatment agency. Termination is authorized for a second offense.

LEVEL 3

Immediate termination is justified for these offenses:

1. Theft of company property or that of other employees.
2. Insubordination or refusing to follow instructions.
3. Intoxication (including the effects of illegal drugs) during working hours or while representing the company.
4. Deliberate destruction of company property.
5. Deliberate injury to another person.
6. Violating a confidence; unauthorized release of confidential information.
7. Other offenses that in the supervisor's or manager's judgment seriously threaten the well-being of the company or any employee.

POLICY ON REPORTING IMPROPER BEHAVIOR

PURPOSE

To provide a means through which employees can report incidents of suspected improper activity.

POLICY

It is the policy of this company to comply with all laws, regulations and principles of ethical conduct which apply to the company and its business. Each employee must observe this policy. Each employee is also responsible for assisting in its application by reporting any instance in which it appears that legal, regulatory or ethical standards have been violated.

The company is responsible for preventing or, if necessary, correcting any such violation. Not only is this a legal obligation, but failure to do so could seriously affect the company's reputation with the public, its customers and government authorities.

PROCEDURE

Any employee who has reason to believe this policy has been violated must report this belief. Normally, the violation should be reported to the employee's immediate supervisor. If that is not practical, or if the employee is dissatisfied with the supervisor's response, the employee should file a written report of the complaint with the Director of Personnel.

Any executive, manager or supervisor who receives a report of possible improper activity shall forward the report immediately to the Director of Personnel. The individual who receives the complaint should immediately begin an investigation to determine the facts of the case. The Director of Personnel may designate some other party to conduct the investigation.

All records of the complaint, including the identity of the employee who filed it, shall be kept confidential and made available only as necessary to conduct a full investigation and to give the accused party a fair opportunity to respond to the complaint. There will be no retaliation in any form against any employee who in good faith reports a violation, even if the investigation determines there has been no violation.

OUTSIDE PUBLICITY

Failure to observe this policy is itself a serious offense. An employee who reports suspected wrongdoing to any party outside the company, without first reporting it as required by this policy, will be subject to discipline up to and including discharge.

POLICY ON EQUAL EMPLOYMENT OPPORTUNITY

PURPOSE

This policy affirms the company's policy of non-discrimination.

POLICY

The company maintains a policy of non-discrimination in all phases of employment and complies in full with all applicable laws. The company will continuously monitor its performance in these basic areas and take action where necessary to comply with applicable requirements:

a. Recruit, advertise, hire, transfer and promote without regard to race, religion, color, national origin, physical handicap, sex, age or any other legally protected classification.

b. Base all decisions relating to every level of employment solely on the individual's qualifications for the job to be filled, particularly when considering promotions.

c. Administer all other personnel actions without regard to race, religion, color, national origin, sex or age. In the case of sex and age, there may be an exception based on a bona fide occupational qualification. If any doubt arises whether a bona fide occupational qualification does exist with respect to either of these two categories, direct the inquiry to the Director of Personnel. Personnel actions in this category include but are not limited to:

    i. Compensation
    ii. Benefits
    iii. Transfers
    iv. Layoffs and recalls
    v. Training
    vi. Tuition assistance
    vii. Company-sponsored social and recreational programs.

d. To comply with this policy, the person responsible for each company facility will appoint an equal opportunity program coordinator. This coordinator will be identified in a notice posted for all employees. The coordinator is responsible for conducting periodic reviews within the framework of this program, making changes where appropriate and taking the initiative to promote effective equal opportunity in any manner. The Personnel Department is responsible for conducting periodic reviews of the program at each facility, working with the equal opportunity program coordinator.

PUBLICITY AND COMMUNICATION

Activities to publicize this policy and gain understanding by all employees will include:
a. Information in employee publications on provisions of this policy and articles on how it is being implemented.
b. Information in corporate reports and news releases.
c. Meetings with corporate executive officers and staff members to clarify the policy and its application.
d. Meetings with local managers and staff members to clarify this policy and its application. This is the responsibility of each facility's equal employment program coordinator. Guidance for these meetings should be obtained from the Personnel Department. The meetings should be conducted according to these guidelines:
   i. Instruct local management to discuss the information in these meetings with employees, including the fact that the company will continue to comply with all applicable laws and regulations. The continuing policy of hiring members of minority groups in all departments and specialities will be emphasized.
   ii. Post a copy of the President's statement of policy on bulletin boards.
   iii. Post all notices required by law or regulation.
   iv. Make the equal opportunity program coordinator responsible for notifying the corporate equal employment program coordinator in writing of the dates and results of any reviews, official complaints or other government action relating to equal opportunity.

RECRUITING AND EXTERNAL COMMUNICATION

Acquaint all recruiting sources with the company's policy. Emphasize use of minority group referral services.
a. Inform employment agencies, training agencies and temporary employment agencies in writing of the company's policy. This is to be done by the equal opportunity program coordinator at each facility. The coordinator will be responsible for reviewing the performance of recruiting sources for adequate compliance with applicable laws and regulations.
b. Include the phrase "An Equal Opportunity Employer" in all recruitment advertising.
c. Identify and advertise in media which have significant minority group audiences in an effort to acquaint prospective employees from these groups with the company's policy. When employees are pictured in consumer or recruitment advertising, some minority group members should be shown.
d. Identify and contact minority group sources such as minority organization, community agencies, community leaders, schools and colleges to inform them of the company's policy and to encourage applications. Continue an active liason with these resources.

e. Participate in local functions such as industrial fairs and exhibitions so as to promote employment and training of minority group members.

f. Incorporate an equal opportunity clause in all purchase orders, leases and contracts.

g. Send all contractors and subcontractors the assurances required by federal law. Insure that these are properly filed and renewed when required.

h. Use available opportunities to publicize the company's policy whenever the opportunity arises. The equal opportunity program coordinator will write to all media in which the company regularly advertises expressing the company's policies and stating that the company will not accept responsibility if the medium's method of job classification does not comply with state and federal laws.

Note: The coverage of the Americans with Disabilities Act includes employers with 15 or more employees, including part-timers, working for 20 or more calendar weeks in the current or preceding calendar year.

The definition of "employer" includes persons who are "agents of the employer, such as managers, supervisors, foremen, or others who act for the employer, such as agencies used to conduct background checks on candidates." Therefore, you, as the employer, are responsible for actions of such persons that may violate the law.

POLICY ON AMERICANS WITH DISABILITIES ACT

It is the policy of this company to abide by both the letter and spirit of the law in all aspects of the Americans with Disability Act. That Act prohibits discrimination in all employment practices, including job application procedures, hiring, firing, advancement, compensation, training, and other terms, conditions, and privileges of employment. It applies to recruitment, advertising, tenure, layoff, leave, fringe benefits, and all other employment-related activities.

The company prohibits all employment discrimination against "qualified individuals with disabilities." This includes applicants for employment and employees. An individual is considered to have a "disability" if he or she has a physical or mental impairment that substantially limits one or more major life activities, has a record of such an impairment, or is regarded as having such an impairment. We also forbid discrimination against persons because they have a known association or relationship with an individual with a disability.

COVERED EMPLOYEES

The ADA applies to impairments that substantially limit major life activities such as seeing, hearing, speaking, walking, breathing, performing manual tasks, learning, caring for oneself, and working. An individual with epilepsy, paralysis, HIV infection, AIDS, a substantial hearing or visual impairment, mental retardation, or a specific learning disability is covered, but an individual with a minor, non-chronic condition of short duration, such as a sprain, broken limb, or the flu, generally would not be covered.

We consider a qualified individual with a disability as a person who meets legitimate skill, experience, education, or other requirements of an employment position that he or she holds or seeks in our organization, and who can perform the "essential functions" of the position with or without reasonable accommodation. The company requires the ability to perform "essential" functions to assure that an individual with a disability will not be considered unqualified simply because of inability to perform marginal or incidental job functions. If the individual is qualified to perform essential job functions except for limitations caused by a disability, we will consider whether the individual could perform these functions with a reasonable accommodation.

MEDICAL REQUIREMENTS

The company will not ask or require a job applicant to take a medical examination before making a job offer. And we will not make any preemployment inquiry about a disability or the nature or severity of a disability. But we may ask questions about the ability to perform specific job functions and may, with certain limitations, ask an individual with a disability to describe or demonstrate how he or she would perform these functions.

We will condition our job offer on the satisfactory result of a post-offer medical examination or medical inquiry, since this is required of all entering employees in the same job category.

We retain the right to use that post-offer medical examination to disqualify an individual if it demonstrates that the individual would pose a "direct threat" in the workplace (i.e., a significant risk of substantial harm to the health or safety of the individual or others) that cannot be eliminated or reduced below the "direct threat" level through reasonable accommodation.

We also retain the right to conduct employee medical examinations where there is evidence of a job performance or safety problem, examinations required by other Federal laws, examinations to determine current "fitness" to perform a particular job, and voluntary examinations that are part of employee health programs.

Information from all medical examinations and inquiries will be kept apart from general personnel files as a separate, confidential medical record, available only under limited conditions.

Note: Tests for illegal use of drugs are not medical examinations under the ADA and are not subject to the restrictions of such examinations. We reserve the right to conduct them according to company policy and current federal, state and local laws.

DISABILITY ACCOMMODATION

We consider reasonable accommodation to be any modification or adjustment to a job or the work environment that will enable a qualified applicant or employee with a disability to participate in the application process or to perform essential job functions. Reasonable accommodation also includes adjustments to assure that a qualified individual with a disability has employment rights and privileges in our company equal to those of our other employees without disabilities.

As examples of reasonable accommodation, we will consider making existing facilities used by employees readily accessible to and usable by an individual with a disability; restructuring a job; modifying work schedules; acquiring or modifying equipment; providing qualified readers or interpreters; or appropriately modifying examinations, training, or other programs. Reasonable accommodation also may include reassigning a current employee to a vacant position for which the individual is qualified, if the person is unable to do the original job because of a disability even with an accommodation. However, we are under no obligation to find a position for an applicant who is not qualified for the position sought. We will not lower quality or quantity standards as an accommodation; nor are we obligated to provide personal use items such as glasses or hearing aids.

While the company will offer accommodation when practical, we will not make an accommodation if it would impose an "undue hardship" on the operation of our business. "Undue hardship" is defined as an "action requiring significant difficulty or expense" when considered in light of a number of factors. These factors include the nature and cost of the accommodation in relation to the size, resources, nature, and structure of the employer's operation.

If a particular accommodation would be an undue hardship, we will try to identify another accommodation that will not pose such a hardship. Also, if the cost of an accommodation would impose an undue hardship on the company, the individual with a disability will be given the option of paying that portion of the cost which would constitute an undue hardship or providing the accommodation.

APPLICATION OF DISABILITY POLICY

Our established attendance and leave policies will be uniformly applied to all employees, regardless of disability. We will not refuse leave needed by an employee with a disability if other employees get such leave. We may also make adjustments in leave policy as a reasonable accommodation, and all our leave policies will integrate with the Family and Medical Leave Act.

Note: Individuals who currently engage in the illegal use of drugs are specifically excluded from the definition of a "qualified individual with a disability" protected by the ADA when the employer takes action on the basis of their drug use.

A test for the illegal use of drugs is not considered a medical examination under the ADA; therefore, we may conduct such testing of applicants or employees and make employment decisions based on the results.

If the results of a drug test reveal the presence of a lawfully prescribed drug or other medical information, such information will be treated as a confidential medical record.

An alcoholic is a person with a disability and is protected by the ADA if he or she is qualified to perform the essential functions of the job. While we provide an accommodation to an alcoholic, we retain the right to discipline, discharge or deny employment to an alcoholic whose use of alcohol adversely affects job performance or conduct. Per our current policy, we prohibit the use of alcohol in the workplace and require that employees not be under the influence of alcohol.

The company will inquire into an applicant's Workers' Compensation history before making a conditional offer of employment. But after making a conditional job offer, we may inquire about such a history in a medical inquiry or examination, as is required of all applicants in the same job category at our firm. We will not base an employment decision on the speculation that an applicant may cause increased Workers' Compensation costs in the future. But we will refuse to hire, or we may discharge, an individual who is not currently able to perform a job without posing a significant risk of substantial harm to the health or safety of the individual or others, if the risk cannot be eliminated or reduced by reasonable accommodation.

POLICY ON PROBATIONARY PERIOD FOR NEW EMPLOYEES

The probationary period for new employees is normally 90 days. It is intended as a period of learning adjustment and an opportunity for the company to evaluate the new employee's suitability.

On the recommendation of the supervisor, the Personnel Department may extend the probationary period beyond the normal 90 days if that is considered necessary.

During the probationary period, the new employee is expected to meet or exceed the established performance standards for new employees in that position and to learn and observe standard procedures and work rules. During this period, the employee can be terminated at any time if it becomes apparent that the employee will not be able to meet the requirements of this position.

Before terminating a probationary employee, the supervisor should make every effort to counsel and assist the employee in meeting the appropriate standards. Any decision to terminate the employee must be ratified by the Personnel Department.

An employee who successfully completes a probationary period shall continue to be employed subject to all policies and regulations applicable to regular employees. The end of a probationary period does not in any way restrict the company's authority to discharge, discipline or reassign the employee.

POLICY ON OVERTIME AVAILABILITY

1. Due to fluctuations in demand, all employees must be advised that they may be requested to work overtime.

2. Non-exempt employees are not to work before, beyond or outside their normal hours unless authorized by their immediate supervisors. Exempt employees may work overtime at their own discretion or when requested to do so by their immediate supervisors.

3. Supervisors should request or authorize overtime work a minimum of four hours before the scheduled end of the work day.

4. Under no circumstances will any non-exempt employee on a continuously moving line or operating a machine be requested or allowed to work more than 12 hours in one day. Other employees may be asked or allowed to work for more than 12 hours in one day, but this practice is discouraged and should not occur repeatedly.

5. Supervisors will monitor time cards each month to insure that authorized overtime is being correctly reported.

6. Non-exempt employees may take work home and qualify for overtime pay only with the approval of their supervisors. This practice is discouraged and only permitted in special circumstances.

7. Payments to non-exempt employees will be made according to state or federal wages and hours laws or the union contract.

POLICY ON ORIENTATION

GOALS

Introduce employees to the job and company, inform them of applicable policies, benefits and job requirements and avoid excessive legal liability.

PROCEDURE

The normal orientation program is conducted in four major phases:

1. An opening meeting with management and personnel representatives.
2. A briefing by the supervisor.
3. An extended formal briefing in the early weeks on the job.
4. Follow-up activities as needed.

THE WELCOME

A Personnel Department representative will conduct the opening session. It should include the following:

- A welcome from the Personnel Department representative.
- Necessary forms for payroll, personnel records, insurance coverage and other purposes.
- A copy of the company's organizational chart. Mention where the employee fits into the organization. Give the employee a map of the building.
- A description of the performance review system, with an emphasis on what will be expected during the probationary period.
- An explanation of the basic details of the pay system. Refer the employee to further information in the employee handbook.
- A copy of the employee handbook and, if available, the latest edition of the company newspaper.
- Discuss subjects, such as parking, that will be of immediate concern to the employee.
- Give the employee a chance to ask questions about the material covered.
- Escort the employee to their department to meet the supervisor.

SUPERVISOR'S BRIEFING

The Personnel Department representative should introduce the new employee to his or her supervisor. The supervisor should be prepared to greet the new employee by name—and should know how to spell and pronounce it correctly.

The supervisor should brief the employee on:
- The names and duties of fellow staff members.
- The group's major responsibilities and how they relate to the overall operation.
- Working hours, including shift assignments, breaks, holidays and overtime policies.
- Where to find lockers, cafeteria, rest rooms, elevators and staircases.
- What to do in case of illness or if the employee is unavoidably late for work.
- Pay policies, including the details of when, how much and in what form: check, cash or direct bank deposit. Also include details of any incentive or bonus plans.
- Details of job duties.
- Whom to see for information or help with problems.
- General policies, such as dress code, safety requirements and responsibility for tools and supplies.
- What kind of performance will be expected during the probationary period.

FOLLOW-UP

A follow-up process should begin the next day. The supervisor should conduct a brief meeting with the employee. It should cover these points.

- Answer any questions the employee might have about the previous orientation sessions.
- Discuss in detail what the employee will be expected to accomplish during the probationary period. Set performance goals to be met within 90 calendar days. Add milestone figures to chart the employee's progress at the 30-day mark.

FULL-SCALE ORIENTATION

Some time within the employee's first month, Personnel should conduct a formal, half-day session for all newly hired employees. The exact scheduling can depend on the number of new people hired. The ideal time is about two weeks after the employee has started work. The objectives of this session include:

- Build spirit and pride in the organization.
- Reiterate the policies and procedures that have been explained earlier.
- Explain employee benefits.
- Explain recognition programs.

A suggested agenda:

- Introduce the highest-ranking available executive. This leader should give a brief welcoming speech that makes the new employees feel important.
- Introduce other members of top management and key department managers.
- Explain the company's history, its products and services, its goals and its self-image. Show how each part of the organization contributes to the overall goals. A senior manager is a good choice to conduct this part of the program.
- Provide basic information on pay, the performance evaluation, training programs and advancement opportunities.
- Describe employee benefits, including vacations, holidays, sick leave, pensions and insurance, and special benefits such as educational aid.

POLICY ON EMPLOYING RELATIVES

POLICY

An employee is not permitted to work in a position where his or her supervisor, or a supervisor's supervisor, is a relative. A relative includes a father, mother, brother, sister, husband, wife, son, daughter, grandfather, grandmother, grandson or granddaughter.

PROCEDURE

No person should be hired for a position when to do so would violate this policy. If such a situation is created through promotion, transfer or marriage, one of the affected employees must be transferred or terminated within two weeks after the relationship is established or becomes known. Termination is to be a last resort. No employee who meets current standards of performance and behavior shall be terminated if a transfer is possible.

POLICY ON TERMINATION

PURPOSE

This policy states the company's philosophy with respect to terminations of employees and provides uniform guidelines for the administration of this policy.

POLICY

It is the policy of this company to retain to the extent consistent with company requirements, the services of all employees who perform their duties efficiently and effectively. However, it may become necessary under certain conditions to terminate employment for the good of the employee and/or company. The types of terminations that exist are layoff, discharge due to performance, disciplinary discharge, retirement and resignation.

GENERAL

The definition of the types of termination are as follows:

1. "Layoff" means termination of employment on the initiative of the company under circumstances, normally lack of work, such that the employee is subject to recall. He/she may be reinstated without loss of seniority if recalled within one year of the date of layoff.

2. "Discharge due to performance" means termination of employment on the initiative of the company under circumstances generally related to the quality of the employee's performance, whereby the employee is considered unable to meet the requirements of the job. In this case, the employee is not subject to recall or reinstatement.

3. "Discharge, disciplinary" means termination of employment on the initiative of the company for reasons of misconduct or willful negligence in the performance of job duties such that the employee will not be considered for re-employment.

4. "Retirement" means termination of active work by the employee at the age or under the conditions set forth in the company's retirement plan, under which the employee receives retirement pay and may enjoy other benefits.

5. "Resignation" means termination of employment on the initiative of the employee. Employees are expected to give no less than two weeks notice of resignation. An employee who resigns will retain no reinstatement or re-employment rights.

6. "Resignation requested" means termination of employment, for cause, on the initiative of the company. "Mutual agreement" terminations must be further identified as either discharge due to performance or discipline for purposes of severance pay eligibility. For pay purposes, terminations are effective on the last day worked, unless otherwise specified by the Department Head.

GUIDELINES FOR DISCHARGE DUE TO PERFORMANCE

In keeping with the company's concern for all employees, termination of employment on the initiative of the company under circumstances generally related to the quality of the employee's job performance deserves special consideration. The company would like to insure that every reasonable step has been taken to help the employee continue in a productive capacity. It is the responsibility of each manager and supervisor to develop the people working for him/her. In cases of unsatisfactory job performance, which may lead to termination of employment, each manager and supervisor should consider the following:

A. Has the employee been made aware of the problem in specific terms?

B. Have the suggestions as to how these problems can be eliminated been put in writing?

C. Has assistance been offered to the employee to help the employee remedy the situation?

D. Has the employee been given a sufficient amount of time and help to remedy the situation? If a situation related to poor job performance has just come to a manager's or supervisor's attention, joint evaluation between the employee and the manager is recommended. The manager should try to determine the cause of the problem. Is it lack of experience in the job, education, motivation, the employee's personal problems or personality conflict?

Once the cause is identified, the employee should be given time, if possible, to remedy the situation. The manager should also consider ways to remedy the situation and to improve the individual's performance.

Other alternatives are:

- Changing the employee's responsibilities in his/her present job.
- Reassignment to a different job in the department.
- Encouraging the employee to bid into an area where his/her chances of success are felt to be better.
- Changing to a position of lesser responsibility. If, after sufficient time and consideration of the above, the employee does not remedy the situation, the supervisor should then proceed with the termination of the employee. (See Termination Procedure below).

GUIDELINES FOR DISCIPLINARY TERMINATIONS

The termination of any employee for disciplinary causes must follow the procedures as set forth in the Policy on Discipline.

TERMINATION PROCEDURE

It is the responsibility of the manager to:
- Notify the Payroll Department and the Personnel Department of the cause and date of the termination.
- Notify the employee of the cause and date of termination.
- Prepare a Personnel Action Form stating the reason for termination and forward this to the Personnel Department.

It is the responsibility of the Personnel Department to:
- Provide the terminating employee with Termination Procedure Forms.
- Contact the terminating employee and set up an appointment for an exit interview (preferably on the last day of work).
- Review Termination Procedure Forms for completeness and required clearance signatures.
- Notify the Payroll Department and Credit Union of the termination.
- Provide appropriate Unemployment Compensation information and forms to the terminating employee.
- Forward all Termination Procedure Forms to the Personnel Department record room.

It is the responsibility of the Payroll Department to:
- Verify that the terminating employee has no outstanding financial liabilities to the company.
- Issue and mail a final paycheck upon completion of all termination procedures and receipt of a copy of the Personnel Action Form.

POLICY ON SAFETY AND HEALTH

POLICY

All employees are responsible for observing safe working practices and for observing the requirements of this policy and of all applicable laws and regulations. It is also the responsibility of each employee to preserve his or her health and to advise their supervisor or manager about any major change in its condition.

RESPONSIBILITY

The Director of Personnel shall coordinate all safety activities including:

1. Establishing procedures for promoting safe working conditions.
2. Conducting safety meetings and training programs.
3. Investigating accidents and recommending measures to eliminate safety and health hazards.
4. Working in conjunction with government authorities including occupational safety and health agencies, our insurance carrier's risk managers and the Workers' Compensation carrier.

Executives, department heads and supervisors are responsible for:

1. Incorporating safe working practices and good housekeeping into the day-to-day activities of their departments.
2. Taking action when necessary to correct and prevent hazards.

A Safety Committee will be made up of a representative of each department, appointed by the department head. The committee will meet monthly. The committee will be responsible for:

1. Reporting health, safety and housekeeping problems to management.
2. Monitoring programs to correct reported hazards.
3. Promoting interest and awareness of safety among all employees.

MEDICAL EXAMINATIONS

1. Job applicants will be required to take a pre-employment medical exam. The examination will be administered by a physician designated and paid for by the company.

2. Every applicant must complete a medical history form completely and honestly. Withholding or changing information can result in termination.
3. Employees being transferred or promoted may be required to have a physical examination. Declining performance or increased absenteeism may also justify a medical exam.
4. Medical examination results are company property and will be released to applicants, employees or doctors only when required by law.
5. All employees are required to report to their jobs in appropriate mental and physical condition, ready to work. If an employee may be impaired because of taking medication according to a doctor's prescription, he or she is expected to discuss it with the supervisor before commencing work that day.
6. Employees who have an alcohol/drug abuse problem should be encouraged to seek treatment. When work performance is affected, the use of a treatment program does not preclude appropriate action by the company.

ACCIDENTS AND INJURIES

1. Any employee who suffers any work-related injury must undergo a medical examination and drug test within 24 hours or face disciplinary action which can include discharge.
2. Employees who suffer work-related injuries or illnesses on the job must report them immediately to their supervisors. The company will arrange transportation of injured or sick employees to a physician or hospital.
3. Following treatment for injury or illness, an employee must:
   a. Complete a Workers' Compensation report as required.
   b. Keep medical appointments as scheduled.
   c. Return to work when cleared by a physician. Employees returning must provide certification from a physician indicating they will be able to work satisfactorily and safely. Employees who fail to return to work after receiving medical clearance may be discharged.
4. In certain cases the company may offer modified duty on a temporary basis to returning injured or sick employees. If the company elects to do so, and the employee is cleared for modified duty, he or she must accept it or face discipline, up to and including discharge.
5. An employee may be granted a medical leave of absence for illness or injury that is expected to require more than two weeks away from work. (See the Policy on Sick Leave).

SAFETY RULES

Each department head and supervisor is responsible for establishing necessary safety rules within his or her department and for taking appropriate corrective or disciplinary action when rules are violated. Safety rules will be posted conspicuously on bulletin boards located in each department.

HIRING AND ORIENTATION

No person shall be hired to do a job which he or she is not physically or mentally able to perform in a safe manner. This policy must not be implemented in any way which violates Equal Employment Opportunity laws or regulations of the American with Disabilities Act.

The orientation of every new employee must include a full discussion of the rules and techniques for safe performance of the employee's job.

TRAINING AND EDUCATION

All managers and supervisors should be alert to the need to provide training, education and motivational materials to improve safety within their departments. The Director of Personnel is responsible for developing and providing necessary programs and training materials.

ACCIDENT REPORTS

Supervisors will report all accidents within their departments to Personnel. Personnel will provide assistance as necessary to investigate the accident, determine its cause, and recommend and help implement preventive measures.

FACILITIES AND INSPECTIONS

The company shall maintain all safety and health facilities to meet all applicable standards with regard to:
- First aid
- Fire extinguishers, hoses and fire axes
- Exits, exit signs, corridors, walkways, fire escapes
- Fire doors and smoke detectors
- Parking lots
- Heating, lighting, ventilation, air conditioning
- Electrical and plumbing installations
- Adequate restrooms
- Lighting and other environmental factors

Engineering, manufacturing and maintenance activities will be carried out to prevent or correct hazards due to defective equipment or facilities.

Department heads and supervisors will conduct regular inspections of their work areas at least weekly to prevent or correct safety and health hazards. They will cooperate fully with inspectors from the company insurance carrier's risk managers, OSHA and the Workers' Compensation carrier.

CORRECTING DEFICIENCIES

Any safety or health hazard discovered at any time, through any means, will be corrected as soon and as effectively as possible.

POLICY ON DRUG AND ALCOHOL ABUSE

PURPOSE

To protect the health and well-being of the company and its individual employees.

DISCUSSION

The abuse of drugs and alcohol is a serious threat to both the company and its employees. Management and employees are equally responsible for maintaining a safe and healthy working environment. For that reason, the company has adopted these policies:

1. The possession, use or sale of alcohol, unauthorized or illegal drugs or the misuse of any legal drugs on company premises or while on company business is prohibited and will constitute grounds for termination.
2. Any employee under the influence of drugs or alcohol which impairs judgment, performance or behavior while on company premises or while on company business will be subject to discipline, including termination.
3. The company has a number of jobs which present special safety considerations to employees. These include the use of moving machinery, transportation of goods and persons and the handling of _____. The company will require that all employees on jobs which involve special safety considerations be tested periodically for the use of drugs. An employee with positive test results may be disqualified to work in such a job.
4. Each employee is responsible for promptly reporting to company health personnel any use of prescribed drugs which may affect the employee's judgment, performance or behavior.

The company will establish such procedures as it finds necessary to effectively enforce this policy. That may include a requirement that employees cooperate in personal or facility searches when there is reason to believe drugs or alcohol are present, when their performance is impaired or when their behavior is erratic. Refusing to cooperate with these procedures may be cause for disciplinary action, including termination.

The company strongly urges employees to use the community health and counselling facilities for help with alcohol or drug problems. It is each employee's responsibility to seek assistance before the problem affects judgment, performance or behavior.

GUIDELINES FOR SUPERVISORS

Supervisors are responsible for taking appropriate action any time an employee's behavior or performance raises any question about the employee's physical condition or ability to do the job properly and safely.

The performance of each employee is important to the company. Supervisors should be aware that to ignore or avoid a performance problem, whatever the cause, is contrary to the best interests of both the company and the employee.

A supervisor should never try to diagnose an employee's condition. This should be reserved for qualified professionals. Confine your actions and your remarks to the specific performance and behavior problems you personally have observed. Do not speculate as to their causes, which can include illness, worries and other problems as well as substance abuse. Never refer to an employee as being "drunk" or "on drugs" and never use any other term which might suggest those conditions. Do not discuss the problems of individual employees with other members of the organization unless there is a business reason to do so.

No two cases are alike, and supervisors should be flexible in their responses. Some cases call for immediate action; others are long-term. Supervisors should use the following guidelines in planning their actions.

Identifying Immediate Problems

These performance and behavior problems might indicate a problem with drugs or alcohol, particularly if they represent a significant change from the employee's past behavior.

1. The employee appears confused or exhibits erratic behavior.
2. The employee has trouble getting along with other employees.
3. The employee exhibits paranoia, slurred speech or behavior that is obviously irrational or unsafe.
4. The employee has been involved in an on-the-job accident or has had a series of safety-related incidents which raise questions about his or her physical and emotional state.

Procedures to follow

When an employee exhibits such behavior and appears unfit to work, the supervisor should follow these procedures:

1. Take the employee off the job. Do this immediately if the condition may affect the safety of others. Otherwise, arrange for at least one other supervisor to observe the employee and confirm your impressions. Begin a written record of

the incident, including the date, time, location, name of the other supervisor and a brief description of the event and circumstances.

2. Give the employee a chance to explain. Select a private location, out of hearing of other employees. If a union representative or some other third party is required, make the necessary arrangements. Do not ask about drug or alcohol use. Confine your questions and statements to specific performance and behavior. Remind the employee of an obligation to report any medical problems or prescribed medication that may affect behavior.

3. If, after the explanation, you still believe the employee is unfit to perform the job, request that the employee accompany you to a medical facility. (Note: This can be a company facility, a private physician or a hospital.)

4. If the employee refuses to answer questions or to go to the medical facility, tell the employee that this refusal can be grounds for discipline, up to and including termination. Do not attempt to restrain the employee or use physical force. If the employee continues to refuse, make a memo of that fact and take appropriate disciplinary action. Arrange for transportation home if that appears necessary.

5. If the employee gives his or her consent, the medical facility may make appropriate tests for the presence of drugs, alcohol and other substances. The results may be released to the facility manager and the employee relations manager only with employee consent. Employee consent must be in writing. If the employee refuses to give it, the supervisor should inform the employee that the refusal could be grounds for disciplinary action.

Identifying long-term problems

These performance and behavior problems might indicate a problem with drugs or alcohol if they continue or intensify over a period of time:

1. Substandard performance, particularly if there is a pattern of decline.
2. Excessive absences or lateness.
3. A tendency to take excessive risks.
4. Continued problems getting along with other workers.
5. Difficulty in concentrating.
6. An excessive number of accidents or close calls.
7. Poor quality of work.

Procedures to follow

When an employee exhibits such behavior, the supervisor should discuss the performance problems with the employee. Do not attempt to diagnose the cause, and do not suggest that the employee is under the influence of alcohol or drugs. Set an appropriate schedule and performance standards for improving the employee's behavior. Inform the employee that he or she can be discharged if the performance does not improve. Make a record of the discussion.

POLICY ON SMOKING

PURPOSE

This company recognizes the need of its employees to work in an environment free of tobacco smoke. The company also respects the rights of employees who choose to smoke to make personal decisions without interference, as long as these decisions do not interfere with the rights of other workers.

POLICY

Smoking is allowed only in places where it is specifically permitted. There will be no smoking in any other areas. Areas where smoking is permitted will be designated by signs.

Department managers are responsible for designating smoking and non-smoking areas in the facilities under their control. They should base these designations on the criteria listed in the next section.

DESIGNATION CRITERIA

No smoking will be allowed in any area where that practice would create a recognized hazard under the Occupational Safety and Health Act or where, in the manager's judgment, smoking would be unsafe.

No smoking will be allowed in public areas or where groups of people frequently gather. These include reception areas, conference rooms, training centers, auditoriums, rest rooms, medical facilities, stairwells and elevators.

In other work areas, managers should determine smoking policies by balancing the needs and desires of the employees. Options include:

1. Permitting no smoking in the area.
2. Allowing smoking in the entire area.
3. Designating portions of the area as no-smoking zones.

Employees who are the sole occupants of fully enclosed offices may designate their offices as smoking or non-smoking zones, as they wish. These designations will apply to any visitors to these offices.

POLICY ON AIDS

POLICY

It is this company's policy to hire, or to continue to employ, individuals who have AIDS or are suspected of having AIDS as long as they are able to meet the normal standards of performance for their jobs. The company's intent will be to provide maximum employment opportunities to AIDS victims while preserving the safety and morale of all other employees.

STANDARDS FOR EXISTING EMPLOYEES

A victim of AIDS or any of its preliminary or related stages will be treated exactly as any other employee who suffers from a serious illness. All medical benefits will be available as provided in the company's medical insurance plan, and all accrued sick leave will be available on the conditions normally applied to all employees.

An AIDS victim will also be treated as a handicapped employee. If, except for the handicap, the employee is otherwise qualified to perform the job, the company will make every reasonable accommodation to the handicap.

No AIDS victim who remains qualified to do his or her job will be denied continued employment. If the employee is no longer able to perform, the company will make every reasonable effort to transfer the employee to a position that is within the employee's ability. The employee will be terminated only if no such position is available but will remain eligible for all leave and health benefits as described above.

No job action will be taken solely because the employee has been diagnosed as having AIDS or a related ailment, or because the employee is considered to be at high risk of contracting AIDS.

However, if a supervisor or manager should reasonably believe that the continued employment of an AIDS victim entails an unusual risk to other employees, the employee may be transferred, if possible, or terminated, if necessary. Such a decision must be approved by the Director of Personnel and only when a substantial and unusual risk is demonstrated.

HIRING PRACTICES

No otherwise qualified job applicant shall be denied employment because he or she is believed to suffer from AIDS or a related ailment, or because he or she is believed to be a high risk for contracting AIDS.

Pre-employment screening will not include any medical tests designed to indicate exposure to AIDS or any questions about the applicant's private lifestyle.

All job applicants will be evaluated solely on their qualifications for available openings.

WORKPLACE SAFETY RULES

These rules apply to employees of all departments. In addition, department heads and supervisors may establish specific requirements for individual departments.

- Never operate any machine or equipment unless specifically authorized to do so by the supervisor responsible for that equipment.
- Do not use defective equipment or tools. Report defects immediately to your supervisor.
- Obtain full instructions for operating any machine with which you are not familiar.
- Never begin any hazardous job unless you are completely familiar with the proper techniques and precautions which apply to it. Check with your supervisor when in doubt.
- Make sure all guards and other safety attachments are properly installed and adjusted before operating any piece of equipment or beginning any hazardous job.
- Do not operate any piece of equipment at unsafe speeds or in excess of its rated capacity.
- Wear all protective clothing and equipment required for the job. Avoid clothing or other items that would offer poor protection or that might be caught in machinery.
- Never attempt to repair, adjust or lubricate a machine unless you have been authorized to do so. Never attempt to repair, adjust or lubricate a machine while it is in operation. Never attempt to repair or adjust electrical equipment unless the power switch has been properly turned off.
- Put all tools and equipment away when not in use.
- Do not try to lift any item which is too heavy or bulky to be handled by one person. Ask for help.
- Keep all aisles, stairways and exits clear of stored items.
- Do not place equipment or materials so as to block emergency exit routes, fire extinguishers, sprinkler controls, machine controls or electrical control panels.
- Stack all working materials neatly, and make sure the piles are stable.
- Keep your work area and all company facilities which you use clean and neat.
- Do not run, participate in horseplay, or distract fellow workers.
- Never take chances. If you are not sure, ask.

POLICY ON COMPENSATION PRACTICES AND PAY SCHEDULE

PURPOSE

It is the purpose of this policy to provide equitable compensation for employees at every level while conforming to the requirements of the Federal Labor Standards Act (FLSA), as amended, its rules and regulations, and State wages and hours laws as they apply to our company.

RESPONSIBILITY

The Director of Personnel is in direct charge of the compensation system for all employees below the level of corporate officer, except for those covered by the union contract, the terms of which are negotiated periodically. The Board of Directors is responsible for compensation of corporate officers.

GENERAL

1. The compensation system for all employees, whether salaried or hourly (other than those subject to the union contract) is divided into _____ pay grades. The rates for each grade are adjusted periodically to account for inflation, shortages of certain skills, regional differences, etc.
2. Extra pay may be earned by non-exempt employees for authorized overtime during regular hours; authorized work on holidays and weekends will be compensated according to FLSA rules. Extra pay for exempt employees will be awarded upon recommendation of department managers and approved by the corporate officer to which the department reports.
3. To be paid for working on a holiday, the employee must be present on the normally scheduled work days immediately before and after the holiday. Supervisors may make exceptions to this policy for valid reasons such as illness or vacations.
4. Employees and supervisors working the third shift receive a 10% differential in their pay grades.
5. Employees who are promoted will initially receive the base pay of the new grade to which they're promoted. Reassigned employees will receive the base pay of the grade to which they're reassigned.
6. Employees whose jobs normally require them to work outdoors for four or more consecutive hours a day will receive an "inclement weather pay premium" of 10% during the months of December through March.

7. The company does not have an incentive pay plan for employees not under the union contract. Merit pay will be awarded through the pay grade system.

8. Non-exempt employees will be paid by check on Friday afternoon of each week. Overtime pay earned will be included in the following week's pay check. Exempt employees are paid on the 15th and the last day of each month. When those days fall on a holiday or weekend, exempt employees will be paid on the work day prior to the holiday or weekend.

9. Vacation pay of up to two weeks may be requested from Payroll by the employees' supervisors to be paid on the day prior to the beginning of the vacation period.

10. Up to one week's pay may be advanced to employees to cover emergency expenses such as medical, accidents, etc. with the approval of employees' supervisors.

POLICY ON PERFORMANCE REVIEWS

Standards for appraising employees should reflect the basic requirements of the job. Department heads, supervisors and representatives of the Personnel Department should establish or revise the basic requirements at any time the content of the job is significantly changed.

Job requirements and individual performance standards can normally be organized under these general headings:

1. Knowledge—How well the employee knows the requirements of the job.
2. Ability—The level of skill the employee applies to the job.
3. Application—The way the employee is able to apply his or her knowledge and the ability to meet the requirements of the position.
4. Dependability—How well you can rely on the employee to perform the job properly, without close supervision.
5. Communication—How effectively the employee exercises the written and oral communications necessary to the job.
6. Effectiveness. How ably the employee has produced the desired results.

APPRAISAL FREQUENCY

Performance review is a continuing process. Appraisals should be scheduled six months after initial employment and thereafter annually during the anniversary month of employment. Between appraisals the supervisor should keep notes on critical incidents in which the employee demonstrates either significantly good or poor performance. These notes should be kept on file to be used in the next scheduled appraisal.

THE APPRAISAL INTERVIEW

The performance appraisal interview should be primarily a discussion. Its goal is to find mutually acceptable ways to improve employee performance and overcome shortcomings. It should also give recognition for good or superior performance.

The appraisal form should guide the discussion. The interview should take this general organization:

1. Analyze past performance, using the ratings and comments on the review form.
2. Discuss and agree upon the steps to be taken to improve.
3. Discuss and identify standards to be applied for the next appraisal.
4. Give the employee a chance to discuss future training and development opportunities.

STATEMENT OF MANAGEMENT RIGHTS

The company retains the right to change, modify, cancel, suspend or interpret any of its personnel policies and practices without advance notice, within its sole discretion and without statement of cause or justification.

No commitment for employment for any specified duration or condition, including "lifetime" employment or discharge only for cause, shall be binding on the company unless it is expressly set forth in a written document signed by the employee and by the Chief Executive Officer of the Company.

All rates of pay, commission schedules, bonus plans and other forms of compensation are subject to change by the company without advance notice, in the company's sole discretion, and without statement of cause or justification. This provision will not be applied retroactively to deprive any employee of specific amounts already established as due under a salary, commission, bonus plan or other form of compensation.

All employees are required to recognize these rights as conditions of their employment.

GRIEVANCE PROCEDURES

An Employee Grievance Board procedure is available to you as a fair and effective means to resolve work-related complaints and problems. By using the procedure's series of four progressive steps, you can call upon your supervisors, Employee Services, the Employee Grievance Board and Corporate Administration to evaluate your case and decide whether or not you have been treated fairly. You can use the procedure when you feel a work-related decision is not consistent with established company policies and practices, including those outlined in this handbook.

Grievances may include such things as discipline, transfer, job posting selection, unfair assignment of vacation or holiday time, a personal request that was denied, etc. You cannot use the procedure to appeal decisions related to the company's responsibility to determine the number and assignment of employees, to establish rules of conduct, to determine the hours and days of work, starting and quitting times, wages and benefits, etc.

The procedure involves a series of four steps. In most cases, begin with Step One. In cases concerning disciplinary action, begin with Step Two.

Step One

Discuss your grievance with your immediate supervisor within three days after the incident. If you are not satisfied, take your grievance to the next supervisory level if one exists in your department.

Step Two

If your grievance is not settled in Step One, submit your grievance in writing to Employee Services (within three days after the incident if your grievance involves disciplinary action).

Your grievance should be written on a grievance report form, available from Employee Services.

An Employee Services representative will try to resolve your grievance through counseling and advice within two days. If the grievance is not mutually resolved, proceed to Step Three.

Step Three

Within five days of your request, the Director of Employee Services will schedule a meeting of the Employee Grievance Board.

You will be able to select this panel of six employees (three supervisory and three non-supervisory) from a group of 10 employees (five supervisory and five non-supervisory) who have been selected by the Director of Employee Services from a list of qualified volunteers.

The Board will hear and thoroughly investigate the facts of your case and then vote by secret ballot. If there is a tie, the Director of Employee Services will also vote. The results will be posted within three days after the Board hearing.

The decision of the Board is final and binding unless it was necessary for the Director of Employee Services to break a tie vote, and you are not satisfied with the results. In that case, you can proceed to Step Four.

Step Four

In order to appeal your grievance to Step Four, you must submit a second written appeal to Employee Services within three days after the Board's decision has been posted.

A meeting with the Administrative Executive Director and Associate Executive Director (pending their availability) will be scheduled for you within five days after you have submitted the appeal.

After you have had your meeting with the Administration, its decision will be given to you in writing within two days. This decision is, in all cases, final and binding.

POLICY ON PEER REVIEW

PURPOSE

A system of peer review can help prevent errors and misjudgments in imposing discipline and can build employee faith in the disciplinary system.

ORGANIZATION

The Peer Review Board shall consist of three members appointed by management and four employee delegates. The employee delegates will be selected by random drawing from among non-exempt employees. The General Manager will appoint the management representatives from nominees submitted by the department heads. All members will serve two-year terms. In the event any member is unable to serve his or her full term, a replacement will be selected in the same manner as the original appointment and will serve the balance of the previous member's term.

The board shall have full access when necessary to advice and representation by the Corporate Counsel. A President elected by board members will preside at all board functions. The board may also elect other officers to perform other assigned duties.

PROCEDURE

Any employee who is disciplined for an offense in Level 2 or higher, or who is assessed any penalty more severe than a verbal warning, shall have access to the peer review process. The employee must sign a statement agreeing to accept and abide by the board's decision. The supervisor will provide the employee with a notice of this right. The notice should include instructions for requesting a hearing before the board.

On receiving a request from an eligible employee, the board will convene a hearing within seven working days. The complaining employee and management shall each have the privilege of requesting one delay of no more than seven working days. Any further delays must be by agreement of the board and all parties.

The board may make necessary rules for conducting its hearings, consistent with these requirements:

1. The proceedings shall be informal, so an employee can present his or her case without the aid of counsel. However, the employee may choose to use an attorney or other representative.
2. All parties to the case will have a full opportunity to present arguments, testimony, evidence and witnesses on their behalf. Board members may ask questions of any party.
3. All decisions will be by a majority of board members present. The board may uphold, deny or modify the disciplinary action in question.
4. The board must maintain a written record of all its proceedings, including the reasons for its decisions. This record shall be kept on permanent file.

POLICY ON EMPLOYEE ASSISTANCE PROGRAM

PURPOSE

The company seeks to retain valuable employees and maintain productivity by identifying personal problems at early stages and motivating the employees to seek help with these problems. The company has available a list of local service organizations which offer help with personal problems.

These organizations have been able to help individuals when they have problems that are beyond their abilities to cope and which affect performance and behavior on the job. An employee's reputation, job security and opportunities for promotion will not be jeopardized by the use of these service organizations.

These organizations help with personal problems only. Employees should discuss job-related problems with their supervisors.

SELF REFERRAL

The company prefers employees to arrange for assistance during non-working hours. Employees who must get assistance during working hours must obtain their supervisor's approval. Supervisors should normally approve such treatment only when it is not readily available at other times.

The employee's participation in any program offered by a local service organization is strictly voluntary. All contacts with local service organizations must be treated in strict confidence. All records kept by service organizations shall be kept for the exclusive use of those organizations. No employee or manager of the company will have access to those files.

POLICY ON PERSONNEL RECORDS ACCESS

PURPOSE

To guarantee that all personnel file information is consistently maintained in accordance with current personnel practices and applicable state and federal laws.

Also, to make certain that employee personnel file data is properly safeguarded and protected.

Finally, to provide for employee and management access to the data maintained in personnel files in a logical and systematic fashion.

COVERAGE

All employees.

RESPONSIBILITY

1. Every employee is permitted to gain access to the records maintained by the company's Personnel Department which contain personal data regarding that employee. These records may be reviewed only in the presence of a designated Personnel official.
2. In order to make corrections on a personnel record file, the employee must first submit a formal request in writing to the Personnel Department.
3. If the request for a correction is turned down, the employee can then request that his or her statement of disagreement with the personnel files be placed within the file. That statement of disagreement is to be a permanent part of information in the personnel file.

MANAGEMENT ACCESS TO PERSONNEL FILES

Management will be allowed access to these files strictly on a need-to-know basis. Of that access, only information regarding an individual's job performance and skill qualifications will be open for review.

EXTERNAL REQUESTS FOR PERSONNEL FILE INFORMATION

Any external source (i.e. individuals or corporations outside the Company) who requests information from an employee's personnel file, must first receive clearance from the employee before any data is released.

The only exception to this policy is verification of employment requests about active employees.

POLICY ON WAGE GARNISHMENT

POLICY

The company will comply with all applicable laws governing the garnishment of wages.

DEFINITION

A garnishment is a court order that compels an employer to withhold a sum of money from an employee's wages to pay debts, taxes or other legal obligations.

DEDUCTIONS

After income and Social Security taxes have been deducted from an employee's paycheck, the remainder is considered "disposable income." From this amount, the company will withhold garnishments according to this schedule:
- The total amount of a federal tax levy.
- On a non-support order by a court, the amount over $00 will be withheld.
- On other types of garnishments, the withholding will be based on this schedule of weekly income:

Disposable Income	Amount Withheld
Less than $00	$00
$00 to $00	The amount over $00
More than $00	00% of disposable income.

- When more than one garnishment notice is in effect, the company will pay creditors, to the extent funds are available, in the order their notices were received.

EMPLOYEE'S STATUS

a. Under federal law, no employee can be discharged on the basis of a garnishment for any one indebtedness, regardless of its nature. No company representative can make any threats of discharge for garnishments connected with a single debt.
b. The company will take no disciplinary action of any kind on the basis of a single garnishment. In the case of multiple debts, any disciplinary action will be based solely on whether an inadequate sense of responsibility is affecting the employee's work performance.
c. Should the company contemplate disciplinary action on the basis of more than one garnishment, the Controller must first investigate the case and determine that the garnishments in fact represent more than one debt and are not multiple claims arising from the same obligation.

d. Any employee who is the subject of a garnishment should be advised of a local service organization, such as a not-for-profit credit counselling organization, to which he or she can turn for help.

LEGAL CONSIDERATIONS

If any provision of this policy is contrary to applicable local, state or federal law, the company will comply with the law. All provisions of this policy which do comply with the law will remain in force.

(NOTE: Amounts vary by state—check with your state for correct dollar amounts.)

Developing an Effective Wage and Salary Administration Program 9

What are the main purposes of a sound compensation system?

The main goals of a sound compensation system are to attract, hold and motivate good employees. Other purposes include eliminating morale problems caused by inequitable pay, giving your firm a good reputation, improving the quality of employees' performance, and raising their productivity level.

What are typical "traps" to avoid in starting an organized compensation system?

Here are four pitfalls to avoid:

1. Don't begin by trying to see how little you can get away with paying. Employees resent that attitude and good ones will leave.
2. Don't announce the start of a compensation program and then stall for months without acting. That looks like you want to wait until you're forced to begin.
3. Create your own plan. You can learn from other organizations but simply copying one usually results in a poor fit for the unique characteristics of your own company.
4. Don't make compensation a mystery. Answer questions about the program or you'll start destructive rumors flying.

What personnel are needed to design, plan and implement a compensation program?

Most of the work will involve a cooperative effort between your managers, supervisors and employees and the person selected to administer the plan. The entire organization will eventually play a part in the creation of the compensation program.

You need an executive who is a good planner to organize the project. You need another person on the project who is familiar with administration and production management. And you need evaluators who will act as a committee to rank and place monetary values on jobs.

Professional consultants offer services in compensation planning. But using internal personnel who are intimately acquainted with many of the jobs and the structure of your organization frequently produces far better results.

What are the functions of the key people who organize the compensation program?

The executive or manager chosen to head the program is called the Administrator. Many wage and salary plan Administrators have backgrounds in personnel or accounting. However, pick the individual you believe is best qualified for the work.

Select a person who has some background and knowledge of production management as the program's Job Analyst. Much of his or her work revolves around defining jobs and providing information to evaluate their work.

You'll need a committee, known as the Evaluation Committee, which places money values on jobs. The individuals on this committee should be drawn from different functions in the company.

What qualifications should the members of the compensation team have?

That team may consist of the Administrator, the Analyst, a clerical assistant who is familiar with payroll procedures and personnel records, and the Evaluation Committee, usually five. But in smaller companies that number may be reduced by having an individual handle more than one function. Whatever the size of your team, it should possess certain capabilities and skills.

The Administrator should have a thorough knowledge of the operations of your company. He or she should be comfortable working with details and be a good planner and organizer. The Administrator should have the type of personality that encourages cooperation. He or she should be persistent and able to get the answers to questions without being irritating.

The Administrator's primary task is to establish the plan, explain how it should work to the Analyst, verify information as it is gathered and secure the cooperation of line managers, supervisors and staff executives.

The job Analyst is responsible for collection of data. He or she prepares forms and documents including job and position descriptions and current salary schedules. This individual must work well with people and have an in-depth knowledge of the work done in plant and office. The Analyst should also understand tools and machines and be able to describe what workers and operators do.

Members of the Evaluation Committee must have considerable knowledge of the importance of all jobs and positions to the firm. Membership on the Committee should include individuals from the plant, office and staff.

What tool is used to plan the compensation program?

The Compensation Planning Checklist (9-01), located at the end of this chapter, will serve as a good working tool for the person who handles the chores of the Administrator. Expand upon and adapt it to your own needs.

What role does job analysis play in developing a compensation program?

Job analysis is usually the first step in developing a compensation program. It involves gathering detailed information about all jobs and positions to get a clear understanding of how each one contributes to achieving company goals and objectives. Job information tells the Analyst what processes are carried out to turn raw material into a product for sale or to enable a company to offer a service. He or she learns how the jobs relate to other jobs. Job information also helps the Analyst determine what type of person is best able to perform the work.

Analysts also help write job descriptions. They assist in ranking and rating jobs and gathering information about wages and salaries outside the firm, as well as those currently in effect within the company.

See Chapter Three for a full discussion on developing job descriptions.

How are job descriptions used in compensation programs?

The job and position descriptions provide the basic information about the tasks, duties, responsibilities and working environment so the Evaluation Committee can successfully complete its efforts to rank, rate and set money values on jobs.

What approaches can be used to rate the values of jobs?

Evaluation of jobs is not an exact science. The members of the Evaluation Committee can reduce subjectivity, though, by requiring its members to reach unanimity on the values of jobs. Though it's clear that the chief executive's job is worth more to a firm than, say, a clerk's, when you look at jobs or positions that are much more closely related, the differences are not so obvious. Most firms use one of the following approaches:

1. The market value approach. It produces an evaluation of your company's jobs and positions by comparing your company's wages and salaries with the wages and salaries paid by other firms.

2. The internal value approach. It evaluates the firm's jobs and positions by making careful internal comparisons between jobs and ranking them in proportion to their value to the firm.

Many firms use one of these approaches and temper the results with data gathered by the other.

How is a market value approach implemented?

The Administrator selects 5 to 10 companies whose work is similar to his own company's. He contacts the personnel managers at those firms and asks to share information with them about wages and salaries. The Administrator combines what he has learned with wage surveys published by business associations, and then compares the firm's pay schedules with the data gathered.

The market approach usually works well with scientific and professional personnel. But it gives no consideration to internal pay relationships in your firm. Generally, the market approach provides a check or comparison on pay schedules after a company has created its own internal program.

How does the internal value approach to rating jobs work?

This approach to job evaluation uses systems that deal objectively with the relationships that exist among jobs and positions in the firm. Some of these systems are suitable for evaluating all jobs and positions, while others are only useful for lower-level jobs. The first requirement for using this approach is an understanding of the compensable factors.

What are "compensable factors?"

Compensable factors are the requirements, responsibilities and working conditions that affect and determine performance. They are the items the firm pays for, and the amount it pays is directly related to the importance of different compensable factors in each job or position.

What criteria can be used to select the compensable factors for job evaluations?

The following criteria usually determine the selection of the compensable factors:

1. The factor must be understandable and acceptable to all employees (and meet any terms of an employment contract, if applicable).
2. Factors must clearly apply to the job under study. For example, it is fruitless to evaluate a watchman's job on decision-making, a factor with little or no value to that job.
3. A factor that applies equally to two or more jobs cannot be used as a measure since no comparison is possible.
4. Factors should not resemble one another so closely that they measure the same thing. For instance, the factors of education and knowledge should not be used in evaluating the same job.
5. The number of factors should be kept to the minimum needed for strong comparisons among jobs. In most cases, 5 or 10 are sufficient.

When the employee work force numbers in the hundreds, it's advisable to group jobs into classes, such as shop jobs, office jobs, professional jobs, etc. Different compensable factors will apply to different groups. Smaller organizations may find class separation unnecessary.

What are the most common compensable factors used in job evaluations?

There are wide variations in the compensable factors selected by different firms. Tailor your selections based on the nature of your business, the types of jobs and the judgment of the evaluators.

The following factors are among those that would be applicable to a manufacturer for most of its shop and office jobs:

- Education
- Experience
- Complexity of duties
- Supervision received
- Relations to others
- Accuracy
- Accountability
- Mental and visual attention required
- Physical endurance
- Working environment
- Type and extent of supervision
- Staff relations

Whatever factors are chosen must be clearly defined so that all members of the evaluation committee understand what they are evaluating in every case.

How are jobs ranked?

First, establish a separate ranking for each class of jobs, such as those in the shop, in the office, professional, etc. Then, select a broad compensable factor, such as "difficulty." Have each evaluator write the job title on a card for each job to be evaluated. Then each evaluator writes his or her judgment as to the relative difficulty of each job.

The evaluators then sort their cards with the most difficult job listed at the bottom of the stack. Cards are collected and the job titles listed in a vertical column at the left on a large chalkboard. Each member's name is written across the top of the chalkboard and the ranking assigned to each job is entered in the proper location opposite the job title and under the member's name.

The evaluation team then discusses the rankings. The members resolve disagreements until each member's ranking is identical. This simple system works best in small companies.

The factor comparison system is more sophisticated and produces better results in large concerns. It compares one job to another in terms of the degree certain universal factors are present: mental requirements, physical requirements, responsibility and working conditions.

Every job is ranked according to each of these factors, on a scale of 1 to 10, with 10 being the highest. The total points for each job can be used to compare one job to another. Monetary values are assigned to each job and the points are used to determine the pay rates for each.

What are the major determinants used in setting wages?

The current industry average wage for the job is the most useful measure of a satisfactory wage and salary structure. However, keep in mind certain other influences on wages:

1. Cost of living increases become necessary to compensate for losses of purchasing power due to inflation.

2. Productivity is becoming increasingly important in determining limits on compensation costs. Most employers now feel that compensation increases should be linked to productivity gains.

3. Labor supply affects wages. Higher than traditionally-accepted wages may be necessary to attract and hold employees.

How can a company determine what other companies pay?

You can determine the "going" (current) wage in an area by a survey made by your Administrator, personnel manager, or an independent consultant. There are many drawbacks to making or commissioning your own survey. Among them are time, lack of response, difficulties in describing jobs for the benefit of the potential respondees, and designing the questionnaire, among others.

It often makes sense to depend on surveys conducted at regular intervals by business associations to which your firm may belong, or by the state or federal government. Other organizations that commonly conduct wage and salary surveys are:

- Chambers of Commerce and Merchants and Manufacturers Associations.

- Professional societies which conduct surveys of members and show range of compensation.

- Commercial publications, such as magazines for purchasing managers, plant managers, etc.

- Executive search firms—these are usually restricted to high level executives, and they may be biased toward the high end.

- Academic placement offices, which are quite useful in determining entry level pay. They tend to estimate on the high side in their own self-interests.
- Employment agencies—usually for clerical jobs.

What should be done after collecting data on comparable wages outside your organization?

You have the choices of matching your current wages to the comparable wages, retaining your existing wages, or paying above the wages included in the data you've gathered. The determining factor is usually your company's ability to pay.

If ability to pay is not a problem, and your current wages are below market averages, your decision depends on your need for the skills. If you must get and retain individuals with certain skills, you must offer competitive wages.

What negative beliefs must be overcome to make an incentive pay system effective?

Before instituting an incentive pay system, find out if any of the following attitudes are prevalent. If they are, you must overcome them:

1. Incentives are synonymous with working faster.
2. Hourly rates will be cut if individual earnings increase.
3. Standards are not set fairly.
4. Standards will be raised to make them more difficult to meet.
5. Incentive plans disrupt the social relations of the group of workers.
6. Unskilled workers may earn more than skilled workers who are excluded from the plan.

How should standards for incentive pay be set?

You can set standards based on past performance, but this is often unreliable. You can use the services of a trained industrial engineer or an experienced plant manager to develop standards. They may use time and motion studies to do so, though many standards have already been determined and are published in handbooks that cover nearly all industrial operations.

Once you've set a standard for each operation, the incentive plan should meet these requirements:

- The base wage must be adequate.
- Each worker under the plan must deliver improved results. The output must be measurable.

- You must openly recognize and verbally praise high productivity.
- The plan should be so fair and equitable that no individuals feel jealous of others for earning high incentive pay.
- Your management must invest the time and money needed to administer the plan and deliver the rewards promptly to the workers.
- Management must know exactly what it wants to achieve under the plan.

What are group incentive plans?

The technical and organizational requirements of group plans are similar to those of individual plans. The major difference is that under a group plan all employees share with the company in the rewards from cost savings or profit increases. Among group plans in common use, there are different methods of sharing rewards, and plans have many different objectives.

Companies benefit from group incentive plans in part because of peer pressure to eliminate below average effort. The plans also create more awareness by employees about the relationships between jobs, productivity and sales. In most companies with group incentives, grievances have declined and cost savings increased, often dramatically.

How is pay structured for managers and professionals?

Upper-level positions seldom fit neatly into a wage and salary structure. Individuals in such positions have far greater opportunity to innovate, to originate and demonstrate leadership and initiative than lower ranks of employees. Their level of performance is critical to the organization.

Middle managers are paid for organizing ability, leadership, specific knowledge of business functions and problem solving. How well individuals perform in these areas is best determined by setting tangible goals during performance appraisals and then in subsequent appraisals checking how well the manager has performed to achieve the objectives you've agreed on.

Professionals, such as engineers, lawyers, chemists and the like, are paid based on what is the competition in the marketplace for their services. When they act as supervisors of others in the same profession, they must be paid a premium for this extra effort.

For top executives, the minimum and maximum a company pays is best determined through surveys, what the firm needs, and what other firms are paying for similar positions.

Since there are no grades for these levels, upward progression of salaries depends on performance. Some organizations pay regular bonuses which are linked in some fashion to the profits of the company. The profit "pool" is divided among the top level people in proportion to their salaries.

Provision for bonuses should also be made for departments which have outstanding years in contributing to profits, whether by increased revenues or lower costs, even if the overall profit is negligible. The amount of the bonus may be less than if the overall company was profitable, but something should be awarded.

COMPENSATION PLANNING CHECKLIST

	Yes	No	Potential Action
1. Does top management actively support the program?	_____	_____	_____
2. Do all managers and staff executives understand the procedures to be followed and their purpose?	_____	_____	_____
3. Does top management have a realistic under-standing of the objectives of the program within the context of company business objectives and financial conditions?	_____	_____	_____
4. Do supervisors under-stand the part they will play in gathering and verifying job information?	_____	_____	_____
5. Do line and staff managers clearly understand they retain basic respon-sibility for pay decisions in their departments within the framework of the compensation program?	_____	_____	_____
6. Have union officials been fully informed about the objectives and the procedures that will follow as the program develops?	_____	_____	_____
7. Has the union agreed to cooperate in, or at least not hinder, the development of the program?	_____	_____	_____

	Yes	No	Potential Action
8. Do we contemplate the establishment of a piece-work system, or, if we already have one, do we contemplate changes?	_____	_____	_____
9. Do managers under-stand that following installation of the compensation program, the Administrator will audit their performance in carrying out the policies established?	_____	_____	_____
10. Do we have adequate information about the compensation programs of our neighboring firms and our competitors?	_____	_____	_____
11. Do we believe that our existing wage and salary levels contribute to excessive turnover, poor morale or low productivity?	_____	_____	_____

12. Does everyone involved understand the implications and requirements of the following procedures:

	Yes	No	Potential Action
- Job analysis?	_____	_____	_____
- Preparation of job descriptions?	_____	_____	_____
- Setting compen-sation levels?	_____	_____	_____
- Using pay as an incentive?	_____	_____	_____
- Maintaining the program?	_____	_____	_____
- Performance analysis?	_____	_____	_____

	Yes	No	Potential Action
13. Do we know what system we plan to use to compensate sales people?	_____	_____	_____
14. Do we plan extensive revision of executive salaries?	_____	_____	_____
15. Have we prepared an announcement of the program for employees?	_____	_____	_____
16. Are we prepared to summarize data in the form of graphs and tables to indicate pay schedules?			
17. Are we prepared to forecast pay trends for top management?	_____	_____	_____
18. Do we have objective performance appraisals for all levels?	_____	_____	_____

Personnel Management and the Law 10

You've read about the multi-million dollar employee lawsuits that are broadsiding American businesses. Like other business managers, you continually face practical personnel problems of hiring, appraising, motivating, disciplining and occasionally firing employees. All these activities can catapult you headlong into a law, rule, regulation or court decision that may put you and your company on the wrong side of an employment issue and in harm's way.

Inadvertently, you could become a target of a governmental agency. Or, you could find yourself bearing the brunt of a costly legal action by a disgruntled former employee—or even an individual who never made it past initial employment interviews.

That's why it's so important to take a serious look at the employment laws you must abide by. You should be fully aware of the most prominent ones, which are covered in this chapter. It will alert you to potential problems and may stimulate you to seek professional counsel before you get bogged down in expensive claims.

State laws

In addition to federal laws governing employment, each state, some cities, the District of Columbia, Puerto Rico, American Samoa and the Virgin Islands have also gotten into the act. So, even though you may have complied with all federal labor and employment laws, you still may not have met all the requirements of the jurisdiction in which you're located.

What to do? First, call the local government office which handles labor matters in your area (these agencies have different names in various jurisdictions—but they're easy to identify in phone book listings of government offices). Ask for information on wages and hours, fair employment practices and whatever other questions you want to look into. Generally the employees in these offices are quite knowledgeable, eager to please, and will send you useful literature or direct you to other offices for more information.

Second, if you're uncertain about any aspect of local labor law, consult with an attorney who specializes in it. A lawyer's advice on employment matters will be worth the price you pay for it.

The four posters

All companies must post at least four notices to employees:

1. Federal Minimum Wage (Fair Labor Standards Act)
2. Equal Employment Opportunity—Title VII of the Civil Rights Act of 1964 (Note: This poster also includes what should be clearly displayed about the Age Discrimination in Employment Act of 1967 and the Equal Pay Act of 1963)
3. Job Safety & Health (Occupational Safety & Health Act)
4. Employee Polygraph Protection Act

You can get these posters from the Department of Labor just for the asking. They must be clearly displayed at every location where you have employees working and, in some states, you must show the state equivalent in both English and Spanish.

All states with minimum wage statutes (except Hawaii and Massachusetts) require the posting of *their* minimum wage law notices, whether or not you've posted the Federal.

All states except seven require that their fair employment law posters (these have to do with what's referred to as Equal Employment Opportunity at the Federal level) be prominently displayed.

The less finicky seven states do *recommend*, though, that their notices be shown. The seven are: Idaho, Indiana, Iowa, Nevada, Montana, Oklahoma, and Washington. (Note: States are apt to change their minds about requirements, just like people. So even if your state is listed, double check it to make sure they haven't changed the law.)

Wages

If there's any law that is almost universally known among employees, it's what's popularly known as the Federal Wage and Hour Law, though it's officially the Federal Labor Standards Act (FLSA).

If a locality has a higher minimum wage than the federal one, then that wage must be paid. And if the state in which you're located has a minimum wage that is lower than the Federal, you must pay your employees the Federal minimum wage.

Be sure to be fully knowledgeable about the following areas of the FLSA (they're covered on the next pages):

1. What's included for purposes of computing minimum wages?
2. Who's entitled to overtime pay and who's not?
3. Are any employees exempt from minimum wage and overtime?

4. Does FLSA set standards for other benefits like vacations, severance pay, holidays, fringe benefits and the like?
5. What employee wage, hour, pay and personnel records must be kept?

By the early '90s, the minimum pay for covered workers had reached $4.25 an hour. It has changed 17 times since 1938 and Congress is always threatening to raise it once again.

What can you include in your calculation of the minimum? You may consider part of wages the reasonable cost or fair value of board, lodging or other facilities customarily furnished by you for employees' benefit.

You can include in your wage calculation the tips received by those employees who regularly receive more than $30 a month in tips.

You must be able to prove that the combination of direct wages and tips add up to at least the minimum wage.

Exemptions from the minimum wage

An amendment to FLSA scheduled to expire March 31, 1993 added some new wrinkles. One is the training wage. That can be 85% of the minimum wage, but not less than $3.35 an hour. You can pay it for 90 days to employees under age 20, except for seasonal agricultural and migrant workers.

You can also apply for an exemption to pay below the hourly minimum for the employment of learners, apprentices and full-time students working part-time in retail or service establishments, agriculture or institutions of higher education. That wage can be no lower than 85% of the minimum wage. But you'll need to request a certificate from the Wages and Hours personnel in the Department of Labor to take the exemption.

The law also includes handicapped workers in the subminimum wage category. They are individuals whose earning capacity is impaired by age, physical or mental deficiency or injury. The subminimum for them is no less than 50% of the minimum wage.

Pay after 40 hours in a week

Whenever covered employees (known as a non-exempt employees) work more than 40 hours in a week, they are entitled to overtime pay. You can't average a 30 hour week with a 50 hour one to get 40 hours, though. Each workweek stands on its own. You must pay one and one-half times the regular rate for the hours in excess of 40.

There's no exemption from minimum wages or overtime payments by means of paying a weekly or monthly wage, rather than an hourly rate. You must convert the weekly or monthly wage to an hourly rate to calculate overtime. Say, for example, you employ a non-exempt individual at $300 per week for a regular 35 hour schedule. That comes to $8.57 per hour. If that individual works 44 hours, you must pay him or her overtime for 5 hours at the regular rate of $8.57 and for four hours at $12.86 per hour ($8.57 x 1.5 = $12.86).

For workers who are paid piece rates, you must also calculate their earnings on an hourly basis to determine overtime pay. You divide their total weekly earnings by the number of hours worked to get the hourly rate.

Exemptions from both minimum wage and overtime pay

There are exemptions from the wages and hours laws, and you should familiarize yourself with the rules governing them. Because they are narrowly defined, you should carefully check the exact terms and conditions for each.

The first exempt group are executive, administrative and professional employees. Also exempt: **outside** salespersons as defined by the Department of Labor.

Generally, individuals meet the test of exempt **executives** if they receive a salary of $250 per week and manage a department with two or more employees. When executives earn between $155 and $250 a week, they must meet further tests to qualify as exempt employees:

- Manage an enterprise or a department of it;
- Regularly direct the work of two or more employees;
- Have authority to hire or fire, or their recommendations for hiring, firing, promotion, advancement or other changes in status are given weight;
- Exercise discretionary powers customarily and regularly;
- Devote no more than 20% of workweek hours to non-management duties.

Administrative employees, who usually have titles like assistant to the general manager, administrative assistant, assistant buyer and the like, must meet their own set of tests to qualify as exempt employees:

- They must earn not less than $155 a week;
- Their primary duties are office or non-manual work directly related to management or general business operations or administration;
- They customarily and regularly exercise discretion and independent judgment;
- They regularly and directly assist executives or perform under general supervision only specialized work requiring special training, experience or knowledge;
- They devote no more than 20% (40% for retail and service) of their time to functions related above.

Professional employees are those who do work that is predominately intellectual, which requires knowledge of an advanced type, which is generally acquired through prolonged courses of specialized instruction. The time they spend on non-exempt work cannot exceed 20% of their workweek and they must be paid a salary of not less than $170 a week.

Outside salespersons do not have a minimum wage requirement. But they must customarily and regularly work away from the employer's place of business in making sales or taking orders. They must not spend more than 20% of their time doing the kind of work that non-exempt employees of their employers do.

FLSA also exempts certain categories of employees like seamen and casual babysitters. If you need a comprehensive list, ask the wage and hour office in your area for one.

Exemptions from overtime pay

Certain types of employees are exempt from the overtime provisions of the wages and hours laws, though not exempt from the minimum wage standards. They include certain highly-paid commissioned employees of retail or service establishments. They also include auto, truck, trailer, farm implement, boat or aircraft salesworkers and parts-clerks and mechanics servicing autos, trucks and farm implements.

Employees of railroads and air carriers, announcers, news editors and chief engineers of certain metropolitan broadcasting stations are exempt, as are employees of motion picture theatres.

Federally non-regulated practices

The FLSA does not regulate quite a few employment practices. These include:

- Vacation, holiday, severance, or sick pay
- Meal or rest periods, holidays off, or vacation lengths
- Premium pay for weekend or holiday work
- Pay raises and fringe benefits
- Discharge notices, reasons for discharge, or immediate pay-
  ment of final wages to terminated employees

However, states are beginning to dictate practices in this area. California, for example, requires payment of final wages within 72 hours to those who quit. It mandates immediate payment of final wages to employees who are discharged. This is another reason for you to check into your state's labor laws.

Keeping records on wages, hours and other items

The FLSA requires you to keep the following records for non-exempt employees for three years:

1. Personal information including name, home address, sex and
   birth date if under 19

2. Hour and day when the workweek begins
3. Total hours worked each workday and each workweek
4. Total daily or weekly straight-time earnings
5. Regular hourly pay rate for any week when overtime is worked;
6. Total overtime pay for the workweek
7. Deductions from or additions to wages
8. Total wages paid each pay period
9. Date of payment and pay period covered

FLSA's Wages and Hours office is very careful to define two terms: **Workweek** and **Hours worked**. A workweek is a period of 168 hours during 7 consecutive 24-hour periods. It may begin on any day of the week and any hour of the day.

In general, hours worked includes all time the employee must be on duty, or on the employer's premises or any other prescribed place of work. Also included is any additional time the employee is required or permitted to work.

Title VII, The Civil Rights Act of 1964

Few employers in this modern era intend to discriminate in their employment practices among individuals based on age, race, religion, sex, color or national origin. Still, habits, customs, mores and prejudices do affect the workplace, resulting in discriminatory practices.

That's why the Federal government passed the Civil Rights Act of 1964 (since amended a number of times) which includes Title VII and Equal Employment Opportunity (EEO). An enforcement body for the laws banning discrimination in employment, the Equal Employment Opportunity Commission (EEOC), was also created. Be aware that many states and some cities have similar statutes, often under the labels of "fair employment practices" laws. The Federal act, and many of the states' equivalent statutes, require you to prominently display a notice to employees which outlines their rights and privileges under the law. The Equal Employment Opportunity poster is the second of the "four posters."

The activities for which discriminatory practices are banned include hiring, compensation, promotions, discharges, layoffs, and other terms and conditions of employment.

Interviewing—what can be asked

The biggest problems for many employers occur in the initial stages of the hiring process.

The most troublesome area is pre-employment—both the employment application form data asked for and questions typically posed during pre-employment interviews. Lawful Job Application Questions (10-01), located at the end of the chapter, gives examples of different types of inquiries that have been ruled lawful or unlawful. Lawful Interview Questions (10-02) also shown at the end of the chapter, details subjects that are discriminatory to inquire about and how to ask acceptable questions.

Note: Lawful Job Application Questions was compiled by the Human Services Division of the State of New York as a guideline on what is lawful and unlawful from both the state and Federal points of view. The State of New York has one of the most stringent employment laws.

You should also be aware that you can be guilty of discrimination in your employment advertising if you express any limitation as to age, race, sex, national origin, religion or color. For example, you can't advertise for a "stenographer under 35" or for a "young man." Beware of job titles that indicate a preference such as:

Discriminatory title	Substitute
Bell Boy	Bell Hop
Male, female, lady, gentleman	Applicant, candidate, trainee
Steward/stewardess	Flight attendant
Foreman	Supervisor
Draftsman	Drafter

Sexual harassment in the workplace

When Title VII was passed in 1964, its prohibitions against sex discrimination were interpreted to be aimed primarily at banning refusals to hire women for any type of job, creating separate lines of promotion or seniority for women, and making it unlawful to have differing fringe benefits based on sex.

Nowhere in the original law, though, do the words "sexual harassment" appear together. Currently, however, sex in the workplace is not just a matter of gender. EEOC guidelines and many court cases have drawn lines in the office or plant proscribing unwelcome sexual conduct.

You should keep in mind that sexual conduct becomes unlawful when it is unwelcome. It can include:

Verbal: sexual innuendo, suggestive comments, threats, insults, jokes about gender-specific traits, sexual propositions.

Nonverbal: making suggestive or insulting noises, obscene gestures, whistling, leering.

Physical: touching, pinching, brushing body, coercing sexual intercourse, assault.

In a landmark case (Meritor Savings Bank v. Vinson, 477 U.S. 57, 1986), the Supreme Court ruled that conduct that creates "an intimidating, hostile or offensive working environment" that interferes with employees' performance violated their civil rights. In 1991, a Florida Federal district court ruled that display in the workplace of nude or partly nude pictures of women constituted sexual harassment.

With what seems to be a wide open door for claims of sexual harassment, what can you do to end its practice and to protect yourself and your organization? When someone has a complaint, take the time to investigate the complaint as soon as possible. The findings should be turned over to top management or to assigned personnel for action. A thorough investigation may not be a complete defense. But it can help, should a claim be filed.

Take the following steps (pronouns could be male or female in these steps):

Step 1. Interview complainant. What does she say happened? Who does she name as harassers? Where and when did incident take place? How did she react? Witnesses? Was it an isolated incident or part of a series? Has she spoken to anyone else about incident?

Step 2. Interview accused harasser(s). Stay objective, assume nothing. Put every statement in writing (your notes may end up in court).

Step 3. Interview witnesses. Phrase questions so you don't give information. Better to say, "Have you heard anyone say something to so-and-so that made her uncomfortable?"

Step 4. Weigh evidence. Consider credibility of each party. Are there any previous complaints against the accused?

Step 5. Take action. Write a detailed report. If harassment did occur, you must take strong action based on your discipline policies.

Preventing sexual harassment

There is no absolute cure for sexual harassment in the workplace. But you must take preventive measures. That means that you cannot expect that merely posting notices or drawing up policies on sexual harassment is enough. Active, intensive and vigorous efforts must be taken for the purpose of eliminating offensive and unwelcome sexual conduct and also to protect your company against claims. Your company may be found responsible for sexual harassment whether you knew about it or not if you've done nothing to stop it.

Top management must make a practice of raising this issue regularly with its managers, supervisors and employees and emphasize how strongly it disapproves. Top management must establish a regular procedure for resolving complaints and publicize it frequently. Beware of making the procedure such that the complainant must first complain to a direct superior who may be the offender. Victims should be encouraged to come forward and be assured of confidentiality.

You should have a written policy against sexual harassment such as the Policy on Sexual Harassment (8-13) found in chapter 8. Make sure that it is kept up to date and in the hands of every manager and supervisor. You should also publish in the employee handbook (or distribute in a leaflet to every employee) the rules governing sexual harassment. The Sexual Harassment Statement (10-03), shown at the end of this chapter, can be adapted for your use.

Religious discrimination

Basically, the prohibitions of discrimination in hiring apply equally to internal personnel decisions such as training, promotions, transfers and fringe benefits. When opportunities are available, they must be available regardless of age, sex, religion, color, race or national origin.

With regard to religion, the law says that you must reasonably accommodate the religious practices of employees. When you're notified by an employee that, for example, to work on a certain day would violate his or her beliefs, an alternative should be offered.

Example: an employer accommodated a Saturday sabbath observer by offering (1) shift changes or (2) a job transfer; (3) allowing the employee to use vacation time; or (4) offering floating holidays. In this case the employee refused to cooperate and would take nothing less than having the sabbath off and keeping the same job. The employer, then, was free to discipline the employee without fear of a charge of religious discrimination.

Equal pay for equal work

As mentioned earlier, what is required to be clearly displayed for all employees to see about the Equal Pay Act (EPA) is included in the EEO poster. Employers not covered by Title VII (generally those with fewer than 15 employers) are covered by EPA for which there are no employment limits.

Under EEOC guidelines, to pay different wages to males and females for equal work in jobs that require equal skill, effort and responsibility and are performed under similar conditions is to discriminate based on sex.

Skill includes experience, training, ability and education measured by the performance requirements of the job. If skill is not required to perform the job, it can't be used as a basis for paying a male more than a female—or vice versa.

Effort is concerned with the measurement of the physical or mental exertion for the performance of a job. You may be able to justify a pay difference by demonstrating the greater physical or mental effort required to do the job.

Responsibility refers to the degree of accountability required in the performance of the job. Example: an administrative assistant who is responsible for scheduling computer operators, finding temps to replace sick ones, and evaluating performance has more responsibility than the operators working under him or her and should be paid higher wages.

Nothing in the EPA, however, prevents you from setting up a seniority system, a merit system or a system which measures earnings by quantity or quality of output.

The third of the "four posters"—safety and health

The federal government offers more free help to small businesses through the Occupational Health and Safety Administration (OSHA) than it does for any other kind of regulatory matters affecting employer and employee working relationships.

In addition to a wealth of advice on how to manage safety and protect employees from health hazards in the workplace provided in published materials, OSHA tells employers how to obtain free, on-site consultations by safety and health professionals. State government agencies deliver these consultative services which are funded substantially by OSHA. All you need do is contact a state office. All states have their own equivalent of the federal occupational and safety health laws.

Basic OSHA record-keeping requirements

OSHA requires you, as an employer, to comply wih safety and health standards covering operations in the workplace and to maintain it free from recognized hazards. It requires employers to record occupational injuries and illnesses that result in death, loss of consciousness, transfer to another job, restriction of work or motion, or medical treatment beyond first aid. You keep this record in a log, OSHA Form 200.

The log must be retained at your company for a period of five years. If you have more than one location, you must keep a separate log for each. OSHA Form 101 must be used to record additional information about each illness or injury.

Every year an annual summary of injuries and illnesses must be reported on OSHA Form 200, posted no later than February 1, and kept posted until March 1. A good place to display it is next to the Job Safety & Health poster (this is another mandated posting, and OSHA advises you also to tack up both its notice and your state's equivalent poster).

You must keep these forms for five years. You don't submit them to OSHA or to any other agency, but they must be available for inspection by OSHA, the Department of Health and Human Services and the Bureau of Labor Statistics, as well as by certain state agencies.

Because some types of businesses have a very low incidence of job injuries and health hazards, they are exempt from the annual record-keeping requirements. These include:

1. Retail trade, except for general merchandise, food, building materials and garden supply retailers.
2. Real estate, insurance and finance companies.
3. Service, except for hotels, amusement parks, recreational services and health services.

Additional sources of safety help

Many Workers' Compensation carriers and liability and fire insurance companies conduct periodic inspections and visits to evaluate safety and health hazards. Contact your carrier to see what it has to offer.

Some trade associations and employer groups offer services on safety and health. Even if you are not a member of such a group, you can find out what kinds of information these groups are circulating to their members.

Some trade unions and employee groups have safety and health expertise that they are willing to share.

The National Safety Council has a broad range of information available. You can reach it at 1121 Spring Lake Drive, Itasca, IL 60143.

Professional associations, such as the American Society of Safety Engineers, American Industrial Hygiene Association, and American Conference of Governmental Industrial Hygienists provide additional resources.

A self-inspection safety and health program

The best way to identify hazards is to conduct your own safety and health inspections. The Safety Checklist (10-04), found at the end of the chapter, will help you get started. Keep in mind that this list is only a start and you must add to it, both through your own knowledge of your workplace and with the help of outside sources such as your insurance carrier and trade associations.

Virtually all businesses are covered by OSHA, though, as mentioned, some are exempt from the record-keeping and reporting requirements. Also excepted: self-employed individuals, farms on which only the owner and members of his family work, and some workplaces (such as mines) which are covered by other Federal agencies.

Workers' Compensation

Workers' Compensation (WC) has close ties to safety, for the leading causes of compensation payments are injuries sustained in the workplace. Companies are experience-rated. That is, the premiums for WC insurance they pay take into account how many claims are paid for injuries on the job.

As an employer, you pay the whole premium for workers compensation coverage—no deductions from employees' pay. All 50 states and some other legal jurisdictions have workers' compensation laws. Only three states allow elective coverage (New Jersey, Texas and South Carolina).

Most employers buy WC coverage from private insurers, though self-insurance is allowed by some states for employers who can prove financial ability. Injuries that are settled under the WC laws of the state free you from liability from personal injury litigation. Not the least important benefit: Injured employees get prompt and reasonable medical and income benefits regardless of fault.

Unemployment insurance

The individual states also administer unemployment insurance. Your company pays unemployment taxes to the federal government (Federal Unemployment Tax Act —FUTA) and to the states in which your employees work. New Jersey and Alaska tax employees, too.

You'll often be contacted by the state when an unemployed former employee makes a claim. The unemployment people want to ascertain whether the individual quit voluntarily, was discharged for misconduct or refused an offer of suitable work. The states will deny claims if any of these conditions caused the individual's unemployment. You have the right to protest any claim that's unjustified and should do so to help control your unemployment insurance costs.

Employee Polygraph Protection Act

This Act also requires you to post in plain view a Notice to employees describing its protections. Like many other Federal statutes, the Act does not preempt any state or local law or any collective bargaining agreement which is more restrictive with respect to lie detector tests.

The law prohibits the use of lie detectors for most private employers either in pre-employment screening or during the course of employment. You cannot discharge, discriminate against or discipline an employee for refusing to take such a test. You can't discriminate against a prospective employee, either, for his or her refusal to submit to a polygraph examination.

The Act permits polygraph tests, subject to restrictions, of certain prospective employees of armored car, alarm and guard service firms, and also of pharmaceutical manufacturers, dispensers and distributors. It also permits such tests, subject to certain restrictions, of employees who are reasonably suspected of involvement in a workplace incident (theft, embezzlement, etc.) that has resulted in economic loss to the employer.

Employees are given some rights when polygraph tests are permitted. They include:

1. The right to written notice before testing.
2. The right to refuse or discontinue a test.
3. The right not to have the results of the test disclosed to unauthorized persons.

Age discrimination

The Age Discrimination in Employment Act of 1967 (ADEA) fine tunes Title VII. For example, it eliminates the upper limit of age 70 from the classification of "protected group."

When enforcement of ADEA was transferred to the EEOC, it set forth rules that these personnel records had to be kept for one year:

- Job applications, resumes or other replies to job advertising
- Records pertaining to promotion, demotion, transfers, selection for training, layoffs, recalls, discharges

- Job orders to an employment agency
- Test papers for employment tests
- Records pertaining to physical exams
- Job advertisements and job postings

Older Workers Benefit Protection Act

Amending ADEA, this Act deals with discrimination by age in employee benefits. For employees 65 and older, group health plans are required to be provided under the same terms and conditions as for those under 65. One new item is the "equal benefit or equal cost principle." That means that if you don't provide, for example, the same face amount of life insurance for those over age 65 as you do for those under that age, then you must at least spend as much money for life insurance on an employee over 65 as you spend on those under that age.

Hiring the handicapped

Title VII of the Civil Rights Act of 1964 gave civil rights protection to individuals so that it is unlawful to discriminate on the basis of race, sex, color, religion, age or national origin. The Americans with Disabilities Act (ADA) provides similar protections to those with disabilities.

The Act became effective July 26, 1992 for organizations with 25 or more employees. Employers with 15 or more employees were covered beginning July 26, 1994.

The law defines an "individual with a disability" as a person who has a physical or mental impairment that substantially limits one or more major life activities, has a record of such impairment, or is regarded as having such an impairment. For example, an individual with epilepsy, paralysis, a substantial hearing or visual impairment, mental retardation, or a learning disability is covered. One with a minor, nonchronic condition—a sprain, infection, or a broken limb—generally is not covered.

An individual with a history of cancer that is currently in remission is covered by the law, as is a person with a history of mental illness.

Individuals who are treated as though they have a substantially limiting disability—say a severely disfigured, but qualified, individual—cannot be denied employment because the employer fears the "negative reactions" of others.

ADA says that you must provide "reasonable accommodation" to a qualified handicapped individual so that he or she can perform the job functions. You don't need to hire a person with a disability who types 50 words per minute over another person without a disability who types 75 wpm if typing speed is needed for the job. Conversely, if the disabled person types 75 wpm but needs a special typing surface so that he or she can continue to be seated in a wheelchair while typing, you should provide such a facility and hire the better qualified typist who has a disability.

On the other hand, the accommodations you make should not impose an undue hardship on your business, defined as an action requiring significant difficulty and expense.

You can't ask about disabilities on your application form or during an interview. But you can ask if the individual can perform particular job functions. You're not discriminating when you fail to hire an individual who can't perform the job functions. However, you can't require a disabled person to undergo a medical exam as a condition of employment unless you ask all applicants for similar jobs to be medically examined.

You can refuse to hire an applicant who is illegally using drugs. Such individuals are specifically excluded by ADA in its definition of a qualified individual with a disability. If you test for illegal drug use, make sure you test not only the disabled but all applicants. Congress passed the Drug Free Workplace Act in 1988. It applies to employers who have Federal contracts worth $25,000. It requires such employers to publish a policy statement covering drug use, to establish a drug awareness program, and to discipline employees convicted of drug use.

Congress intended the ADA to protect persons with AIDS and HIV disease from discrimination.

See the ADA personnel policy in Chapter 8.

Pregnancy on the job

In 1978, the Pregnancy Discrimination Act made it unlawful to fail to hire, promote or otherwise discriminate against women based on pregnancy, childbirth or related medical conditions. You must treat pregnant applicants and employees the same way as you treat others—your decisions must be based on their ability or inability to do the work, not on what you or someone else in your organization may think about pregnant women at work.

When you have an employee who is unable to perform her job because of pregnancy related conditions, you must treat her in the same manner as you do other temporarily disabled persons. That means modifying tasks, giving alternative assignments, offering disability leave, or leave without pay.

If you keep jobs open for the return of temporarily disabled workers, then you must keep open a job for a woman who left to bear her child.

Whatever fringe benefits you provide for other employees on leave, must be provided on account of pregnancy leave.

Family and Medical Leave Act

The Act applies to companies with 50 or more employees. A worker must be employed for one year and have at least 1,250 hours of service in the 12 months prior to requesting leave. Leave can be taken for the birth of, or the placement for adoption or foster care of, a child or the serious health condition of the employee, their spouse, child or parent. A serious health condition involves a physical or mental condition which requires in-patient care or continuing treatment by a health care provider, as well as the employee being unable to perform necessary job duties.

The Act allows for 12 weeks of unpaid leave per 12-month period with the employee to receive continued health care coverage as if they were still working. Spouses working for the same employer get a total of 12 weeks for the birth or placement of a child or for the care of a sick parent. When possible, the employee must give 30 days' advance notice before taking leave. The employer may require a doctor's certification and future recertification of the employee's condition, if necessary. The employee may be required to use accrued paid leave as part of the 12 weeks. During leave, the employee does not accrue any benefits or seniority.

After the leave ends, the employee must be reinstated to the same or an equivalent position with similar pay, benefits, responsibilities, and other terms and conditions of employment. If the employee does not return, the employer may recover health care premiums paid. The highest paid 10% of the work force may be exempt if leaving will cause the employer serious economic harm. Intermittent leave or a reduced leave schedule is also allowed. The employer can also temporarily transfer an employee to a position for which they are qualified.

See the Policy on Family and Medical Leave in Chapter 8.

Immigration Reform and Control Act

The Immigration Reform and Control Act of 1986 (IRCA) prohibits employers from knowingly hiring, recruiting or referring for a fee aliens who are not authorized to work in the United States because they have entered the country illegally or their immigration status does not permit employment. The law also prohibts employers from continuing the employment of individuals they know are unauthorized aliens.

When you hire an applicant, you must get him or her to fill out Form I-9, Employment Eligibility Verification. Then you must sign the form attesting that you've examined the appropriate documents which verify the individual's identity and authorization to work in the U.S. *Everyone* hired after November 6, 1986 must complete the form and have it verified, by the employer, no matter what size or type of company.

Benefits—non-cash compensation

Employers for many years were free to give non-cash benefits. But abuses occurred when they used them to discriminate in favor of certain individuals. As a result, Congress passed the Employee Retirement Income Security Act (ERISA).

It soon became clear, however, that ERISA wasn't restricted to retirement plans. The other types of benefit plans that ERISA covers include a surprisingly broad range of plans such as medical, hospital, surgical, disability, death benefits, accident benefits, prepaid legal services, day care centers and others.

ERISA requires that employers interpret and apply benefit plans or programs, whether written or unwritten, in a consistent and uniform manner. Employers run into problems when they make exceptions for certain employees and provide them with fewer or more benefits than allowed in a particular plan or program.

For example, if you give one employee (perhaps out of sympathy for his or her physical, mental or family condition) severance pay of 10 weeks, you're likely to find, as one employer did, that a court will determine that you must provide *all* severed employees with the same 10 weeks severance pay.

Reporting and disclosure for ERISA

You must prepare and furnish to each participant in a benefit plan a Summary Plan Description.

You must provide participants with a summary of material modifications to the plan within a specified time after they occur.

If you reduce benefits, you must notify participants six months before the plan year when the reduction goes into effect.

For pension plans, you must provide a statement at least once a year of accrued and vested benefits. Within 60 days of a request from an active participant, you must provide such a statement—though not more than once every 12 months.

ERISA doesn't tell you what type of benefits you have to give to employees. Some states, however, are getting involved in this area and requiring employers to provide coverage for certain medical conditions.

Members of management must be very careful when describing or responding to questions about benefits. Some employers have been required to honor promises they made to induce an individual to take a job, or to reassure an anxious employee. Let the plan documents speak for themselves whenever possible. When amplification or interpretation is needed, have the manager best versed in benefits handle this chore.

COBRA

COBRA (Consolidated Omnibus Budget Reconciliation Act of 1986) mandates that employers offer laid-off or terminated workers and their dependents the option to continue their group health plan coverage (medical, dental, vision, prescriptions — but not life insurance and disability plans) for 18 months after their employment ends. In the case of dependents of individuals who become eligible for Medicare (which may cause dependents to lose coverage under employers' plans) employers must offer to continue their group health insurance for up to 36 months.

You can charge former employees up to 102% of the costs of their coverages. You must offer individuals continuation, and explain the terms, when their employment ends. The COBRA Employee Information Letter (10-05), shown at the end of this chapter, can be used to advise employees of their rights to coverage.

Former employees have 60 days to notify their employer of their election to continue. An employer can't demand payment for the coverages sooner than 45 days after they have elected to get them.

COBRA does not include employers with fewer than 20 employees.

Employment at will

The doctrine of employment at will says that unless an employee is hired for a specific length of time, his employment may be terminated upon appropriate notice. However, statutes and case law have established exceptions to what used to be a common practice of allowing employers to fire employees without consequence. For example, in certain circumstances (e.g. where an employee has engaged in an act of "whistle blowing" on his employer), termination of the employee might be considered an act against public policy and thereby result in a claim by the employee.

Another exception to the employment at will doctrine is civil rights legislation that more recently has given protection to minorities and other disadvantaged groups against termination, where discrimination has been shown against the protected individual. In another type of case, the simple statement by a manager to a job applicant about job security—"as long as you do the job, you'll have a job"—was construed by a court to mean lifetime employment. And ambiguous statements in personnel handbooks have been construed against the employer. Further, some states are outlawing firings other than those for just cause and with good faith and fair dealing.

Terminating an employee

There's no perfect way to terminate an employee without some risk that the discharge will come back to haunt you. Still, you'll avoid most of the potential trouble if you follow these steps:

A. Corrective action: When discharging due to shortcomings in the employee's performance, be sure you're following all the procedures in your performance appraisal policy. When you're firing for disciplinary reasons, be sure you're following all the steps in your discipline policy. Forms for each are found in Chapter Eight (8-32 and 8-17).

B. Documentation: Fully document all events and actions that lead to discharge, including all dates and circumstances. Include policies violated, corrective and disciplinary steps taken and previous rule breakings.

C. Approvals required: Even though managers or supervisors have the rights to hire and fire in their job descriptions, make them submit recommendations with the documentation to a higher level of management before they do the hiring or firing. In the termination procedure, involve individuals from the Personnel or Human Resources department. Their charter: making sure that all the requirements of the company for termination have been observed.

Another safeguard includes having a termination policy. See the Policy on Termination (8-25) in chapter 8. The Separation Agreement Letter (11-45) in Chapter 11 tends to deflect potential legal liabilities that can result from terminations.

JOB APPLICATION QUESTIONS

SUBJECT	UNLAWFUL	LAWFUL
Age	How old are you? What is your date of birth? What are the ages of your children?	Are you 18 years of age or older? If not, state your age.
Arrest record	Have you ever been arrested?	Have you ever been convicted of a crime? Give details.
Birth control	Inquiry as to capacity to reproduce, advocacy of any form of birth control or family planning.	None
Disability	Do you have a disability? Have you ever been treated for any of the following diseases? Do you have now, or have you had, a drug or alcohol problem?	None

(It is unlawful to inquire, either directly or indirectly, about an applicant's disabilities. You may inquire only whether a prospective employee can perform specific tasks in a reasonable manner.)

| Marital status | Do you wish to be addressed as Miss, Mrs., or Ms.? Are you married, single, divorced, separated? What's the name of your spouse? What does your spouse do? | None |

SUBJECT	UNLAWFUL	LAWFUL
National origin	What's your ancestry, national origin, parentage, or nationality. Nationality of applicant's parents or spouse.	None
Race or color	Complexion or color of skin	None
Religion	Inquiry into religious denomination affiliations, parish, church, religious holidays observed. Applicant may not be told "This is a (Catholic, Protestant or Jewish) organization."	None

(Nothing in the law on religion shall bar any religious or denominational institution or charitable organization which is operated, supervised or controlled by or in connection with a religious organization from giving preference to persons of the same religion or denomination.)

SUBJECT	UNLAWFUL	LAWFUL
Sex	Inquiry as to gender.	None
Address or duration of residence	How long a resident of this state or city.	Applicant's place of residence.

SUBJECT	UNLAWFUL	LAWFUL
Birth date	Birthplace of applicant. Birthplace of applicant's spouse or other close relatives.	None
Citizenship	Of what country are you a citizen? Whether an applicant is naturalized or a native-born citizen; the date when the applicant acquired citizenship. Requirement that applicant produce naturalization or first papers. Whether applicant's parents or spouse are naturalized or native-born citizens of the U.S.; the date when such parents or spouse acquired such citizenship.	Are you a citizen of the United States? If not a citizen of the U.S., do you intend to become a citizen of the United States? If not a citizen, have you the legal right to remain permanently in the U.S.? Do you intend to remain in the U.S.?
Driver's license	Requirement that applicant produce a driver's license.	Do you possess a valid driver's license?
Education	Year(s) of attendance; Date(s) of graduation.	Inquiry into applicant's academic, vocational or professional education and the public and private schools attended.

SUBJECT	UNLAWFUL	LAWFUL
Language	What is your native language? How did you acquire your foreign language abilities?	Inquiry into languages applicant speaks or writes fluently.
Military	Inquiry into applicant's military experience other than in the Armed Forces of the U.S. or in a state militia. Did you receive a discharge in other than honorable circumstances?	Inquiry into applicant's military experience in the Armed Forces of the U.S. or state militia. Inquiry into service in a particular branch of the U.S. Army, Navy, Air Force, etc. Did you receive a dishonorable discharge? (must be explained that a dishonorable discharge is not an absolute bar to employment)
Name	Original names of an applicant whose name has been changed by court order or otherwise. If you have ever worked under another name, state name and dates. Maiden name of a married woman. If yes, explain.	Have you ever worked for this company under a different name? Is additional information relative to change of name, use of an assumed name or nickname necessary to enable a check of your work record?
Notify in case of emergency	Name and address of person to be notified in case of emergency.	None

SUBJECT	UNLAWFUL	LAWFUL
Organizations	List all clubs, societies and lodges to which you belong.	Inquiry into membership in organizations the applicant considers relevant to his or her ability to do the job.
Photograph	Affix a photograph to the application form.	None

LAWFUL EMPLOYMENT INTERVIEW QUESTIONS

CATEGORY	IT IS DISCRIMINATORY TO INQUIRE ABOUT	EXAMPLES OF ACCEPTABLE INQUIRIES
Name	The fact of a legal name change. Maiden name.	Whether the applicant has ever worked or been educated under another name (allowed only when the information is needed to verify applicant's qualifications).
Birthplace and residence	Birthplace of applicant. Birthplace of parents. Any requirement that the applicant submit a birth certificate, naturalization papers or a baptismal record.	Citizenship data as necessary to comply with alien hiring laws.
Religion	Applicant's religious affiliation or church membership. Religious holidays observed.	None
Race	Applicant's race. Color of skin, eyes or hair.	None
Photographs	Submission of photographs with application or at any time before hiring.	None

CATEGORY	IT IS DISCRIMINATORY TO INQUIRE ABOUT	EXAMPLES OF ACCEPTABLE INQUIRIES
Age	Applicant's age or date of birth. Indications that might bar workers under or over a certain age. Driver's license number (code may reveal age).	Applicant may be asked if he or she is over age 18.
Foreign	Applicant's native tongue. Language commonly spoken in applicant's home. How applicant acquired the ability to speak or read a foreign language.	Foreign language skills when required by the job.
Relatives	Name and address of any relative. Number, names, addresses and ages of applicant's spouse, children or relatives not employed by the company.	Name of applicant's relatives already employed by the company.
Military	Military experience in other than U.S. armed forces. National guard or reserve units to which applicant belongs. Draft classification or other eligibility for military service. Applicant's whereabouts during periods of war. Date, type or conditions of discharge.	U.S. military experience as part of employment history. Whether applicant has received a notice to report for active duty.

CATEGORY	IT IS DISCRIMINATORY TO INQUIRE ABOUT	EXAMPLES OF ACCEPTABLE INQUIRIES
Organizations	Any clubs, social fraternities or sororities, lodges or similar organizations to which the applicant belongs.	Membership in a union, professional society or other job-related organizations.
References	The name of a pastor, rabbi or other religious leaders.	The names of persons who are willing to provide personal or character references.
Sex and marital	Any question whose answer could be used to determine the applicant's sex or marital status. Number of children or other dependents.	None
Arrests and convictions	Number of arrests or the charges involved.	Convictions which relate to the job and which have not been expunged or sealed by a court.
Height and weight	Any inquiry into the applicant's height or weight.	None

CATEGORY	IT IS DISCRIMINATORY TO INQUIRE ABOUT	EXAMPLES OF ACCEPTABLE INQUIRIES
Disabilities	Any inquiry as to physical or mental disability which lacks a direct bearing on satisfactory performance of the job in question (for example, asking a wheelchair-bound applicant about mobility when the job is normally performed in a single location).	Does the applicant have any condition to prevent him or her from performing in a satisfactory way (for example, a hearing impairment in a person applying for a position as a telephone operator).
Education	Whether the applicant is a high school graduate.	Highest grade completed. Details of educational background.

SEXUAL HARASSMENT IN OUR WORKPLACE

This company believes that each individual employed has the right to be free from harassment because of age, color, religion, creed, national origin or sex. Sexual harassment is defined as including:

- Unwelcome physical contact.
- Sexually explicit language or gestures.
- Uninvited or unwanted sexual advances.
- Offensive overall environment, including the use of vulgar language, the presence of sexually explicit photographs or other materials, and the telling of sexual stories.

This company will not tolerate any form of sexual harassment. Should you feel you are being harassed, please follow these guidelines to help us remedy the problem:

Harassment by other employees should be brought to the attention of your manager immediately. The manager will investigate the matter, and if the allegation is sustained, the responsible employee will be disciplined, up to and including discharge.

A second proven charge of sexual harassment against any employee will result in immediate discharge.

Should you feel that your manager has not investigated the matter to your satisfaction, contact [name or title] immediately.

Should the harassment originate from your manager, you are to contact [name or title] immediately.

SAFETY SELF-INSPECTION CHECKLIST

_____ Are emergency telephone numbers posted where they can be quickly found?

_____ Are all exits clearly marked?

_____ Are you recording all occupational injuries and illnesses, except minor injuries requiring only first aid, on OSHA Form 200?

_____ Is one person clearly responsible for the safety and health program?

_____ If medical facilities are not nearby, do you have at least one employee currently qualified to render first aid?

_____ Are first aid kits readily accessible, periodically inspected and replenished as needed?

_____ If you have a fire alarm system, is it certified as required?

_____ Is your fire alarm system tested at least annually?

_____ Are sprinkler heads protected by metal guards when exposed to physical damage?

_____ Are fire extinguishers mounted in readily accessible places?

_____ Are approved safety glasses required to be worn at all times where there is risk of eye injuries?

_____ Are hard hats provided and worn where danger of falling objects exists?

_____ Where lunches are eaten on premises, are they eaten in areas which are free of exposure to toxic materials or health hazards?

_____ Are spilled materials cleaned up immediately?

_____ Are covered metal waste cans used for oily and paint-soaked materials?

_____ Are all work areas adequately illuminated?

_____ Are pits and floor openings covered or adequately guarded?

_____ Are aisles and passageways kept clear?

_____ Are materials and equipment stored so that sharp projections will not interfere with the walkway?

_____ Are guardrails provided wherever aisle surfaces are elevated more than 30 inches above any adjacent floor or ground?

_____ Is the glass in the windows, doors, glass walls, etc., which are subject to human impact, of sufficient thickness and type or the condition of use?

_____ Do all stairways having four or more risers equipped with handrails?

_____ Are stairway handrails capable of withstanding a load of 200 pounds or more applied from any direction?

_____ Are steps on stairs provided with a surface that makes them slip-resistant?

_____ Are signs posted, when appropriate, showing the elevated surface load capacity?

_____ Is a permanent means of access and egress provided to elevated storage and work surfaces?

_____ Is material on elevated surfaces piled, stacked or racked in a manner to prevent it from tipping, collapsing, rolling or spreading?

Safety Checklist (10-04) *continued*

___ Are all exit signs illuminated by a reliable light source?

___ Are doors that aren't exits or access to exits marked NOT AN EXIT, TO BASEMENT, STOREROOM, etc?

___ Are all exits kept free of obstructions?

___ Are there sufficient exits to permit quick escape in emergencies?

___ Are exit doors openable from the direction of exit travel?

___ Are ladders maintained in good condition?

___ Are portable metal ladders legibly marked with signs reading CAUTION - DO NOT USE AROUND ELECTRICAL EQUIPMENT?

___ Are worn or bent tools replaced regularly?

___ Are appropriate safety glasses, face shields, etc. used while using hand tools or equipment which might produce flying materials or be subject to breakage?

___ Are grinders, saws and similar equipment provided with safety guards?

___ Are rotating or moving parts of equipment guarded to prevent physical contact?

___ Is each electrically operated tool effectively grounded?

___ Are power-actuated tools stored in locked containers when not being used?

___ Is there a power shut-off switch within reach of each operator for each machine?

___ Are all emergency stop buttons colored red?

___ Are only trained personnel allowed to operate industrial trucks?

___ Is adequate ventilation assured before spray operations are started?

___ Are NO SMOKING signs posted where appropriate?

___ Are hazardous substances which may cause harm identified?

___ Are local exhaust ventilation systems operating properly?

___ Are employees' physical capacities assessed before being assigned to lifting heavy objects?

___ Are restrooms and washrooms kept clean and sanitary?

___ Is approved hearing protective equipment available where needed?

COBRA Employee Information Letter (10-05)

COMPANY NAME
ADDRESS
CITY, STATE ZIP

Date

Dear _____:

In accordance with the provisions of the Consolidated Omnibus Budget Reconciliation Act of 1985 (COBRA), you may elect to continue your Major Medical and dental coverage at group rates through (insurance company name) for a period of up to 18 months.

To do so, you must reimburse the company each month for no more than 102% of actual costs, the 2% being an administration fee allowed by the law.

At the present time, the rates are as follows. Please note that these rates may change. When they do, you will be advised via your monthly invoice. Payment is due on the 5th of each month.

		Major Medical	Continue? (Yes/No)
Single	$	_____	_____
Husband/wife	$	_____	_____
Family	$	_____	_____

		Dental	
Single	$	_____	_____
Family	$	_____	_____

Please let us know of your decision, whether it is yes or no, as soon as possible, by returning the enclosed copy of this letter with your reply written on it. For your convenience, we have enclosed a self-addressed stamped envelope.

Sincerely,

___Yes, I wish to continue my insurance as indicated above.

___No, I do not wish to continue my insurance.

_____   _____
Employee signature   Date

Record Keeping 11

Record keeping is the foundation of any personnel department. This chapter contains the key forms, organized by subject for easy access. The forms may be easily customized to fit the needs of your company.

Attendance. These forms include absentee and lateness reports, vacation requests and schedules, time sheets and leave of absence forms.

Benefits. This group of forms includes applications for group life and profit sharing, forms dealing with benefits eligibility requirements and a statement of plan benefits.

Discipline. One of the most sensitive areas, this section contains two important forms: employee warning notice and disciplinary report.

Injury and illness. A critical subject for all companies, this section includes an illness and accident report as well as disability forms.

Job postings and salary increases. Forms for posting jobs and evaluating employee applicants are found in this section, as is a form for a salary increase recommendation.

Payroll. This group of forms deals with a wide range of payroll and salary issues.

Temporary personnel. This section contains forms for requisitioning temporary help and tracking personnel agencies as well as temporary personnel.

Employee transfers. From an employee transfer request to the actual transfer, these forms cover the entire process.

Employee separation. This section provides forms for the separation process, from a separation notice to a personnel action form advising the personnel department of the final disposition.

Miscellaneous. An employee suggestion submittal form and an employee referral form comprise the last section.

EMPLOYEE ATTENDANCE RECORD

Month _____   19 _____

Employee Name _____

Employee Number _____

Code:
U = Unexcused absence   L = Late (show no. of minutes late)
E = Excused absence   J = Jury duty
V = Vacation   S = Sick

Week	Mon	Tue	Wed	Thu	Fri	Sat
1						
2						
3						
4						
5						

Total late time for month: _____ hours _____ minutes

Total days absent: _____Sick _____Excused _____Unexcused

EMPLOYEE LATENESS REPORT

Department _____ Date _____

Employee _____ Employee No _____

Time Due At Work _____

Actual Arrival Time _____ Total Time Missed _____

Did employee notify company? ___Yes ___No

Person Notified _____ Title _____

Action Taken: ____ None ____ Deduct Pay
____ Make Up Time ____ Other (Specify below)

_____
_____

Comments: _____
_____
_____

Signed _____ Date Signed _____
Title _____

EMPLOYEE ABSENTEE REPORT

Date _____

Name of Employee _____

Report received by _____

Expected No.   Expected Date
of Days Absent _____   of Return _____

Time of report _____

Report phoned to _____

Reported by   ( ) Self   ( ) Other Relative
                ( ) Spouse   ( ) Friend
                ( ) Supervisor   ( ) Other _____

Reason

( ) Sick   ( ) Illness in family

( ) Injury on job   ( ) Outside injury

( ) Transportation ( ) Death in family

( ) Jury duty   ( ) Military duty

( ) Other: _____
_____
_____

Signature _____

Departmental Absentee Report (11-04)

DEPARTMENTAL ABSENTEE REPORT

Department _____ Date _____

The following were absent from work today:

Employee	Employee No.	Reason for Absence
_____	_____	_____
_____	_____	_____
_____	_____	_____
_____	_____	_____
_____	_____	_____
_____	_____	_____
_____	_____	_____
_____	_____	_____
_____	_____	_____
_____	_____	_____
_____	_____	_____
_____	_____	_____
_____	_____	_____
_____	_____	_____
_____	_____	_____

Signature _____

OVERTIME AUTHORIZATION FORM

Department _____ Date _____

Employee _____ Employee No _____

Hours Authorized _____

Reason:

_____

_____

_____

Requested by _____ Title _____ Date _____

Approved by _____ Title _____ Date _____

Departmental Overtime Report (11-06)

DEPARTMENTAL OVERTIME REPORT

Department _____ Date _____

Employee	Employee No.	Overtime Authorized
_____	_____	_____
_____	_____	_____
_____	_____	_____
_____	_____	_____
_____	_____	_____
_____	_____	_____
_____	_____	_____
_____	_____	_____
_____	_____	_____
_____	_____	_____
_____	_____	_____
_____	_____	_____
_____	_____	_____
_____	_____	_____

Total _____

Signature _____

DEPARTMENTAL VACATION RECORD

Vacation begins on week number
(Circle week)

Employee

Jan	Feb	Mar	Apr
1 2 3 4 5	1 2 3 4 5	1 2 3 4 5	1 2 3 4 5
1 2 3 4 5	1 2 3 4 5	1 2 3 4 5	1 2 3 4 5
1 2 3 4 5	1 2 3 4 5	1 2 3 4 5	1 2 3 4 5
1 2 3 4 5	1 2 3 4 5	1 2 3 4 5	1 2 3 4 5
1 2 3 4 5	1 2 3 4 5	1 2 3 4 5	1 2 3 4 5
1 2 3 4 5	1 2 3 4 5	1 2 3 4 5	1 2 3 4 5

Employee

May	Jun	Jul	Aug
1 2 3 4 5	1 2 3 4 5	1 2 3 4 5	1 2 3 4 5
1 2 3 4 5	1 2 3 4 5	1 2 3 4 5	1 2 3 4 5
1 2 3 4 5	1 2 3 4 5	1 2 3 4 5	1 2 3 4 5
1 2 3 4 5	1 2 3 4 5	1 2 3 4 5	1 2 3 4 5
1 2 3 4 5	1 2 3 4 5	1 2 3 4 5	1 2 3 4 5
1 2 3 4 5	1 2 3 4 5	1 2 3 4 5	1 2 3 4 5

Employee

Sep	Oct	Nov	Dec
1 2 3 4 5	1 2 3 4 5	1 2 3 4 5	1 2 3 4 5
1 2 3 4 5	1 2 3 4 5	1 2 3 4 5	1 2 3 4 5
1 2 3 4 5	1 2 3 4 5	1 2 3 4 5	1 2 3 4 5
1 2 3 4 5	1 2 3 4 5	1 2 3 4 5	1 2 3 4 5
1 2 3 4 5	1 2 3 4 5	1 2 3 4 5	1 2 3 4 5
1 2 3 4 5	1 2 3 4 5	1 2 3 4 5	1 2 3 4 5

LEAVE OF ABSENCE INFORMATION SHEET

Name _____

Department _____

1. Letter Requesting Leave
   Submit a Leave of Absence Request Form and a Disability Certificate, if applicable, to your supervisor who will forward it to the Human Resources Manager for approval.

2. Vacation Pay
   If you have not taken your earned vacation prior to your leave, you may:
   a. Withhold your vacation pay, enabling you to take your vacation when you return from leave; or
   b. Be paid for vacation earned as of your last working day in increments of 40 hours. You will receive your vacation pay on the first payday following the date your leave begins. Indicate the chosen option on your Letter Requesting Leave. Vacation time will continue to accrue during an approved leave of absence, provided you return to work.

3. Sick Pay Benefits
   Sick pay benefits will be paid to you while on a disability leave of absence for either the length of the disability or until all sick hours accrued are used, whichever occurs first. Should the dates of disability change during your leave, you must submit a revised Disability Certificate. You will receive sick pay benefits through your normal pay method.

4. Health Insurance Benefits
   If you are eligible for benefits under the terms of the hospital and surgical plan, or if you are enrolled in a Health Maintenance Organization, there will be no change in the status of your coverage while you are on a leave of absence.
   NOTE: You will need to make arrangements with the Employee Benefits Department to make the applicable contribution to covered benefits, if any.

5. Life Insurance Benefits
   There will be no change in the status of your regular life insurance coverage while you are on leave of absence.
   NOTE: You will need to make arrangements with the Employee Benefits Department to pay the applicable premiums for supplemental group life insurance and voluntary accidental death and dismemberment coverage.

6. Profit Sharing Thrift Plan (401K)
   Your status will be changed to "active non-contributory" at the time you are no longer receiving a paycheck. Contributions to the profit sharing thrift plan (401K) will resume upon your return to work.

7. Stock Purchase Plan
   Your status will be changed to "active non-contributory" at the time you are no longer receiving a paycheck. At the end of the option period, fewer shares may be purchased for you, reflecting the missed payments. Contributions to the stock purchase plan will resume upon your return to work provided the duration of your leave does not exceed six months. If you do not return to work within six months, your options to buy stock will end and your money, together with the interest earned, will be refunded to you.

8. Address Change
   Your address will be automatically changed when you begin your leave of absence; you will receive your statements at home.

9. Returning from Leave
   You should confirm the date of your return with the Human Resources Department approximately one month prior to your anticipated return in order to facilitate placement. The company cannot guarantee that any employee will return to his or her previous job, salary or location. However, every effort will be made to place employees returning from leave in available positions suitable to their abilities and qualifications. If an employee requests a work schedule change, placement may not be possible.

10. If You Decide Not to Return
    Please notify the Human Resources Department as soon as you have made your decision not to return. At that time, you should submit a letter of resignation and the separation process will begin.

LEAVE OF ABSENCE REQUEST FORM

To: Personnel Department   Date: _____

From: _____   Through _____
            Name   Supervisor

_____
      Department

____   DISABILITY LEAVE OF ABSENCE

Attached is a Disability Certificate completed by my physician approximating the
dates of disability to be from _____ to _____. I will be
returning to work on_____.
(Should your physician change the dates of your disability, you must submit a
revised Disability Certificate.)

Sick pay benefits will be paid only:
a) Upon receipt of a statement from your physician specifying the dates of actual
disability.
b) For the period of disability or until all sick hours accrued are used, whichever
occurs first.
As of_____you have_____hours of sick pay benefits accrued.

____   NEWBORN CHILD CARE LEAVE Newborn Child Leave starts when your disability
leave, as stated by your physician, ends.

I would like to request a Newborn Child Care Leave (up to four months unpaid leave
of absence) of _____ (indicate length of leave). I plan to return to work
on_____.

____   LEAVE OF ABSENCE (other than disability)

I would like to request a leave of absence beginning_____ and
ending_____. My reason(s) for this request
is (are)_____
_____.
I plan to return to work on_____.

Leave of Absence Request Form (11-09) *continued*

If you have not taken your vacation prior to your leave, you may:
  a) withhold your vacation pay, enabling you to take your vacation after you return from leave, or;
  b) be paid for vacation time earned as of your last working day in increments of 40 hours. You will receive your vacation pay on the first pay day following the date you start your leave. As of _____you have _____ hours of available vacation.

Vacation pay option elected: a___ b___

Signature _____

Vacation Request Form (11-10)

VACATION REQUEST FORM

Name_____   Date of hire _____

My first choice for two weeks' vacation is:
    From _____   Through _____

My second choice is:
    From _____   Through _____

(If a holiday occurs during your vacation, please request any extra days below.)

_____

_____

_____

I request to split my vacation:
    First week: From _____   Through _____
    Second week: From _____   Through _____
    Third week: From _____   Through _____
    Fourth week: From _____   Through _____

Vacation
Approved by _____   Date _____

Split vacation
Division head approval _____   Date _____

WEEKLY TIME SHEET—HOURLY EMPLOYEES

Fill in hours and minutes for each employee and each day worked. Enter X for days not worked.

Week of _____, 19___

	Mon	Tue	Wed	Thu	Fri	Sat	OT	Total Hours
Fill in date:	____	____	____	____	____	____	____	_____

===

Employee

_____ ___ ___ ___ ___ ___ ___ ___ ____

_____ ___ ___ ___ ___ ___ ___ ___ ____

_____ ___ ___ ___ ___ ___ ___ ___ ____

_____ ___ ___ ___ ___ ___ ___ ___ ____

_____ ___ ___ ___ ___ ___ ___ ___ ____

_____ ___ ___ ___ ___ ___ ___ ___ ____

_____ ___ ___ ___ ___ ___ ___ ___ ____

_____ ___ ___ ___ ___ ___ ___ ___ ____

_____ ___ ___ ___ ___ ___ ___ ___ ____

_____ ___ ___ ___ ___ ___ ___ ___ ____

_____ ___ ___ ___ ___ ___ ___ ___ ____

_____ ___ ___ ___ ___ ___ ___ ___ ____

_____ ___ ___ ___ ___ ___ ___ ___ ____

_____ ___ ___ ___ ___ ___ ___ ___ ____

_____ ___ ___ ___ ___ ___ ___ ___ ____

_____ ___ ___ ___ ___ ___ ___ ___ ____

Weekly Time Sheet—Salaried Employees (11-12)

WEEKLY TIME SHEET—SALARIED EMPLOYEES

Department _____ Week ending _____ 19____

Employee	Hours on Job	Hours out of office			Total Hours
		Vacation	Sick	Other	

APPLICATION FOR GROUP LIFE INSURANCE
BASIC NONCONTRIBUTORY COVERAGE

Name of Employee (Please print)

_____

Last   First   Middle Initial

Social Security Number _____

Marital Status
_____ Single   _____ Separated
_____ Married   _____ Divorced
_____ Widowed

Sex
_____ Male   _____ Female

Date of Birth: Month _____ Day _____ Year _____

If married, name of spouse

_____

Spouse's Date of Birth: Month _____ Day _____ Year _____

Name of Beneficiary

_____

Last   First   Middle Initial

Relationship of Beneficiary to Insured

_____

Date Employed Full-time: Month _____ Day _____ Year _____

I request insurance under the (company name) Group Life Insurance Plan, as now or hereafter applicable to me. I am actively at work at least 20 hours per week.

Signature of Employee _____

Date Signed _____

Application for Profit Sharing Benefits (11-14)

APPLICATION FOR PROFIT SHARING BENEFITS

TO: The Administrative Committee/Profit Sharing Thrift Plan

Company Name _____

Address _____

RE: Application for Benefits

I hereby make application for the benefits available, if any, from the Profit Sharing Thrift Plan for Employees of _____:

Basis of Application:

____ Retirement ____ Disability ____ Termination of Service
(Age 62 or later) (Effective date:_____)

Name (Please print) _____
Social Security Number _____
Date of Birth _____
Other names used (Maiden, Married, etc) _____

Request for Payment

When: ____ Now* How: ____ Lump Sum**
____ July 1st after attaining ____ Payment over (i)____
age 59 1/2 (number of years) or
____7-1-_____* (ii) $_____
per month until
account is fully
distributed***

Federal Income Tax Withholding:

____ Please withhold ____ Please do not withhold
for taxes for taxes

_____ _____
Date Participant's Signature

_____ _____
Company Name Street Address

_____ _____
Department City, State, Zip

Consent of Spouse – If no spouse, write "None."

_____ _____
Date Signature of Spouse

Application for Profit Sharing Benefits (11-14) *continued*

To be Completed by the Administrative Committee:

Approved _____   Disapproved _____

Reason _____

_____

Modifications _____

_____   _____

Date   by Administrative Committee

* If the payment is taken prior to age 59 1/2 and the taxable portion is not rolled over to an Individual Retirement Account, the taxable portion may be subject to a 10% excise tax. The 10% additional tax does not apply to distributions for death or disability, and certain other classifications. The distribution must commence no later than July 1st nearest age 70 1/2.

** Any taxable portion is eligible for a tax-free rollover to an Individual Retirement Account or alternatively, if age 59 1/2 and a plan participant for 5 years, to the special five-year forward averaging method. Special ten-year averaging may also be available to those participants attaining age 50 prior to January 1, 1986.

*** May be subject to a 10% excise tax if taken prior to age 59 1/2 except for death or disability, and certain other classifications.

ELIGIBILITY REQUIREMENTS FOR BENEFIT PROGRAMS

PLAN	ELIGIBLE AFTER
a. Group life insurance plan	Date of employment*
b. Medical and major medical	Three months of service**
c. Long term disability	Six months of service
d. Group voluntary accidental death and dismemberment plan	Date of employment
e. Retirement plan	One year of service and age 21
f. Profit sharing plan	Six months of service on January first
g. Employee stock purchase plan	Two years of service on January first

* Supplemental coverage available after three months of employment.
** Officers and exempt employees are covered as of the date of employment.

All employees of the company, including part-time employees, are eligible to participate in the following company employee benefit plans after they have completed the required amount of continuous service.

EMPLOYEE BENEFIT PLAN COVERAGES

A. Group Life Insurance Plan

_____
_____
_____

B. Hospital and Surgical

_____
_____
_____

C. Long Term Disability Insurance

_____
_____
_____

D. Group Voluntary Accidental Death & Dismemberment Plan

_____
_____
_____

E. Retirement Plan

_____
_____
_____

F. Profit Sharing Thrift Plan (401K)

_____
_____
_____

G. Employee Stock Purchase Plan

_____
_____
_____

Pension Plan Statement of Estimated Benefits (11-17)

PENSION PLAN
STATEMENT OF ESTIMATED BENEFITS AS OF: _____

A Personal Retirement Benefit Statement for: _____

******** ESTIMATED MONTHLY BENEFITS AT NORMAL RETIREMENT DATE ********

Your Monthly Benefit from the Retirement Plan: $ _____

Your Monthly Primary Social Security Benefit: $ _____
    Social Security estimates are based on current laws and the assumed
    continuation of your present salary to your normal retirement date. Actual Social
    Security benefits will be based on your actual wage history and Social Security
    laws in effect when you retire.

Your Total Monthly Retirement Income: $ _____

    ***** ESTIMATED MONTHLY ACCRUED RETIREMENT BENEFIT *****
    Your monthly accrued benefit is the amount of the benefit earned as of the date
    of this statement. It will give you an idea of your current status as to Plan
    benefits, but it is not a guarantee that such benefits are or will become payable.
    If your Plan participation were to terminate as of the date of this statement and
    you were fully vested, the accrued benefit would be payable monthly, for your
    lifetime, commencing on your normal retirement date.

Your Total Monthly Accrued Benefit to date: $ _____

    As of the date of this statement, you were ____% vested in your accrued benefit.
    The Pension Plan provides a vested benefit after five years of service.

Date of Hire _____

****

    THIS STATEMENT WAS PREPARED ON THE BASIS OF THE ABOVE DATA AND
THE CURRENT TERMS OF THE PLAN. SOME OF THE FIGURES ARE NECESSARILY
APPROXIMATE. WHEN THE TIME COMES FOR YOU TO RECEIVE A BENEFIT, THE
AMOUNT YOU RECEIVE WILL BE BASED ON THE PROVISIONS OF THE PLAN IN
EFFECT AT THAT TIME. IF ANY OF THE EMPLOYEE DATA SHOWN IS INCORRECT,
PLEASE CONTACT THE BUSINESS OFFICE.

Employee Warning Notice (11-18)

EMPLOYEE WARNING NOTICE

Employee _____ Employee No. _____

Date of Warning _____ Shift _____ Time _____

Date of Violation _____ Time _____

Location of Violation _____

Nature of Violation

( ) Substandard work   ( ) Inappropriate conduct

( ) Carelessness   ( ) Disobedience

( ) Clocking out   ( ) Clocking out
    ahead of time   wrong time card

( ) Tardiness   ( ) Absenteeism

( ) Intoxication or   ( ) Other: _____
    substance abuse

Comments _____
_____
_____
_____

Employee's Signature _____ Date _____

Supervisor's Signature _____ Date _____

Personnel Manager's Signature _____ Date _____

Disciplinary Report (11-19)

DISCIPLINARY REPORT

Department _____ Date _____

Employee _____ Employee No. _____

Description of Infraction _____

Date of Infraction _____ Time _____

Location of Infraction _____

Reported by _____ Title _____

Witnessed by _____

Comments _____

_____

_____

Supervisor's Signature _____

Employee's Signature _____

===

Disciplinary Action Taken _____

_____

_____

Recommendation _____

_____

_____

A copy of this disciplinary report has been placed in the employee's personal file.

Personnel Dept. Signature _____ Date _____

ILLNESS REPORT

Employee _____   Date _____

Age _____   Male ( )   Female ( )
Shift _____   Employee No. _____
Dept. _____   Foreman _____

Is illness related to employment? Yes ( )   No ( )

Date of initial diagnosis _____

Describe the illness:

_____
_____
_____

If employee left work, time of leaving _____

Did employee return to work?   Yes ( )   No ( )

If yes, at what time? _____

Name and address of physician _____
_____

If hospitalized, name and address of hospital _____
_____

Comments _____
_____
_____

Supervisor's signature _____   Date _____

Accident Report (11-21)

ACCIDENT REPORT

Employee _____

Age _____   Male ( )   Female ( )
Shift _____   Employee No. _____
Dept. _____   Foreman _____

Date of accident _____   Time _____

Location of accident _____

Nature of injuries _____
_____
_____

Cause of accident _____
_____

If employee left work, time of leaving _____

Did employee return to work?   Yes ( )   No ( )

If yes, at what time? _____

Name and address of physician _____
_____

If hospitalized, name and address of hospital _____
_____

What is being done to avoid such accidents in the future?
_____
_____

Comments _____
_____
_____

Supervisor's signature _____   Date _____

ATTENDING PHYSICIAN'S STATEMENT OF DISABILITY

Name of Patient (Please print) _____
                                Last   First   Middle initial

Date of Birth _____   Date of Employment _____

Address _____

City _____   State _____   Zip _____

Company Name and Address

_____
_____
_____

The patient is responsible for the completion of this form without expense to the Company. Space is available on the reverse side if you wish to amplify your answers.

1. HISTORY
   (a) When did symptoms first appear or accident occur?
       Mo._____Day_____19_____
   (b) Date patient ceased work because of disability
       Mo._____Day_____19_____
   (c) Has patient ever had same or similar condition?
       Yes_____ No_____
   (d) Is condition due to injury or illness arising out of patient's employment?
       Yes_____ No_____ Unknown_____

2. DIAGNOSIS
   (a) Diagnosis: _____
   (b) Date of last examination   Mo._____Day_____19_____
   (c) Subjective symptoms:

       _____
       _____
       _____

   (d) Objective findings (including current X-rays, EKG's, Laboratory Data and any
       clinical findings):

       _____
       _____
       _____

3. DATES OF TREATMENT
   (a) Date of first visit   Mo._____Day_____19_____
   (b) Date of last visit   Mo._____Day_____19_____
   (c) Frequency   Weekly_____ Monthly_____
                             Other (specify)_____
                             _____

4. NATURE OF TREATMENT (Including surgery and prescribed medication, if any):
   _____
   _____
   _____

5. PROGRESS
   (a) Has patient
       Recovered_____   Improved_____
       Unchanged_____   Retrogressed_____
   (b) Is patient
       Ambulatory?_____   House confined?_____
       Bed confined?_____   Hospital confined?_____
   (c) Has patient been hospital confined? Yes_____ No_____
   If yes, give name and address of hospital
   _____

   Confined from _____ through _____

6. CARDIAC (if applicable)
   (a) Functional capacity (American Heart Assn.)
       Class 1 (No limitation)_____
       Class 2 (Slight limitation)_____
       Class 3 (Marked limitation)_____
       Class 4 (Complete limitation)_____
   (b) Blood Pressure (last visit) _____
                                   Systolic/Diastolic

7. PHYSICAL IMPAIRMENT
   (*as defined in Federal Dictionary of Occupational Titles)
   _____ Class 1 - No limitation of functional capacity; capable of heavy work* No
           restrictions (0-10%)
   _____ Class 2 - Medium manual activity* (15-30%)
   _____ Class 3 - Slight limitation of functional capacity; capable of light work*
           (35-55%)
   _____ Class 4 - Moderate limitation of functional capacity; capable of clerical/
           administrative (sedentary*) activity (60-70%)
   _____ Class 5 - Severe limitation of functional capacity; incapable of minimal
           (sedentary*) activity (75-100%)

Remarks:

_____

_____

_____

8. MENTAL/NERVOUS IMPAIRMENT (if applicable)

   (a) Please define "stress" as it applies to this claimant.

   _____

   _____

   (b) What stress and problems in interpersonal relations has this claimant had on the job?

   _____ Class 1 - Patient is able to function under stress and engage in interpersonal relations (no limitations)

   _____ Class 2 - Patient is able to function in most stress situations and engage in most interpersonal relations (slight limitations)

   _____ Class 3 - Patient is able to engage in only limited stress situations and engage in only limited interpersonal relations (moderate limitations)

   _____ Class 4 - Patient is unable to engage in stress situations or interpersonal relations (marked limitations)

   _____ Class 5 - Patient has significant loss of psychological, physiological, personal and social adjustment (severe limitations)

   Remarks:

   _____

   _____

   _____

9. PROGNOSIS

   (a) Is patient now totally disabled for...

   PATIENT'S JOB: Yes_____ No_____

   ANY OTHER WORK: Yes_____ No_____

   (b) What duties of patient's job is he/she incapable of performing?

   _____

   _____

   _____

   Do you expect a fundamental or marked change in the future? Yes_____ No_____

   If yes, when will patient recover sufficiently to perform duties?

   1 Mo._____ 1-3 Mo._____ 3-6 Mo._____ Other_____

   If no, please explain:

   _____

   _____

   _____

10. REHABILITATION
    (a) Is patient a suitable candidate for further rehabilitation services? (i.e.,
        cardiopulmonary program, speech therapy, etc.)
        Yes_____   No_____
    When could trial employment commence:_____
    Would vocational counseling and/or retraining be recommended?
    Yes_____ No_____

11. Additional remarks _____
    _____
    _____
    _____

(Please print the following information)

_____
Name (attending physician)   Taxpayer ID No.

_____
Address

_____
City   State   Zip   Telephone

_____
Signature   Date

DISABILITY CERTIFICATE

To be completed by employee

Employee's name _____ Home phone _____
Home address _____

I authorize the physician to release necessary information to [company name] regarding my condition while under his/her care.

Employee's signature _____ Date _____

===

To be completed by attending physician:
Date disability began _____
Expected return to work date _____

Nature of disability, including complications _____
_____
_____

Work restrictions _____
_____

Date(s) seen _____
_____

If hospitalized, name of hospital _____
    Dates: From _____ To _____
    Date of surgery, if any _____ Procedure _____

If pregnancy, expected date of delivery _____

Physician's name _____ Signature _____

Address _____

Phone number _____ Date _____

Return to:
Human Resources Department

Job Posting Sheet (11-24)

JOB POSTING SHEET

Post Date _____

===

Position _____ Department _____
Experience _____ Education _____
Skills _____ Salary _____
Person to Contact_____ Date Available _____

===

Position _____ Department _____
Experience _____ Education _____
Skills _____ Salary _____
Person to Contact_____ Date Available _____

===

Position _____ Department _____
Experience _____ Education _____
Skills _____ Salary _____
Person to Contact_____ Date Available _____

===

Position _____ Department _____
Experience _____ Education _____
Skills _____ Salary _____
Person to Contact_____ Date Available _____

===

Position _____ Department _____
Experience _____ Education _____
Skills _____ Salary _____
Person to Contact_____ Date Available _____

===

Position _____ Department _____
Experience _____ Education _____
Skills _____ Salary _____
Person to Contact_____ Date Available _____

===

Position _____ Department _____
Experience _____ Education _____
Skills _____ Salary _____
Person to Contact_____ Date Available _____

===

Position _____ Department _____
Experience _____ Education _____
Skills _____ Salary _____
Person to Contact_____ Date Available _____

===

EVALUATION OF EMPLOYEE FOR POSTED JOB

Name _____

Position applied for _____

Current position:

Title_____ In position from_____ to_____

Previous positions in company:

Title	Position	From	To
_____	_____	_____	_____
_____	_____	_____	_____
_____	_____	_____	_____
_____	_____	_____	_____

	Does not meet	Meets	Exceeds
Required experience	_____	_____	_____
Required education	_____	_____	_____
Skills	_____	_____	_____

Comments _____
_____
_____

Interviewer _____ Date _____

Salary Increase Recommendation (11-26)

SALARY INCREASE RECOMMENDATION

Employee _____ Employee No. _____

Job title _____ Dept. _____

Employment date _____ Time in present job _____

Age _____ ( ) Male   ( ) Female

Attendance past 12 months:

_____ Paid absences _____Non-paid absences _____Late days

Explain any periods of absence, including leave of absence:

_____

_____

_____

Present salary _____

Range of increase _____

Recommended increase _____

Recommended new salary _____

Status after increase: ( ) Exempt   ( ) Non-exempt

( ) Promotion - Show qualifications under Reason

  Date promoted _____

  Former job title _____

  Former salary range _____

( ) Merit increase

  (Merit increases must be based on increased productivity, improved quality,
  reduced costs and/or additional responsibility.)

Reason _____

_____

_____

Recommended by _____ Date _____

===

For salary administration and payroll use

	Per hour or pay period	Annual
Present Rate	_____	_____
Increase	_____	_____
New Rate	_____	_____

Approved by _____ Date _____

Employee Payroll Form (11-27)

PAYROLL FORM

Employee _____   Employee No. _____

Social Security Number _____

Department _____   Period Ending _____

Gross Pay $ _____

Deductions
  Federal Withholding $ _____
  State Withholding   _____
  FICA   _____
  Insurance   _____
  Pension Plan   _____
  Dues   _____
  401K   _____
  Other   _____

Total Deductions $ _____
Net Pay $ _____

Prepared By _____   Date _____

Departmental Payroll Form (11-28)

DEPARTMENT PAYROLL RECORD

Department _____

Period Beginning _____ Period Ending _____

Employee	Hours Reg	OT	Pay Rate	Wages Reg	OT	Total Wages
_____	___	___	___	___	___	___
_____	___	___	___	___	___	___
_____	___	___	___	___	___	___
_____	___	___	___	___	___	___
_____	___	___	___	___	___	___
_____	___	___	___	___	___	___
_____	___	___	___	___	___	___
_____	___	___	___	___	___	___
_____	___	___	___	___	___	___
_____	___	___	___	___	___	___
_____	___	___	___	___	___	___
_____	___	___	___	___	___	___
_____	___	___	___	___	___	___
_____	___	___	___	___	___	___
_____	___	___	___	___	___	___
_____	___	___	___	___	___	___
_____	___	___	___	___	___	___
_____	___	___	___	___	___	___
_____	___	___	___	___	___	___
_____	___	___	___	___	___	___
Totals	___	___	___	___	___	___

Payroll Department Data Form (11-29)

PAYROLL DEPARTMENT DATA FORM

Employee Name	Current Annual Salary	Biweekly Pay	Exempt Yes/No	Withholdings	
				State	Federal

AUTHORIZATION AGREEMENT FOR PAYROLL DEPOSITS

I (we) hereby authorize and request the company named below, hereinafter called COMPANY, to initiate credit entries and to initiate, if necessary, debit entries and adjustments for any credit entries to my (our) account indicated below and the depository named below, hereinafter called DEPOSITORY, to credit and/or debit to such account.

DEPOSITORY NAME _____

DEPOSITOR ACCOUNT NO. _____

This authority to remain in full force and effect until COMPANY and DEPOSITORY have received written notification from me (or either of us) of its termination in such time and in such manner as to afford COMPANY and DEPOSITORY a reasonable opportunity to act on it.

CUSTOMER NAME _____

SOCIAL SECURITY NO. _____

Employee No. _____ Date _____ Signed _____

TO BE COMPLETED BY THE COMPANY

COMPANY NAME _____ Company ID NO. _____

Depositor account number information:

Bank
Code   Transit routing number   Transit/ABA
                                              check digit
I__I__I   I__I__I__I__I__I__I__I__I__I   I__I

Account number information
I__I__I__I__I__I__I__I__I__I__I__I__I__I__I

DEPOSITORY VERIFICATION

The above information has been verified.

DEPOSITORY _____

OFFICER'S SIGNATURE _____ Date _____

Employee Information Form (11-31)

EMPLOYEE INFORMATION FORM

TO ALL EMPLOYEES:
Please print all information. Use capital letters. Place only one character in each box.

NAME: |_|_|_|_|_|_|_|_|_|_|_|_|_|_|_|_|_|_|_|_|_|_|_|_|_|_|_|_|_|_|_|_|_|_|_|_|_|_|_|_|_|_|_|

FIRST ADDRESS LINE: |_|_|_|_|_|_|_|_|_|_|_|_|_|_|_|_|_|_|_|_|_|_|_|_|_|_|_|_|_|_|_|_|_|_|_|

SECOND ADDRESS LINE: |_|_|_|_|_|_|_|_|_|_|_|_|_|_|_|_|_|_|_|_|_|_|_|_|_|_|_|_|_|_|_|_|_|_|

CITY: |_|_|_|_|_|_|_|_|_|_|_|_|_|_|_|_|_|_|

STATE: |_|_|

ZIP CODE: |_|_|_|_|_| - |_|_|_|_|

TELEPHONE NUMBER: |_|_|_| - |_|_|_| - |_|_|_|_|

SOCIAL SECURITY NUMBER: |_|_|_| - |_|_| - |_|_|_|_|

SEX (F|M): |_|

BIRTHDATE (YYMMDD): |_|_| - |_|_| - |_|_|

MARITAL STATUS (M|S): |_|

NAME OF SPOUSE: |_|_|_|_|_|_|_|_|_|_|_|_|_|_|

EMERGENCY CONTACT: |_|_|_|_|_|_|_|_|_|_|_|_|_|_|_|_|_|_|_|

EMERGENCY TELEPHONE NUMBER: |_|_|_| - |_|_|_| - |_|_|_|_|

EMPLOYEE JOB HISTORY

Employee name

Position	Date	Reason for Change	Grade	Depart- ment	Salary
1.					
2.					
3.					
4.					
5.					
6.					
7.					
8.					
9.					
10.					

EMPLOYEE SALARY HISTORY

Employee _____

Starting Date _____   Starting salary _____

Position	Date	Salary Increase	Type of Increase: Merit/ promotion/ other
_____	_____	_____	_____
_____	_____	_____	_____
_____	_____	_____	_____
_____	_____	_____	_____
_____	_____	_____	_____
_____	_____	_____	_____
_____	_____	_____	_____
_____	_____	_____	_____
_____	_____	_____	_____
_____	_____	_____	_____
_____	_____	_____	_____

Temporary Personnel Requisition (11-34)

TEMPORARY PERSONNEL REQUISITION

Job Title _____

Supervisor _____ Department _____

Dates Desired: From _____ Through _____

Hours Desired: From _____ To _____

Job Duties _____
_____
_____
_____
_____
_____
_____
_____

Supervisor's Signature _____ Date _____

Approved by _____ Date _____

TEMPORARY AGENCY WORKER LOG

Agency Name _____   Contact _____

Address _____   Phone _____

City, State, Zip _____

Type of personnel _____

==

Date _____   Job Performed _____

Name of Temp _____   Use Again?___Yes ___No

Department _____   Supervisor _____

==

Date _____   Job Performed _____

Name of Temp _____   Use Again?___Yes ___No

Department _____   Supervisor _____

==

Date _____   Job Performed _____

Name of Temp _____   Use Again?___Yes ___No

Department _____   Supervisor _____

==

Date _____   Job Performed _____

Name of Temp _____   Use Again?___Yes ___No

Department _____   Supervisor _____

==

Date _____   Job Performed _____

Name of Temp _____   Use Again?___Yes ___No

Department _____   Supervisor _____

==

Date _____   Job Performed _____

Name of Temp _____   Use Again?___Yes ___No

Department _____   Supervisor _____

==

Date _____   Job Performed _____

Name of Temp _____   Use Again?___Yes ___No

Department _____   Supervisor _____

==

Date _____   Job Performed _____

Name of Temp _____   Use Again?___Yes ___No

Department _____   Supervisor _____

==

EMPLOYEE TRANSFER REQUEST

Employee _____   Employee No. _____
Current position _____   Department _____
Supervisor's name _____   Phone ext. _____
Attendance record _____   Time in position _____

Describe present job duties and responsibilities:
_____
_____
_____

Indicate the position desired and the department:
_____

Describe your skills, education and experience which you feel will be useful in
evaluation for the position desired:
_____
_____
_____

Specify your reason for requesting a position change:
_____
_____
_____

Employee signature _____   Date _____

SUPERVISOR'S TRANSFER REQUEST EVALUATION FORM

Employee's name _____ Employee No. _____

Position/location desired _____

Date of hire _____

Employee's attendance record _____

Comment on the employee's job performance with attention to technical knowledge and competency, quality of work and accuracy:

_____
_____
_____

Evaluate the employee's performance in the areas of:

Dependability _____

Cooperation _____

Skills _____

Time required to learn new jobs _____

Do you recommend this employee for position requested?

_____ Yes _____ No

Please comment:

_____
_____
_____

Supervisor's signature _____ Date _____

Reviewed by _____ Date _____

SUPERVISOR'S CHECKLIST FOR TRANSFERRED EMPLOYEES

Review each item on this checklist with the transferred employee when he or she reports for work. When the review is complete, both supervisor and employee should sign and date the form.

_____ Organization of the
      department
_____ Purpose of department work
_____ Relationship to other depts.
_____ Review of job description
_____ Department procedures
_____ Hours of work
_____ Breaks and lunch schedule
_____ When absent
_____ Review of grade and salary
      level

_____ Telephone usage
_____ Confidential data
_____ Security procedures
_____ Opportunities in dept.
_____ Introduction to manager
_____ Location of washroom
_____ Location of time clock
_____ Employee parking areas

_____
Employee's signature

_____
Date

_____
Supervisor's signature

_____
Date

(Upon completion, please return to the Human Resources Division)

TRANSFER NOTIFICATION FORM

To be completed by the department from which the employee is transferring and sent to the new department.

Employee _____ Social Security No. _____

Department transferring from _____
          Date of hire _____
          Last day worked _____
          Previous periods of employment _____
          _____

Department transferring to _____
          Date of transfer _____
          Accrued vacation _____
          Accrued sick leave _____

Other information _____
_____
_____

Completed by _____ Date _____

PERSONNEL ACTION FORM

NOTICE OF EMPLOYEE SEPARATION

The following employee was separated TODAY

Employee: _____   Employee No. _____

Social Security No. _____

Job Title _____

Reason for Separation:
(Check one and explain under remarks)

_____   Layoff   _____   Retirement
_____   Discharge due to performance   _____   Resignation
_____   Discharge, disciplinary   _____   Resignation requested

Remarks: _____
_____
_____

Remuneration paid after separation:

Vacation pay: ___ Yes   __ No
Severance pay: ___ Yes   __ No

This separation is issued by _____
                                              Name

_____   _____
            Title   Date

LETTER OF RESIGNATION

To: Human Resources Department   Date _____

From _____

Department _____

I hereby submit my resignation as an employee of Acme Corporation.

My last working day will be: _____

My reason(s) is (are):

_____

_____

_____

Any further correspondence after my termination may be forwarded to the following address:

                                    _____

                                    _____

                                    _____
                                    Telephone number

_____
Signature

RETIREMENT CHECKLIST

Employee _____ Department _____

1. Letter of Resignation—
   Submit a Letter of Resignation, indicating your upcoming retirement to your
   supervisor who will forward it to the Human Resources Department. Please
   including your forwarding address in your letter.

2. All vacation earned but not taken prior to retirement will be included in your final pay.

3. Address change—
   Your address will be automatically changed when you retire and you will receive
   your statements at home.

4. Employee Benefits—
   Contact the Employee Benefits Department for information concerning your benefit
   coverage.

5. Company Property
   If you have been issued any of the following, return them to your supervisor:

   _____ Security badge   _____ Supervisor's manual
   _____ ID badge   _____ Keys
   _____ Other _____

SEPARATION CHECKLIST

Employee _____ Department _____

1. Letter of resignation—
   If you have not already done so, please submit a Letter of Resignation, indicating your upcoming termination, to your supervisor who will forward it to the Human Resources Department for processing.

2. Forwarding address—
   Notify the Human Resources Department regarding a forwarding address or address change; otherwise the address of record will be used.

3. Final pay—
   The last regular payroll check will be (date)_____. The final pay will be in the form of a check which will be mailed to you at your forwarding address on (date)_____. If you prefer to pick up your check in person, contact the accounting department at extension____, to make appropriate arrangements. If you have completed one year of service, all vacation earned but not taken prior to termination will be included in your final pay.

4. Profit sharing plan or stock purchase plan—
   Contact the Employee Benefits Department at extension____, if you are participating in these plans.

5. Optional medical coverage—
   Should you wish to apply for Optional Extended Medical Coverage, contact Employee Benefits or contact your Health Maintenance Organization if you are covered under an HMO.

6. Employee guide and benefit program books—
   Please return these books to the Human Resources Department.

7. Company property—
   If you have been issued any of the following, please return them to your supervisor:

   _____ Supervisor's manual   _____ Security badge
   _____ ID card and badge   _____ Keys
   _____ (Other) _____

SEPARATION NOTICE

Department _____   Effective Date _____

Employee _____   Employee No. _____

Reason for Separation:

____ Discharged   ____ Illness
____ Quit   ____ Layoff
____ Other (Specify)

_____
_____
_____

Comments _____
_____
_____

Signed By _____   Title _____
Date _____

SEPARATION AGREEMENT LETTER

Date _____

Name _____

Address _____

_____

Dear _____

    This letter will confirm the substance of our conversation of [date]. You were told that we had decided to terminate your employment.

    You were also told that the company wants to make your transition to a new employer as easy as possible. For that purpose, we agreed that you would resign as an alternative to termination and that you could state to other employers that you had left the company voluntarily.

    We also discussed severance pay, continued benefits and other topics. We agreed that in addition to the pay and benefits to which you normally would be entitled under current company policies, the company would provide the following additional pay and benefits:

[List additional benefits]

_____

_____

_____

    In return for the listed additional pay and benefits, you acknowledge that this agreement is the full and final settlement of any and all claims resulting from your employment with the company. These claims include but are not limited to claims under contract, tort or the provisions of state or federal statutes that you may have now or in the future. You also agree that the company owes you no further liability or obligations beyond those described in this agreement.

    We agreed that your termination will be effective [date]. All pay, benefits and other entitlement from your employment will be computed on that basis unless we have agreed on some other arrangement as one of the additional benefits listed above. We also agreed that before you receive any additional pay or benefits, you will return the following property to the company:

[List property]

_____

_____

_____

You are free to examine this document in full and to consult an attorney, if you wish, before signing it.

I am pleased that we have been able to reach this agreement and are able to part amicably. I wish you the best in finding new employment. The terms of this letter will be treated in confidence.

(Signed)	Date	Title

I have read this letter and agree that it accurately states our understanding and agreement.

(Employee)	Date

EMPLOYEE SUGGESTION SUBMITTAL FORM

PART A

Employee _____ Employee No. _____

Department _____ Phone No. _____

Is this a group submittal?   ____Yes ____No
(If yes, give names of all
submitters and obtain their
signatures on the reverse side.)
Have you submitted a
suggestion before?   ____Yes ____No

PART B

WHAT IS THE SITUATION OR PROBLEM? BE SPECIFIC. ATTACH ANY
ADDITIONAL INFORMATION.

_____

_____

_____

WHAT IS YOUR SOLUTION TO IMPROVE THIS SITUATION OR PROBLEM? BE
SPECIFIC. ATTACH SAMPLES IF APPLICABLE.

_____

_____

_____

WHAT TYPE OF BENEFITS, SAVINGS AND IMPLEMENTATION COSTS CAN BE
EXPECTED FROM THIS SOLUTION? EXPLAIN HOW YOU CALCULATED THESE
SAVINGS.

_____

_____

_____

I have read and understand the rules and regulations governing the Suggestion System
and agree to be bound by them. I understand that the Corporation has the sole
discretion whether to make an award, if any, and that it may use a suggestion without
giving an award. I understand that the maximum amounts for tangible and intangible
awards are $5,000 and $100 respectively. I agree to these limitations even if the
savings the Corporation might realize from my suggestion may far exceed the amount

of any award. In consideration of the Corporation's evaluation of my suggestion, I hereby assign all patent, copyright and trademark rights, and all other proprietary rights which may exist in my suggestion to the Corporation. I agree that the Corporation shall have the exclusive right to determine all questions regarding eligibility of participants and suggestions, designations and amounts of awards. I also agree to maintain my suggestion confidentially after submission.

(Note: In the event of a group submittal, all members of the submitting group must attach the information requested in Part A and sign the submittal form. Additional signature may be provided on the back.)

Signature _____ Date _____

I wish to remain anonymous during the evaluation:

_____ Yes _____ No

Employee Referral Form (11-47)

EMPLOYEE REFERRAL FORM

Employee Making Referral _____

Employee No. _____ Department _____

Individual Referred _____

For (specify position) _____

Address _____

Years Known _____ Relationship to Employee _____

Qualifications _____
_____
_____

Employee Signature _____

Alphabetical Index

Index by Subject

Boldface numbers indicate document numbers and the pages on which they are located.

A

Accident report **(11-21)**, **329**
Age discrimination, 286-287
Age Discrimination in Employment Act of 1967 (ADEA), 286-287
AIDS. *See also* Americans with Disabilities Act (ADA)
    hiring person with, 287
    personnel policy regarding **(8-31)**, **250**
Americans with Disabilities Act (ADA), 287-288
    personnel policy regarding **(8-22)**, **229-232**
Applicant. *See also* Interview; Job application; References
    checking references of, 26-27
    comparison of, following interview, 27
    job offer letter **(2-11)**, **44**
    methods of screening, 25-26
    predicting future performance of, 4
    rating form **(2-10)**, **43**, 27
    rejection letter **(2-12)**, **45**, 28
    role of interviewer in judging abilities of, 4-5
Application. *See* Job application
Appraisal. *See* Performance appraisal

Attendance
    departmental absentee report **(11-04)**, **309**
    employee
        absentee report **(11-03)**, **308**
        lateness report **(11-02)**, **307**
        record **(11-01)**, **306**
    personnel policy regarding **(8-02)**, **191-192**
    weekly time sheet
        hourly employees **(11-11)**, **318**
        salaried employees **(11-12)**, **319**
Attitude survey. *See* Employee attitude survey
Authorization for release of prior employment information **(2-08)**, **40-41**
Automation, effects of, on manpower planning, 171-172

B

Behavior-oriented interview questions **(1-02)**, **14**, 4-5,
Behavior, reporting improper, personnel policy regarding **(8-20)**, **224**
Behavior scale, in performance appraisal, 114
Benefit programs
    application for profit sharing in **(11-14)**, **321-322**
    eligibility requirements for **(11-15)**, **323**

lawful interview questions **(10-02)**, **297-300**, 280-281
and pregnancy, 288
in recruitment advertising, 281
religious, 282
Dress, personnel policy regarding **(8-15)**, **219**
Drug and alcohol abuse, personnel policy regarding **(8-29)**, **246**

E

Educational assistance program
forms for reimbursement **(4-09)**, **111**; **(4-10)**, **112**
inclusion in training program, 95
Employee(s). *See also* New employee
communicating results from employee attitude surveys to, 153
expectations from performance appraisal, 117-118
policy regarding relatives of **(8-26)**, **238**
referral of **(11-47)**, **360**
requisition for new **(2-01)**, **30-31**, 23
resistance to change in, and retraining of, 87
responsibilities, in personnel policies, 184
Employee assistance program, personnel policy regarding **(8-38)**, **259**
Employee attitude survey
action plans for implementing changes **(6-11)**, **166**, 153
commitment of line managers in introducing, 140
communicating results to employees, 153
company concerns in introducing, 139-140

comparing norm differences, 148-149
defining objectives of, 141
developing trend data from successive, 148
effective use of data acquired in, 139
in exit interview **(7-02)**, **177-178**, 171
follow-up and feedback **(6-09)**, **164**, 150-151
group interviews in **(6-02)**, **157**, 142-143
handling sensitive issues from, 152
interpretation of results in **(6-05)**, **160**, 147, 149
mail survey for, 146-147
neutral responses on, 148
objectives of meeting in presenting results, 151-152
organization of survey items, 147
planning analysis of data, 147
questions used in **(6-01)**, **154-156**, 142
reinforcement of survey efforts, 153
reporting results of, 147
response scales used in, 143-144
responsibility for following up on, 141-142
responsibility for interpreting, 150
scheduling, 144
scope and size of survey **(6-03)**, **158**, 144-145
script in communicating instructions for **(6-04)**, **159**, 146
set-up of committee for, 141
sharing results from, 151
solutions for problem areas revealed by **(6-10)**, **165**, 152-153
stages in process of, 140
strategies for following up on **(6-06)**, **161**; **(6-07)**, **162**; **(6-08)**, **163**,

141, 150-151
techniques for tabulating data, 145-146
Employee discipline
personnel policies regarding (8-18), 222; (8-19), 223
report on (11-19), 327
warning notice regarding (11-18), 326
Employee Polygraph Protection Act, 286
Employee Retirement Income Security Act (ERISA), 289-290
reporting and disclosure for, 290
Employee selection system, ingredients of reliable, 25. *See also* Hiring process
Employment at will doctrine, 290
Employment reference response form (2-07), 39, 27
Equal employment opportunity, personnel policy regarding (8-21), 226, 283
Equal Pay Act (EPA), 276, 283
Essay performance appraisal, 114
Ethics and personal conduct, personnel policy regarding (8-13), 215, 184
Exempt employees. *See* Legal considerations
Exit interview
attitude survey in (7-02), 177-178, 171
performance appraisal in (5-10), 138, 124

F

Family and Medical Leave Act (FMLA), 288-289
policy regarding (8-05), 195-202
Federal Labor Standards Act (FLSA), 276-277

policy regarding (8-33), 252-253
record keeping requirements, 279-280
Federal Wage and Hour Law. *See* Federal Labor Standards Act (FLSA)
Feedback
from employee attitude survey (6-09), 164, 150, 151
from performance appraisal
corrective, 119-120
improving techniques in, 120-121
negative, 120
purpose of, 119
Focus groups, in developing training programs, 84, 92
Future performance, use of past experience in predicting, 4

G

Grievance procedures, personnel policy regarding (8-36), 256-257, 183, 185
Group interviews, in employee attitude surveys (6-02), 157, 142-143
Group life insurance, application for (11-13), 320

H

Handicapped workers. *See also* AIDS
compensation for, 277
hiring of, 287-288
Health. *See* Safety and health
Hiring process. *See also* Interview; Recruitment
differences between executive and lower-level jobs, 27
evaluation of resume, 26
handling rejected candidates, 28
importance of, 1

and determination of interrelationships of the job, 60
interview form for **(3-04)**, **66-68**, 61
questionnaire
preparation of **(3-05)**, **69-72**, 61
role of, in developing wage and
salary administration program, 253
role of, in conducting job interviews,
61
techniques of, 60
worksheet for **(3-03)**, **64-65**
Job application
disclaimer and acknowledgment **(2-
04)**, **35**, 26
form **(2-03)**, **33-34**, 25-26
lawful questions on **(10-01)**, **292-
296**
update form **(2-05)**, **36**
Job description. *See also* Job description
program
example of **(3-02)**, **63**, 58-59
format for **(3-01)**, **62**, 57
Job description program. *See also* Job
analysis; Job description
benefits of, 58
gaining employee cooperation in
starting, 59
job requirements glossary **(3-09)**,
79-81
need for, 57-58
preparation guides, 61
for managers **(3-08)**, **76-78**
for supervisors **(3-07)**, **75**
for workers **(3-06)**, **73-74**
in wage and salary administration
program, 253
Job evaluation
compensable factors in, 266-267
internal value approach to, 266
market value approach to, 266

methods of ranking values in, 267-
268
Job immersion, 93. *See also* Training
programs
Job interview. *See* Interview
Job offer
information included in, 27-28
interview for, 7
letter for **(2-11)**, **44**
Job performance
identifying causes of poor, 83-84
use of performance appraisal in
correcting poor, 118
Job posting sheet **(11-24)**, **323**
Job profile **(2-02)**, **32**
definition of, 25
use of, 25
Job requirements glossary **(3-09)**, **79-81**
Job rotation, 93, 95
Jury duty, personnel policy regarding **(8-
04)**, **194**

L

Leaves of absence. *See also* Family and
Medical Leave Act; Mater-
nity leave; Military leave;
Sick leave
information sheet **(11-08)**, **313-314**
personnel policy regarding **(8-06)**,
203-204, 195-196
request form **(11-09)**, **315-316**
Lectures, in classroom training, 89
Legal considerations
age discrimination, 276, 286-287
Age Discrimination in Employment
Act of 1967 (ADEA), 286-
287
Americans with Disabilities Act
(ADA), **(8-22)**, **229-232**, 287-
288
benefits, 277

Overtime
    authorization form for **(11-05)**, **310**
    availability, personnel policy
        regarding **(8-24)**, **234**
    compensation for, 277-278
    departmental report for **(11-06)**, **311**
    exemptions from pay for, 278-279

P

Panel discussions, in classroom training,
    89. *See also* Training pro-
    grams
Panel interview, 7
Part-time employee letter of understand-
    ing **(2-18)**, **51-52**
Peer appraisal, in performance appraisal,
    117
Peer review, personnel policy regarding
    (8-37), **258**
Performance appraisal
    choosing appropriate method for,
        117
    combining with salary reviews, 121
    critical incidents method in **(5-01)**,
        125, 115-116
    employee expectations, 117-118
    evaluation of system, 122-123
    for exit interview **(5-10)**, **138**, 124
    feedback
        purpose of, in, 119
        techniques in, 119-121
    form for **(5-02)**, **126-128**, 116
    goals and standards in **(5-04)**, **130**,
        118-119
    interview report **(5-03)**, **129**
    maintaining a program for, 122
    management-by-objectives approach
        to, 116, 117
    management preparation for ap-
        praisal interview **(5-05)**, **131**,
        119

methods for, 114
objectives of good system, 113
peer appraisal in, 117
rating scales in, 114-115
record keeping for, 123
responsibility in performing, 116-
    117
steps in, 118
training of supervisors and managers
    in **(5-08)**, **134-135**; **(5-09)**,
    136-137, 123-124
use of, to correct poor performance,
    118
use of, in promotion discussions,
    121
Performance reviews, personnel policy
    regarding **(8-32)**, **242**
Personnel file checklist **(2-16)**, **49**
Personnel policies
    AIDS **(8-31)**, **250**
    Americans with Disabilities Act
        (ADA) **(8-22)**, **229-232**, 287-
        288
    attendance and punctuality **(8-02)**,
        191-192
    compensation practices and pay
        schedule **(8-33)**, **252-253**,
        184
    disciplinary offense descriptions
        (8-19), **223**; **(8-20)**, **227**
    dress **(8-15)**, **219**
    drug and alcohol abuse **(8-29)**, **246**
    employee assistance programs
        (8-38), **259**
    employee discipline **(8-18)**, **222**;
        (8-19), **223**, 197
    employing relatives **(8-26)**, **238**
    equal employment opportunity
        (8-21), **226-227**, 283
    ethics and personal conduct **(8-13)**,
        215-216